Wild Blue Yonder

Wild Blue Yonder

Glory days of the US Eighth Air Force in England

Martin W Bowman

CASSELL

Cassell
Wellington House, 125 Strand
London WC2R 0BB

British Library Cataloguing-in-Publication Data
A catalogue record for this book is available from the British Library

Martin Bowman has asserted his right to be identified as the Author of this Work.

ISBN 0-304-36466-5

Designed by Rod Teasdale

The re-enactment shots posed by models
in this book are purely representative
of events of World War Two.

Printed and bound in Italy

Contents

Introduction 6

Going Over 8

Somewhere in England 16

Overpaid, Oversexed and Over here 40

Religion 66

Pursuits 72

Fields of Little America 80

Nudes, Names and Numbers 92

'This is London' 100

The Tour 122

Failed to Return 140

Death 152

R & R 158

A Comfortable Blend of War and Peace 174

Flak happy isn't the word for it 182

Yuletide 190

Romantic Interludes 196

Happy Days Ahead 204

Twelve O'Clock High 216

Acknowledgements 220

Glossary 221

Select Bibliography and Further Reading 222

American troops, or 'GIs' as they were known because of their own derisive term of 'Government Issue', began arriving in war-weary Britain in the months immediately after Pearl Harbor. The 'Yanks' came from the big cities and the backwoods, upstate and downtown: from California to Connecticut, Delaware to Dakota, 'Frisco to Florida; Midwest to Maine, the mighty Mississip' to Missouri; New York, New England, Ohio and Hawaii; the Pacific, Philly and the Rockies to the Rio Grande; from Texas to Tallahassee; Wyoming, Wisconsin, the Windy City and way beyond. The English locals, and the Americans themselves, were in for a culture shock. Some things though never change. Boston, Cambridge, Ipswich, Manchester and Norwich were the same in any language, on both sides of the 'pond'.

Bomber and fighter groups made a particular impact. The young Americans, with their well-cut uniforms, new accents and money, created a colourful and heroic chapter in the lives of the British people that is still remembered today.

On 22 February 1942, 8th Bomber Command was formally activated in England under the command of Major General Ira C. Eaker. Eaker and his chiefs in Washington believed that the B-17 Flying Fortresses and B-24 Liberators were so heavily armed that they would not require fighters to escort them to their targets. The theory was that they could penetrate even the strongest defences in broad daylight without high losses. They also aimed to match the bombing accuracy that bombardiers had achieved in the clear skies of Texas and the southern states. But by September losses were on the increase. The RAF, and even some personnel in the USAAF, were of the opinion that bombing in daylight was suicidal – and it was on occasions – but the Americans continued regardless. US escort fighters arrived albeit late in the war, and by spring 1944, the P-51 Mustang was accompanying the US 'heavies' to Berlin and back. Ultimately, the round-the-clock

Left: *Crew of* The Old Squaw, *303rd BG, at Molesworth in 1943. Standing: Captain Claude W. Campbell, pilot; Miller, Ririe, William A. Boutelle, bombardier. Kneeling: Howard Hernan, Wilson, Quick, Kraft, Backert. (Hernan Coll)*

Right: *The 'Yanks' came from the big cities and the backwoods, upstate and downtown: from California to Connecticut, Delaware to Dakota, 'Frisco to Florida; Midwest to Maine, the mighty Mississip' to Missouri; New York, New England, Ohio and Hawaii; the Pacific, Philly and the Rockies to the Rio Grande; from Texas to Tallahassee; Wyoming, Wisconsin, the Windy City and way beyond. (MWB)*

Far right: Big Beautiful Doll *and a US staff car during a sojourn at Old Buckenham. (MWB)*

bombing by the RAF at night and the 8th Air Force by day helped to achieve victory.

The 8th Air Force, and the villagers and townsfolk of East Anglia, shared a close attachment that only wartime can create. England 1942–45 was a battlefront. All the civilians were involved in the war effort: as shipyard and factory workers, Red Cross and Land Army volunteers, farmers and firemen. Above all they were determined fighters who had already endured more than three years of war. Into their lives came the sights and sounds – particularly the jargon – of the men from Idaho, New York, California and the rest, as they went on flak leave, R&R, and pubbing missions. The impressions they made were profound.

The stirring deeds of these gladiators-of-the-air filled the newspapers and magazines of the period. Their exploits were crystallized in the minds of the population with movies such as William Wyler's wartime epic *Memphis Belle*; a poignant feature screened on both sides of the Atlantic about the lives of a B-17 crew who flew the ship on twenty-five missions. More than half a century after the war this immortal period of Anglo-American history is still being commemorated – with new films and books, and with celebrations for returning US veterans and the English families who had opened their hearts and homes to them so long ago.

Those Second World War years are recalled here by a cast of characters no movie director could ever hope to assemble. Their stories tell of laughter, friendship, death, fear, exhilaration, stupidity, superstition, discipline and indiscipline, lust and love, respect, disrespect, and outrage. Not to mention the sheer horrors faced mission after mission by the 'boys in the sky', along with the deprivations experienced by the British men, women and children. These are their memories.

Martin W Bowman, Norwich, England

Left: 'At the end of June the first American heavy-bombardment group was on its way – by air. Not without loss. Three B-17s were forced down on a Greenland icecap.' Target Germany. (MWB)

Going Over

'Over There, Over There, we're going over, Over There'

Lines from the wartime song 'Over There'

At the end of June, the first American heavy-bombardment group was on its way – by air. Not without loss. Three B-17s were forced down on a Greenland icecap. One of the crews managed to survive by cutting off the blades of one twisted propeller with a hacksaw, then using that engine to furnish heat for the plane and power for the radio generator until a navy flying boat, landing under extraordinarily hazardous conditions, rescued them. The other crews were also saved – one from a small island and the other from the sea. Two other Fortresses, caught by bad weather off Greenland, were forced down. Again, both crews were rescued.

Target Germany. The B-17s, including *My Gal Sal*, from the 97th BG, were en route to England on 26 June 1942

Below: *Wendover Field, Utah.*
(USAF)

The orders finally came directing the Group to prepare to move out because we had completed the first phase of training. The entire thirty-day training period was spent on detached service and was followed by a move to Wendover Field, Utah. Here, the Group was to receive the balance of its air crews and ground personnel. This was the beginning of the

Above: Queen Mary. *(MWB)*

second phase of training. Wendover Field wasn't the kind of base that you might look forward to being assigned to. It was a dreary base, with no shrubs or trees of any kind. The only thing green on the whole base was the airplanes and they were olive drab. The town of Wendover was nothing more than a train watering-stop, with a gas station, a couple of houses, and a hotel straddling the Utah-Nevada State Line. The State Line ran down the center of the hotel so it was possible to gamble on the Nevada side, but not on the Utah side.

Crew 64, **Staff Sergeant Gene Gaskins, Wendover Field, Utah, 1943**

We ground echelon stood in awe – in respect and wonder – for there alongside the pier in Brooklyn stood that magnificent ship the *Queen Mary*! As Lieutenant West of the 66th Bomb Squadron said: 'My God! What a big ******* target!' There were five days of unique experiences whilst aboard the 'queen of the seas'. For instance: delicious meals so elegantly served; those royal sleeping accommodations; exciting social and activity programs on deck; restful campouts that provided such invigorating and cherished celestial

observations; and windswept breezes from the North Atlantic. The pride of the British Cunard Line was truly a lady! She transported us to the shores of our to-be homeland for the duration. She did a marvellous job for freedom. God blessed the 'queen' and she carried many service personnel and priority passengers safely to and fro during those dreadful years. A lady – with dignity and charm!

Tom J. Shepherd, 44th BG

Our Flying Fortress crew boarded the *Queen Mary* in October 1943. Sometime after sunset, the 17,000 or more American troops were lined up more than three or four deep on the *Queen's* railings as we sailed past 'The Lady' on our way to the Narrows and on to the open sea. As improbable as it now may seem, a GI standing next to me said, 'Don't I know you?' to which I replied, 'You must be from Minnesota. That voice sounds like home.' It turned out he was from the Sherburn area and we had on occasion seen each other in Fairmont and Fox Lake. I've often thought about what may have happened to that young man in the months that were to follow.

Stanley Peterson, 96th BG, navigator, Ingram's crew

Above: *America – the arsenal of democracy. Vega-built Fortresses at Burbank, California. 42-39871, being hoisted above the others, served in the 652nd BS, 25th BG and the 305th BG and was lost on 28 May 1944. 42-39873 became* Stormy Weather *in the 615th BS, 401st BG, and failed to return on 1 August 1944. 42-39869 (right) became* Heaven Can Wait *in the 412th BS, 95th BG at Horham, and failed to return with Lt. Richard P. Bannerman and crew on 11 April 1944. 42-39875 (off-centre) became* Buzz Blonde, *later* Helen Highwater, *and finally* Through Hel'en Hiwater; *in the 303rd BG at Molesworth and was lost on 15 January 1945. 42-39876 (centre) became* Gloria Anna *in the 569th BS, 390th BG. 42-39892 was assigned to the 401st BG and was lost on a mission to Berlin in March 1944. Lockheed-Vega built 2,750 B-17s in WWII. (Lockheed-California)*

We flew our own B-24 overseas in early September 1943 from Bangor, Maine, to England, on the transatlantic route. Snow, blizzard conditions and ice had closed in along the sub-arctic route and we were told to proceed to Greenland rather than to the designated stopover at Iceland. The navigator took a celestial reading but we also had to resort to radio communications with ground stations. For hours we sought an opening to BW-1, a base bounded by a glacier of ice where only one pass at the runway was possible. We knew we had but one chance and we took it. As we came in up a long fjord leading to the single runway, the navigator suddenly announced we were about to land but the leading wire antenna was still out and it was too late to fully retract it. I frantically cranked it in – but not in time. We hit the runway and raced down it. The weight at the end of the wire snapped off and flew through the air like a projectile in the direction of some Quonset huts which were lining the runway about one hundred yards away. Even before the plane came to a halt on the runway I knew what was coming. I would be reprimanded. I learned the lesson to never have the antenna out as we approached any base from that time on. Luckily, no one in the Quonset huts was hit. I never used the wire antenna again. Ironically I became first radio operator after our original radio operator was shot down.

Technical Sergeant Forrest S. Clark, air gunner, 67th BS, 44th BG

Heading north from Hunter Field we had a brisk tailwind, so we did a lot of sightseeing on the way up the coast. We flew a circle around Norfolk, Virginia, and I was able to pick out my home there. We then flew to Washington, DC and flew around the Capitol Building, staying at about 1,000 feet. We soon found ourselves over New York City and decided to fly around the Statue of Liberty. We were still ahead of schedule, so I suggested to Beiser that we fly around the Empire State Building. Staying at 1,000 feet, we flew rather close to the tallest building on earth at that time. Unfortunately, someone with binoculars could read our tail number,

and when we got to England, a letter of reprimand was waiting for Beiser. He never held it against me for getting him into this minor bit of trouble.

After six hours we arrived at Grenier Field, Manchester, New Hampshire where we spent the night while our plane was refueled and serviced. We spent an extra night and then took off heading to the town of Happy Valley, Labrador. Our field of departure there was Goose Bay. We arrived at about noon and the ground crews got busy servicing the plane. We were scheduled to take off in the early hours after midnight the next day, headed for Keflavik, Iceland. We went to bed early because of this accelerated schedule. Bad weather was expected and it was very bad when we were routed out of bed. It was snowing pretty hard, but the operations people said that the flights were on as scheduled. We were to take off at thirty-minute intervals, go to 11,000 feet and remain at that altitude for the entire trip.

We all went sightseeing in Reykjavik. Iceland didn't have the shortages that one would expect in the States. The shop windows had all kind of goods that were being rationed at home. Many sidewalks in the town were lined with fish heads a couple of feet high, with paths cut through at doorways. The refrigerated fish heads would be removed before they thawed and processed into fish oil that was

Above: *'We were still ahead of schedule, so I suggested to Beiser that we fly around the Empire State Building. Staying at 1,000 feet, we flew rather close to the tallest building on earth at that time. Unfortunately, someone with binoculars could read our tail number, and when we got to England, a letter of reprimand was waiting for Beiser. He never held it against me for getting him into this minor bit of trouble.' Second Lieutenant Richard 'Dick' Johnson (MWB)*

used in paint making and in many other processes.

The next morning, our aircraft having been serviced, we took off for Prestwick, Scotland. We had expected more B-17s to go with us, but two of our group of eight never made it to Iceland. One had tried to go above the storm and running out of fuel had come back down just before running completely out of gas, ditching alongside a ship. Unfortunately the water was so cold that most were lost to hypothermia before they could be picked up. The other lost B-17 had decided to go below the weather when it got daylight, expecting to make an emergency landing on Greenland. They never made it, having to ditch when their fuel ran out. All of these men were lost. Their May Day transmission

was the only clue to their position.

Our flight to Prestwick was uneventful as the weather had improved a little. We were very proud of 'our' brand new Flying Fortress that we thought would be ours to fly all our combat missions in. No such luck. On 12 April, our plane, with the tail number 42-102392, was taken away from us. We had such short notice that we even left some of our gear on board, including our parachutes, binoculars, and a few personal items that we eventually got back.

Second Lieutenant Richard 'Dick' Johnson. The B-17 the crew flew over in was allocated to the 91st BG. It was named *Cool Papa*, and was lost with Lieutenant McCardle's crew on 1 May 1944.

Below: *'On February 28th the group, traveling by boat, boarded the Frederick Lykes, a C-3 freighter, lying at the foot of 38th Street. On the next morning we backed out past the* Queen Elizabeth, *and sailed into the fog beyond the Statue of Liberty …'* Allan Healy (MWB)

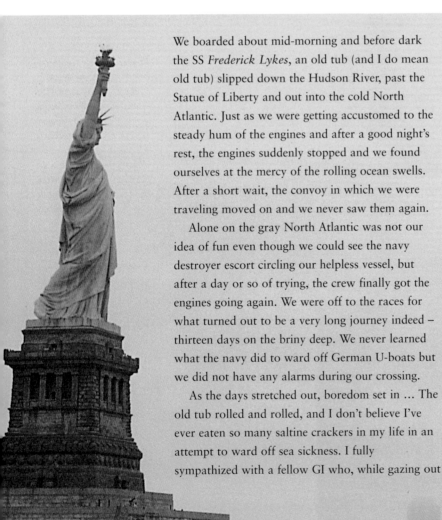

We boarded about mid-morning and before dark the SS *Frederick Lykes*, an old tub (and I do mean old tub) slipped down the Hudson River, past the Statue of Liberty and out into the cold North Atlantic. Just as we were getting accustomed to the steady hum of the engines and after a good night's rest, the engines suddenly stopped and we found ourselves at the mercy of the rolling ocean swells. After a short wait, the convoy in which we were traveling moved on and we never saw them again.

Alone on the gray North Atlantic was not our idea of fun even though we could see the navy destroyer escort circling our helpless vessel, but after a day or so of trying, the crew finally got the engines going again. We were off to the races for what turned out to be a very long journey indeed – thirteen days on the briny deep. We never learned what the navy did to ward off German U-boats but we did not have any alarms during our crossing.

As the days stretched out, boredom set in … The old tub rolled and rolled, and I don't believe I've ever eaten so many saltine crackers in my life in an attempt to ward off sea sickness. I fully sympathized with a fellow GI who, while gazing out

over the gray North Atlantic, remarked to me one day, 'It will be great to be back on terra firma, and the more firma the less terra!'

The men were getting antsy and rumours flew that someone had seen land off the starboard side. Then, all of a sudden, the heaving and rolling of the ocean stopped, and the old tub glided like a luxury liner up into the Firth of Clyde. The men crowded the decks to see double-decker buses moving up and down the streets lined with old brick buildings.

Late the night of the thirteenth day, our long, long voyage came to an end in a dock area deep in Glasgow. To the unfamiliar high whistle of the small freight engines, we disembarked and headed straight for our train, which was to take us to Rackheath. Unlike any train we had ever seen, each row of seats had a door. And the seats did not adjust for sleeping. Sleeping in the sitting-up position, we looked out the little windows on a darkened nation. About mid-morning, the train stopped on a track at Salhouse. We were there even if it meant jumping off the train to the ground five feet below.

Rackheath here we come!

Francis (Frank) W. Stokes, 467th BG

12

Below: *'Many of the crews had had their new bomber painted stateside at Mitchell Base with these beautiful Varga or Petty girls. They spent much of their own money and were very disappointed when at Valley they had to relinquish these ships for assignment, never to see them again. Such is war!' Robert H. Tays,* Country Boy – Combat Bomber Pilot. *George Petty's* Esquire *gatefold inspired Tony Starcer's artwork on the 91st BG's* Memphis Belle, *arguably the most famous nose art in WWII.* Memphis Belle *was the first B-17 to officially complete twenty-five missions and her crew were rewarded with a Bond Tour of the USA in 1943 while William Wyler's movie of the same name appeared in 1945. (MWB)*

It came time to leave Grand Island. On a blustery day in March we climbed aboard our pristine B-17G. Chick revved up the engines. We surged down the runway and climbed quickly into the gray overcast, bound for fame and glory at last. Our first stop was Presque Isle, Maine, but, first, Chick decided that we would give his hometown, Poughkeepsie, a buzz job it wouldn't soon forget. Chick was going to fly under the bridge spanning the Hudson River but changed his mind as the air was too turbulent. Then we headed for Chick's house. His mom was out in the backyard waving and yelling at us as we flew low over the house. Chick had called her and told her that we were coming. The townspeople came out in force as we turned Poughkeepsie inside out. (A B-17 flying overseas had buzzed the World Series earlier that year.)

We stopped overnight at Presque Isle and then headed for Goose Bay, Labrador, the first leg of our transatlantic journey. 'Goose,' as it was familiarly

called by the aircrews, was a busy place. It was used by the Air Transport Command and the bomber crews which were flying overseas. Planes were constantly landing and taking off. The bomber crews always left early in the evening so as to arrive on the other side in daylight hours. The snow was falling constantly, and the big base was completely snowed in. Only the tips of the pine trees were showing above the snowdrifts. Streets were cut deep into the ice and snow. The PXs were full of beautiful goods of excellent quality. The ferry command (ATC) people were well-heeled from their little private enterprise operations, and they threw money around like crazy. Some of them finished the war as rich men. They ferried more cigarettes, booze, and silk stockings than anything else. It was the ambition of every flier to get in ATC after his combat tour was ended.

The night we left, there were fifty-five bombers making the passage. We lost only two of them on the flight over. Presumably they went in the drink. Our aircraft was one of the last to leave. By the time we did, there was a lot of snow coming down so we had to make an instrument takeoff. Just as we were airborne the airplane lurched. We had hit something on takeoff but we didn't know what. We circled a few times and decided we were all right. The navigator set a course for Iceland. We would be flying just south of Greenland on the Northern Route. There were DF stations on the other side which could shoot a fix and give one a heading all the way across the ocean. This was my job. It was exciting to shoot fixes, realizing that someone half way around the world was on the other end of the transmission. I had a lot of fun, so much so that I overdid it. We flew all night and watched the big, scarlet sun come up over the ocean. I felt the awesome solitude Columbus must have felt. We were all alone. I could hear a lot of traffic on the radio from the other airplanes, but we could see none of them.

I think the crossing must have taken about twelve hours. Iceland was locked in solid, but with nowhere else to go, we had to do an instrument letdown to Meeks Field. We broke out of the overcast and landed. The mists cleared away, and

the bright sunshine divulged that we had been flying around among some awesomely high mountain peaks. None of us had realized there were any mountains at all on Iceland. We would have been scared silly if we had known what was up there. When we got down, we started to run the props through and discovered pine needles in a section of the wing. So we had hit something after all.

Iceland was nothing but frozen tundra and high mountains. There were no trees or vegetation. We didn't get to go into town – a disappointment. We had heard about the high incidence of alcoholism in Iceland; so we figured there must be alcohol there too. I did get to watch some anti-aircraft batteries practice firing at a tow-target sleeve. It was fascinating to watch their rapid fire and see the pretty little black bursts popping in the sky like Fourth-of-July bombs. I was soon to get my fill of this sight.

The next day we set sail for the United Kingdom. We landed at Stornaway on the Isle of Lewis in the Outer Hebrides. Some of the crews didn't go to Stornaway, but I am glad we did. The place was an anachronism, right out of Robert Burns. We had landed there late in the evening. That night we all went into the little town to a dance, that is, all but Bachman, the flight engineer, who, having taken a

personal proprietorship in the airplane, insisted on maintaining a guard over it all night. I guess he was worried about saboteurs. The rest of us sure weren't. We had a swell time at the dance but could not understand a word the villagers were saying to us, so thick was their dialect. The next morning I had a delightful surprise when I awoke and saw the quaint, thatch-roofed cottages, stone walls and grazing sheep. I was engrossed by the great black ravens, which strode about majestically, for all the world like senators. There was a wee kirk at the end of the lane that might have been 'Alloway's auld haunted kirk.' In truth, I would not have been a whit surprised to see Tam o'Shanter and the Cutty Sark come dancing by, followed by that 'towzie tyke', Old Nick; witches, warlocks, 'auld haggies,' and sundry 'beasties' of every description. It was that kind of place.

We took off from Stornaway at noon on 15 March 1944 and flew to Prestwick, the great transatlantic base, landing at 1:30 p.m. Prestwick was a huge installation, something to see. I assume it was never bombed. I have never understood why. It was the busiest air terminal in the world at that time. Besides the B-17s constantly arriving, there was every kind of aircraft known to the Allies. You name it – it was there.

Above: *'Iceland was locked in solid, but with nowhere else to go, we had to do an instrument letdown to Meeks Field. We broke out of the overcast and landed. The mists cleared away, and the bright sunshine divulged that we had been flying around among some awesomely high mountain peaks. None of us had realized there were any mountains at all on Iceland.'* Chick's Crew, Ben C. Smith (MWB)

We were hardly down and checked in before our new airplane was taken away from us never to be seen again. This was quite a shock, especially to Bachman. We had even named the airplane. Our morale took a nosedive. For the first time the realization began to steal over us that we were not something special. We were not 'Chick's Crew', we were 'fresh meat' – replacements – soon to be gobbled up by the voracious appetite of the air war like all those who had gone before. A chill rain was falling. We huddled together dejectedly, full of gloomy foreboding.

Chick's Crew, **Ben C. Smith**

As a crew, we trained hard flying the famous B-17 bomber, and when we weren't flying we attended ground school classes. Our training was intensive; seven days a week, night and day. Within the three months we trained, each of us realized how important our individual effort was for the survival of the crew. We were always together and as a result we became interested in each other's lives, which caused an occasional personality clash. It was usually forgotten when we stepped into the plane for a practice flight. After a period of training, reality struck; we were ordered to a staging area for overseas assignment. We were still very impressed with our importance as combat crewmembers – a very enviable position to most other GIs.

In September 1943 we were on our way overseas and sailed on the *Queen Mary* from New York along with 15,000 other Army Air Corps personnel. Needless to say, this was a very crowded ship, but after five days we arrived safely and disembarked in Scotland. With twenty-nine other crews we were assigned to a replacement pool and after five days we were rushed to a bomb group as replacement crews for those lost. When we entered our barracks on a cold dreary night all we saw were empty beds. We were told that these were the beds of men who had been shot down a few days before. A very sobering thought for us as a group. Suddenly, flying status was not that appealing, and someone said out loud, 'And we volunteered for this'.

Staff Sergeant Laurence S. 'Goldie' Goldstein, B-17 radio operator on B. J. Kiersted's crew

Above: *'I wanted wings, 'till I got the gol-darn things Now, I don't want them anymore!'* (MWB)

We flew up past the Statue of Liberty to Bangor, Maine, where we were grounded by a snowstorm for a few days. This new B-17 had good heat, but when the engines stopped, that thin aluminum skin was no insulation. The temperature dropped almost instantaneously to Yankee temperature, and us southern members of the crew got a lesson in getting into warm clothes quickly. 18 January took us to Gander, Newfoundland. The snow was as high as the cockpit on each side of the runway! After we had parked and had the wheels chocked, the pilots set the brakes and were idling the engines diluting the oil for this arctic weather. I was folding maps and gathering my gear to deplane when I glanced out the nose. There was a gasoline trailer, minus tow vehicle, parked across our nose. Nothing remarkable about that, except this trailer was coming sideways toward us! It only lacked five feet of impacting the B-17. I dropped everything and headed back through the plane yelling, 'Whoa, whoa.' I was all the way back to the bomb bay when we hit. Of course, the trailer wasn't actually moving, we were skiing on the icy runway. The pilots had their heads down looking at the instruments and hadn't seen the motion start, but when I yelled they cut the switches. The props were still turning when we hit, however, and sliced gaping holes in the trailer. 100 octane spilled everywhere. But by the grace of the Lord there was no fire. Our props were bent, but the Fort next to us was damaged worse than ours from flying metal. We were cleared by the investigation that followed.

In a few days the Fort was repaired and we were ready to tackle the Atlantic Ocean. It was to be a very long flight to Nutts Corner, Ireland. We loaded extra cargo, mostly mail, in the bomb bay and took off at night. We had to fly pretty high (on oxygen)

at first to pass over a nasty weather front. Nutts Corner was full and we were sent on to Ayr, Scotland, without landing. We were at last on the ground after a fourteen-hour flight. True to army style, no sooner had we gotten off the Flying Fortress than they took it and all the new flying gear away from us. We went by truck (lorry) to Glasgow and by train from there to Stone for assignment as a replacement crew. We were there only a few days and we whiled away the time playing poker, getting familiar with pounds, shillings and pence.

The next train dropped us in East Anglia at the Elmswell railroad station, the stop for Great Ashfield.

Second Lieutenant William W. Varnedoe Jr., navigator, Second Lieutenant George H. Crow Jr.'s crew, 385th BG

Right: *The next train dropped us in East Anglia at the Elmswell railroad station, the stop for Great Ashfield.'* Second Lieutenant William W. Varnedoe Jr. (MWB)

Left: *American Red Cross brooch, badge and a 'Doughnut cluster'! (Richards Coll)*

Somewhere in England

'Goodbye GI don't leave us quite alone.
Somewhere in England we must write in stone
How Britain was invaded by the Yanks
And under that "a big and hearty thanks"'

A tribute to the GIs by A. P. Herbert, the famous English historian

'The RAF was decimated. We were on our knees. And the Americans suddenly appeared.'

George Stebbings, a fourteen-year-old Air Training Corps cadet

It was a battered but still defiant Britain that greeted the Americans. The great German aerial Blitz was over; the danger of invasion seemed remote. But on the far fronts of the war things were not going well… More significant still for these apostles of unborn air-power from across the sea, shortly before their arrival the *Gneisenau*, *Scharnhorst*, and *Prinz Eugen*, supposedly

Above right: *The train itself was much smaller than those that cruise the vast distances across the States … Rather than entering at the front or rear of the car, all we had to do was open one of the many doors and step into the small compartment, which had opposing bench-like seats … The train station itself was built on a level with the train right up to within a few inches. So entering was both easy and rapid.' Will Lundy (MWB)*

immobilized at Brest, took advantage of the vile February weather to make a dash through the Channel for their home bases. The RAF took suicidal chances in a gallant and vain attempt to stop them. Critics of air power – ignoring the fact that the German warships had also eluded surface vessels – made the most of the occasion. There were recriminations in Parliament. It was a black week.

The Americans went to London. They had no time for sight-seeing, but they were impressed by many things – by the bomb damage, neatly tidied but still an object lesson in the destructiveness of aerial bombardment; by the blackout; by the stringency of wartime diet; by the calm fortitude of

the British people, who wore the war like an old coat – frayed around the edges, but still nothing of which to be ashamed.

The task facing the seven officers would have appalled anyone – as one RAF officer dryly put it – except Americans. Starting from scratch, they had to build an organization which would, if their theories were sound and if their convictions were correct, eventually become a hammer that, used in conjunction with the RAF, would crack the iron skull of Nazi Germany.

Target Germany, Act I, Scene I (February 1942)

These lines are dedicated to a man
I met in Glasgow, an American.
He was an Army officer, not old,
In the late twenties. If the truth were told
A great deal younger than he thought he was
I mention this ironically because,
After we'd had a drink or two, he said
Something so naive, so foolish, that I fled.
This was December, Nineteen Forty Two.
He said: 'We're here to win the war for you.'
Lines to An American Officer
by Noël Coward

Solid ground! Most welcome, unsinkable, sweet smelling, beautiful foreign solid ground. The *Queen Mary* was a great ship, but I'm really happy that portion of the trip is now but a memory. Like most of my companions, it was our first experience outside of the continental US. Sure, I'd been down across the border to Mexico for part of a day a couple of times, but Scotland is 6000 miles away. So now with every passing moment something new or completely different appeared for comparison or wonder. All conversation was directed toward these foreign sights.

There, up ahead of me, is a railway station with a troop train patiently waiting for the shuttle boats to bring our Group ashore. As each boatload landed the troops gathered their meager belongings and trudged on up to the station. There to greet us were some hardy Scots dressed in kilts and making us feel welcome with lively bagpipe music. The train itself was much smaller than those that cruise the vast distances across the States. In fact the passenger cars are almost toy-like by comparison, but even though much smaller these cars do have some advantages over ours. The first obvious difference is the boarding. Rather than entering at the front or rear of the car, all we had to do was

Above: *'Arriving there, we watched our first bowling on the green. The English take this sport very seriously. They form exclusive clubs, wear special dress, and follow special rules and protocol. It's all very formal, and they make every effort to appear as though they are enjoying themselves. I found this to be true wherever I witnessed a bowling match.'* Robert H. Tays (via Don and Peggy Garnham)

Above: *Shipdham airfield in 1997. (MWB)*

open one of the many doors and step into the small compartment, which had opposing bench-like seats. At the far end of the compartment was a sliding door that provided access to a long corridor running the length of the car. The train station itself was built on a level with the train right up to within a few inches. So entering was both easy and rapid. Soon we were under way, slowly easing out of the station at Greenock, gathering speed and on our way southward toward England.

After several hours of expressing through both small villages and larger cities, we stopped in the midlands of England at Crewe. Why? Calisthenics. Yes, right in the middle of the city's train station. Nearly 900 officers and men fell out. We formed four lines along the platform as best we could and proceeded to jump and flail our arms, etc., much to the wonder and some amusement of the natives. We were told the calisthenics activities were scheduled to get the kinks out, but I rather suspect they had a more immediate reason. Most of us aboard the *Queen Mary* had had no opportunity to take showers or baths, as fresh water was limited to

drinking, etc. Salt water doesn't do much with a bar of soap. So without changing clothes, little cleaning and cramped up in small compartments for many hours, I'm afraid we were more than a little ripe. The exercise mixed us with fresh air, temporarily alleviating the problem.

We slowly made our way back on board, but not before we managed to grab some hot unsweetened tea and 'cakes' which were so freely given to all traveling servicemen. As we were to learn, and appreciated over and over again, almost all train stations had booths or facilities where some type of refreshment was graciously given to us.

Back on the rails southward we rocketed along, occasionally slowing, often hearing the rather haunting sound of our train's whistle as it warned of our approach across roads. As we passed the road, we could see gates closed to prevent bicycles, pedestrians, or an occasional vehicle from crossing. It appeared that these gates were opened and closed manually. No automatic equipment here. Also, by looking ahead, I learned that whenever barrage balloons were flying we soon would be entering a city. The more numerous the balloons, the larger the city. Also, the farther south we went the more the balloons were tethered by heavy cables to discourage low level strafing and dive bombings.

Naturally there was no luxury of a dining car (if any did exist), so out came the 'D' rations. There always has been criticism of the 'D' rations, but when you are hungry you will eat most anything. I must have been in worse shape than I thought because I not only ate all I could get, but it actually tasted good.

As daylight gradually faded, we were introduced to our first blackout instructions. All doors and windows must remain closed with the double covering tightly in place. Absolutely no light can be allowed to be seen outside, no matter how dim the light might be inside. With darkness also came fatigue, irritability, and fitful sleep.

I find it terribly hard to navigate at night with no lights. Sure, I have a brilliant flashlight, but every time I try to use it I get a chorus of 'Mind that torch!', or 'No lights', or 'Mind that light, Yank'. It didn't take the English long to identify any sign of light at night as being the mistake of one of us. After so many years of living in brilliant desert sunshine, my night vision just wasn't. While I was having trouble determining that even buildings existed on the other side of the narrow streets, our English allies could recognize friends. I finally learned to negotiate the darkness by watching the silhouette of buildings against the slightly lighter sky. No matter how many carrots I ate, my night viewing improved little.

Finally orders were received to get ready, as the long train ride would soon be ended. It was long past midnight and an air raid warning was in effect. So we had to use caution – extreme caution – not to show light of any kind, including cigarettes. London was receiving its nightly attack by German bombers about thirty miles away, occasionally circling in our vicinity before or after making their bomb run.

That uncomfortable chill of fear accompanied me as I followed my buddy out into total darkness, as usual toting my worldly goods on my shoulders. Up steps and into a waiting British lorry. As each truck filled, it slowly pulled away, the driver

apparently almost feeling his way along curving, narrow roads as his headlights were only tiny slits cut into covers over each light. Now, finally barracks! Open one door, close it, open the next, close it and you are in a large room full of beds. In a few seconds one of the beds was full of me, as it was 3:30 a.m.. Who cares where I was?

Next morning I awoke to see that we were located in low rolling green hills where barracks were widely separated and sprinkled along country lanes, all suitably camouflaged. Meandering through the general area was a section of the Grand Union Canal, built in the eighteenth century to provide a water route for barges carrying goods

Above: *P-51 undergoing refit at the 8th Air Force repair and replacement centre, Warton, Lancashire. (David Mayor)*

Below: *Calisthenics in a field near dispersals at Rackheath. (Allan Healy)*

to and from London and the industrial Midlands. Bordering the canal and a road over it is a pub! How about that, a fine old English pub right on our base. Where are we? Cheddington aerodrome. And where is that? Near the small village of Tring – an intriguing and musical name, that. Is this going to be our operations base? No, just temporarily until the permanent base is completed. Seems that it was necessary to improve the runways and taxiways at Shipdham to support the heavy weight of our fully loaded B-24s, which should arrive in a few weeks.

With nothing but time on our hands and few coins in our pockets, it's back to basics. Reading of Articles of War, rifle drills, gas mask drills, accustomizing ourselves to new olive-drab woollen gas-resistant clothes (special flaps etc. at openings at wrists, front and fly), orientation meetings, and, of course, the last resort, close order drills by the hours. So much of the latter in fact, that shortly many GI boots began to wear out – and there were

no replacements. Then enterprising officers began utilizing bicycles to save their shoe leather while directing us in more close order drills, until too many boots were holey.

The unlikely combination of a pub bordering a canal, inky blackness, a bridge, and shaky American bike riders, resulted in several unintentional swims in the murky water, as well as some cold underwater explorations for submerged bikes.

Diary entry, Will Lundy, 44th BG

'Rackheath' was the name of the park and small village of the estate of Sir Edward Stracey, Bart. His large Georgian house stood in the center of the park at the end of a long drive coming in from the Norwich–Wroxham road. The entranceway to this drive had a beautiful set of gates brought from Paris and called the Golden Gate. Some of his farms, with thatched cottages and open straw stacks, intermingled with the Nissen huts we used, which

Below: *Rackheath airfield with Sir Edward Stracey's estate in the foreground. In the distance are the Norfolk Broads. (MWB)*

were spotted about in clusters under his tall beeches and chestnuts. Other of the farms and their woods and hedgerows had been leveled for our runways. The airbase was completely mingled with farm, field, and spinney. Pheasants crowed near the barrack sites and rabbits came out in the late evenings about the Operations block. It was a lovely spot, even to homesick Americans.

… I went to a big carnival the other night – English version. August 7 was Bankers [sic] Holiday, the same as our Labor Day, and nobody works anyplace. Everybody hops a train for someplace else to have a good time. We're on a big estate here and the main grounds are apparently used as a park for the occasion, and all sorts of stands were set up. They had the usual milk bottles to knock down, lemonade stands marked 'Minerals', and a fortune teller's tent. The prizes were cigarettes instead of cupie dolls or canes, and money games were completely lacking. Everybody in the family was there. Only the usual rides were missing and the barkers in the stands. Everyone makes as little noise as possible and looks bashful if they win something.

Right: '… the Nissen huts we used, were spotted about in clusters under tall beeches and chestnuts.' Allan Healy (Healy)

The house is about the size of the library at home and is of light-yellow stone. Flowering vines climbing the walls make it quite beautiful. Behind the house, and a part of the house, is a big greenhouse with a large grape arbor completely filling an inside framework. The vines must be well over one hundred years old and are beautifully trimmed. To the rear of this is a large orchard and garden with a tennis court, walled courtyard, and three more greenhouses beside a big fishpond. It's very well-kept as is most of the estate, which in all must cover a couple thousand acres, including several small farmhouses, woodlands, and fields. Still living the life of Reilly – or is it Riley? Anyway, it could be worse. Goodnight/R.
Captain Ralph H. Elliott, pilot, 467th BG, Rackheath, in an early letter home to his wife Vonny in which he describes Sir Edward's estate

22

We were based in Norfolk, inland of that great bulge on the east coast of England directly across the North Sea from Holland – the nearest bomber base to Germany and the hostile shore. Norfolk is rolling wheat country and open farms. It is beautifully treed, and cut by the winding rivers and lakes they call the Broads. Norwich is its heart, a sprawling ancient-modern city lying below Mousehold Heath, with the superb spire of its eleventh-century cathedral rising over red roof and flint-cobbled or half-timbered buildings. Norwich gave only a few of the pleasures of a city, but it was a place to go. Every night our first spring there, the barrage balloons would go up encircling the town. These same balloons later helped to make that long barrier from London to Dover set to tumble the V1s. At night the total blackout made getting about difficult, though it made some other things easy and a couple kissing in a doorway was not an unusual sight. We ceased to be tourists early and took the cathedral for granted, though some came to worship there, and a few to be married. The Cow Tower became just a landmark rather than a relic of an older, walled city. Most visited the castle in an early trip, saw its museum and dungeons, and then took it too for granted. The narrow ways and timbered houses of

Elm Hill testified to the antiquity of Norwich but we soon paid little attention to their quaintness and became like old residents.

The 467th Bombardment Group, **Allan Healy**

It was late 1943 and I had been on a three-day pass to London. I was on my way home by train from Liverpool Street Station and we were pulling into Thorpe Station at Norwich. I could see that there had been an air raid on the city and there were emergency vehicles all over the place. The area about the station apparently was a target. It was one of those dark and dreary days so characteristic of East Anglia. I didn't know what to do because there were no buses or trucks back to the base. So I wandered about until I found myself inside Norwich Cathedral. I sat in one of the pews and in came officers of the RAF and others all seeking some peace in the sanctuary. I must have fallen asleep for a long time because when I awoke the noise of the sirens was over, the sky had cleared a little, and everything was back to normal. Outside the cathedral it was peaceful once again. As peaceful as wartime Norwich could be. As I walked outside I saw the familiar line-up of convoy trucks to take us back to the base.

Below: *'While we were pondering the next move, another sweeping left turn brought dim winks below. Many moving, dancing flickers barely visible. Lights? There shouldn't be any here; total blackout has been a way of life in the UK for years. Then someone said, 'We're over Norwich.' Barely over it, however, at 200 feet. Flashlights, carried by pedestrians, were reflecting on wet pavement in the city and resembled countless, darting fireflies. At that moment of realization I became petrified. Norwich Cathedral's spire is jutting up somewhere, 315-feet high. Pull up, get some more altitude fast! Too late. It just flashed by while we watched. All this in a matter of seconds, but I well remember the unique feeling of simultaneous fear and relief.'* Captain Tommy L. Land, 3rd SAD Mobile Repair Group pilot, Yankee Buzz Bomb, *which he flew out of a field near Cromer after it had crash-landed there on 7 October 1944. He flew it to Watton where the B-24 was repaired and returned to service with the 458th BG. (MWB)*

Once, when on a tour of the cathedral area and the castle, an American airman who had had too many pints of ale remarked, 'I wonder what will happen after the war. They'll probably tear it all down,' referring to the historic landmarks of the region. Of course they didn't 'tear it all down' and much of it is still there.

Many years later I returned to Norwich and went to the cathedral. There I wandered about on a nostalgia trip. I met another man, about my age, and we started to talk about World War Two. He said he had been with the RAF and was based near Norwich. He said he used to come to the cathedral after a particularly trying period of combat. My mind immediately went back to the time I had done the same thing.

We were comrades immediately despite the lapse of so many years. The details of that incident came back and I remembered that I went to an Easter service at Norwich Cathedral. It was in 1944, and inspiring despite there being some bomb damage to the cathedral area. This memory has stayed with me after forty years and may have been a bright spot in my wartime experience.

Sanctuary in Bomb Time, Technical Sergeant
Forrest S. Clark

Right: *'Splasher 5 at Cromer was the familiar place of assembly and return. Great Yarmouth and Lowestoft were our front doors on the North Sea. Beachy Head, Dungeness, Orfordness, Spithead, all became the familiar points from which we would depart for the enemy coast.'*
Allan Healy (MWB)

We were impressed by England's state of siege. The wrecked homes and buildings of Norwich showed the ruthless hand of the German bombing that we were about to return a thousand-fold. Every crossroad had its tank barriers and pillboxes ready for use. We saw how grimly the British citizen was prepared to defend his homeland.

The Luftwaffe had about given up bombing when we arrived. But our first days had alerts. We heard the uneven droning of German planes and went out to look. Some few went to the shelters. The searchlights all about us stabbed the sky and we heard the crack of anti-aircraft fire. On the first two raids, shell fragments fell on our base. It was not

long, however, before the tannoy call of 'Enemy aircraft in area', or even 'Enemy aircraft overhead', only caused us to roll over in our sacks. Each felt a tightening of the stomach, nevertheless, and began to think of the reality of warfare. Many of these nights we heard the RAF going out – a loud hum and roar that filled the sky and went on incredibly long...

Splasher 5 at Cromer was the familiar place of assembly and return. Great Yarmouth and Lowestoft were our front doors on the North Sea. Beachy Head, Dungeness, Orfordness, Spithead, all became the familiar points from which we would depart for the enemy coast.

***The 467th Bombardment Group**, Allan Healy*

MY BONNIE LIES OVER THE OCEAN

I lived at Cromer in 1943 and used often to go to the cliffs between Suffield Park and Overstrand to watch the 8th Air Force return from their missions. The afternoon of 26 July was bright with good visibility, the sea relatively calm. I was first aware of this lone aircraft flying towards the coastline at about 200 feet. It seemed doubtful if it would clear the cliffs and the higher ground inland where a number of Fortresses and Liberators came to grief. The aircraft approached the cliffs at a relatively slow air speed but only in the last mile of the flight did I realize that the pilot was going to ditch. The landing gear was up. I was not certain that any props were 'feathered' but am certain No. 4 engine at least was 'milling'. The aircraft continued to approach the beach and I thought it might attempt to land on the beach itself – the tide was in. The pilot held off longer than I anticipated and soon I could see the prop wash churning up the sea as the aircraft skimmed over it. Eventually the tips of the props caught the water and were instantly bent back around the engine nacelles. Although undoubtedly close to stalling, the pilot lifted the nose at the point of impact and the tail struck the water first and then in a shower of spray the B-l7 was on the water.

As the spray cleared, the aircraft was initially still facing the beach although it eventually turned through about thirty degrees to starboard which may have been the influence of the tide. All the upper wing surfaces were above the water and all the crew climbed out on to the starboard wing. The aircraft was close enough to the shore to enable me to witness the crew congratulating the pilot on a very successful ditch with much backslapping and joviality. I was not at any time aware that the pilot or any other crewmembers sustained any injury. One (or possibly two) dinghies had ejected automatically from the stricken Fortress and after some time the crew climbed into one. The aircraft had by this time turned slightly as described but it seemed feasible that it might be towed on to the beach. However when eventually sea water rose above the wing the aircraft sank rapidly and had gone. I had thought that the aircraft should have been visible at low tide but I believe it was never seen again.

The crew slowly made their way ashore all in one dinghy assisted by a small fishing boat. From nowhere some three or four people congregated on the beach to recover the crew. The dinghy was not making much progress and I waded into the water to assist in beaching it. Before we reached the beach the crew asked me what time the pubs opened and where the local girls met. One of the crew gave me some chocolate about one inch thick, which I enjoyed, but I subsequently believe it was a laxative!

The crew milled about on the beach for some while and we enjoyed American cigarettes. Eventually we were joined by some military types and after a further bout of handshaking the crew were transported off.

Russell A. Reeve describing the demise of Fortress *Wee Bonnie* of the 561st BS, 388th BG, which ditched off Cromer on 26 July 1943. All ten of Second Lieutenant Adalbert D. Porter's crew were rescued. This crew was then lost on 9 September 1943.

We were truly on foreign soil, just in time for tea. So tea it was with people who were glad to see us. For the evening meal, they especially baked a cake decorating it with the American flag to properly top off the day. It took several days to get a repair crew over to fix our brakes. This presented a problem in that the plane was equipped with the secret Norden bombsight, which had to be guarded constantly. I assigned two crewmembers to stay with the plane the first night which was not to their liking; however, the succeeding night all of the enlisted men volunteered for this duty. It seems that the English girls on base were eager to meet these new Yanks.

After the evening meal, Fergie and I decided to go to town, which was Manchester. Arriving there, we watched our first bowling on the green. The English take this sport very seriously. They form exclusive clubs, wear special dress, and follow special rules and protocol. It's all very formal, and they make every effort to appear as though they are enjoying themselves. I found this to be true wherever I witnessed a bowling match.

Went to a bar and was introduced to English beer and girls. Ten o'clock soon arrived when the bars had to close and we proceeded back to the base while the sun was still shining. It took a long time to get used to the sun in the northern latitudes

Above: *English bowls*
(via Don and Peggy Garnham)

and the English double summertime clock schedule. Both Fergie and I were proposed to during this first outing. English girls were desperate to go to America.

Repair of the aircraft did take place in due time, and after a week or ten days, we were off. Knowing that this was a training base with very short runways for a B-24, I garnered all the knowledge of my crew and myself for short field takeoff, made all proper preparations, and proceeded to Valley, Wales. Locking the brakes and with strong acceleration, we cleared the runway in the minimum distance. Every crewmember breathed a sigh of relief. Our original destination was routinely reached ten days later. Many of the crews had had their new bomber painted stateside at Mitchell Base with these beautiful Varga or Petty girls. They spent much of their own money and were very disappointed when at Valley they had to relinquish

these ships for assignment, never to see them again. Such is war!

From Valley, we went to Stone for casual processing and on to Loch Neagh, Ireland for Theatre of Operations indoctrination. The briefings and training included navigation, engineering, meteorology, tactics, evasion, and other specifics and odd peculiarities of the area. The Irish countryside and people were much to our liking: friendly, and glad we were there to help them out. A family troupe of actors performed in a barn with a bar each evening much to our liking. The family members played all different parts in these hero and villain episodes. Good warm Irish beer, a play or two, a little fraternization with locals, and it was time to go back to base while the sun was still high in the sky. Never did get used to that.

Country Boy – Combat Bomber Pilot,
Robert H. Tays

Shortly after I arrived in England I wrote my aunt advising that I was in a nice place and being treated well. So far as I know it is the only letter from me to survive the war. I said, 'Haven't been in action yet. Hope to start soon. It'll be a big show when we get started.' This was putting a brave face on things. The truth is I didn't hope to start soon. I hoped to start never! I would rather have been anywhere than where I was. I cursed myself for letting my pride get me into such a fix, but I had come too far to back down now.

We were in one of the better groups. Molesworth was one of the original four pioneer groups in the Eighth. The accommodations were far better than on many bases. We lived in permanent stucco barracks that had been built by the RAF before Molesworth became an American station. The group had a fine combat record, excellent leadership, and fairly good morale. There was no despair or sloth. The crews were well-trained and high-calibre individuals for the most part. Most of the flight personnel had high IQs and each man was a specialist. All were graduates of flight schools or one of the Air Corps Technical schools, and the standards were high for both. The ground crews were superb with an *esprit de corps* as great or greater than the flight crews.

... Finally it was our turn. We did not fly to our base; we took the train from Bovingdon to a station near Molesworth and were ignominiously carried there in trucks. When we came to our squadron area, we were not greeted by the familiar, 'You'll be sorry,' the customary greeting stateside. The men we saw gave us only a few incurious glances and said nothing to us. Our hearts sank. We were assigned a barracks shared by two or three other crews. Six empty cots gaped at us. These had been occupied by a crew that had not returned from the mission the day before. We were not prepared for this sobering reality.

In progress was a non-stop poker game. The players did not look up or acknowledge our presence in any way. We were accorded a few glum nods from some others who were lying in their sacks reading. About that time the door flew open, and a bevy of uproarious drunks fell inside. It was the lead crew – Captain Brinkley's crew. I had seen many drunks, but this was a different kind of drunkenness. These men were veterans of the great missions of Schweinfurt and Oschersleben. They had seen too much, and it showed. I had the sudden feeling that things were far different from what I had been led to believe. I was right ...

We were not referred to as Lieutenant Cecchini's crew. Instead, we were called the 'new crew,' which continued to be our status until we had flown about eight combat missions. New crews were given the most vulnerable places in the formation and had a way of disappearing after a few missions. We heartily resented this callous treatment; but, after winning our spurs, we were as bad as the rest ...

Chick's Crew, Ben C. Smith

CHUMS WHO GAVE US GUM

There was a faint drumming in the air, a far-off buzzing and we knew they were coming. When the Yanks arrived us youngsters stood open-mouthed as these huge aircraft filled the skies overhead. The noise was tremendous; it was very daunting and quite an awesome sight. We hopped on our bikes and rode off following them to the airfield, to their dispersal point. The end of the aircraft opened as it landed and these crewmen threw out chewing gum and candies for us. They had heard these terrible stories that the English were starving and on rations, we didn't mind playing on it a little bit. Then they threw out a bundle of ten-shilling notes and there was a right free for all.

Eleven-year-old Jim Matsell experiencing the arrival, at Deopham Green, of the 452nd BG. Later his mother did washing for the group and Jim would collect it on his bicycle.

I remember the Americans cycling through Wacton to the Tibenham base, and me, then a cheeky schoolgirl, asking 'Any gum, chum?'

I was so pleased to receive some. Ration books allowed us four ounces of sweets per week. If you ate them the same day you had to wait a week for the coupons to be valid, so a piece of free gum was quite a treat. Another memory was watching Liberators going up in the mornings on missions. With pencil and paper I would make a list of each one. Then, watching them return home in the evenings, sadly not all were ticked off my list to return. The best memory was being collected in army lorries at the school and then being taken to the most wonderful parties at Tibenham given by the Americans. They had hearts of gold to entertain what must have been hundreds of kids. We were shown kindness, which meant a lot during wartime. Sweets were put in every pocket; there were parcels, gifts, film shows and Santa. It was wonderful.

Beryl M. Sutton

The boy stood on the corner of the street. The day was cold and bleak and the winter wind was blowing. He was waiting patiently for his friend to come. What to do he had no idea. They could stay indoors, but they had read their comics; they wanted some chocolate, but their pocket money had been spent. The boy's friend eventually arrived and after a few minutes they decided to go on their bicycles to the US airfield at Thurleigh, the home of the 306th BG, where the Yanks were. Maybe they would find Francis. He was a GI who used to come to the boy's house. When Francis came it was just like Christmas. He brought peaches and other goodies and sometimes a fruit cake that one of the cooks used to bake or a tin of Spam. Maybe if they could find him he'd have some chocolate, but if not they could watch the bombers go out or come back.

'Damn the war,' the boy said. 'Why did it have to happen?' He had heard Francis telling his parents awful things about the war, so again he said, 'Damn the war.'

Where did all these men come from? How did all those juts and those bombers get there they thought, as they propped their bikes up against the fence. A truck was coming towards them so they shouted, 'Got any gum, chum? Hello Yanks. Got any Hershey bars or gum?'

'Here, catch kids,' shouted the GIs and threw them some.

'Bet those Yanks are going to drop bombs on Germany,' the boy said, and they sat watching the war go on behind that fence in the heart of England.

Where would they be when they grew up? Would they be soldiers or would they fly one of those planes? Maybe, they would grow up and get married. They were just one boy and his friend with their bikes, caught up in the humdrum of war, having to put up with it and not knowing where their lives would take them in the years to come. At about the same time, two schoolgirls were also planning their lives one day in a school playground in Milton Ernest. 'Wish we were old enough to marry one of those Yanks,' said one.

Again two kids in the heart of Britain with the GIs not far away. One of the girls used to get some chewing gum by going home from school and boiling two eggs hard and taking them down to two Military Policemen on the gate at 8th Air Force HQ, Milton Ernest Hall.

After school that day they just watched as two or three staff cars came out of the drive of the Hall. One contained the Andrew Sisters. They recognized them because they had seen them in a movie the other day. In another car was Glenn Miller. He was a dance bandleader. They talked to the MPs as they ate their hard-boiled eggs and it must have seemed like *Breakfast at Tiffany's* to eat real eggs. One of the

Above: *Cycle race at Wendling. (Joe Micksch via Ben Jones)*

Right: *Start of cycle race at Wendling. (Joe Micksch via Ben Jones)*

little girls asked about America. Was it wonderful? If they went there could they become film stars? She would be glad when the war was over so she too could get on with her life. It seemed so unfair.

Memories Are Made of This, Connie Richards. Those two 'kids' are now Connie and Gordon Richards.

'I arrived at Midland Road Railway Station in Bedford with a tin hat and a pack on my back. When I first set eyes on the premises I just didn't know where to start! The first time I ran up the Stars and Stripes, two elderly bobbies, much too old for fighting, rushed over and told me in no uncertain terms, 'Well, you had just better take that thing down again, madam. You haven't bloody well conquered us that fast!' I guess it was just that old British sense of humour.'

Anona Moeser, American Red Cross. In premises at Bromham Road, Bedford, she established the first American Red Cross club in England, which became part of the 'morale and recreation' programme for the young, homesick Yanks. Anona recruited local women to help her clean the dilapidated premises and once furnished, she advertised in the *Bedfordshire Times* for 'dancing girls' to visit the premises to partner 'her boys'. Bedford's mayor, Alderman Canvin, who was convinced that the GIs came to England only to dance and woo the women, severely criticized Anona for her bad taste in trying to encourage 'women of ill-repute' into the club. It was only after Lady Michael Bowes-Lyon, who was part of the volunteer kitchen-crew at the club, told her sister-in-law, the Queen, about all the fuss, that her Majesty herself paid the questionable club a visit and decided that the dancing-girl request was well justified.

Above: *Anona Moeser, American Red Cross, in premises at Bromham Road, Bedford. (via Richards)*

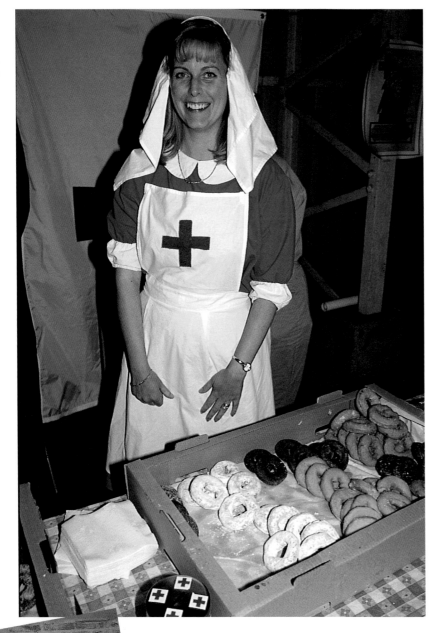

Above: *'At the Red Cross building we had a place one could relax, get coffee and doughnuts and keep extra clothing or supplies. The Red Cross girls were always friendly and cheerful. I can't say enough for the efforts of the Red Cross …' John McClane (MWB)*

'My first mission – holding out the cup of coffee and trying to smile. I was so scared you wouldn't want to smile back. I remember straining to see through the clouds, counting. Then trying not to let anyone see me wipe away a tear when the last one appeared.'

Mary Carroll Leeds, American Red Cross girl, Attlebridge, June 1944 to May 1945

Above: *Red cross at Thorpe Abbotts in the early 1980s. (MWB)*

The Clubmobile was run by the American Red Cross. It was a converted London Transport single-decker bus. The driver was English, and it was manned by two American girls. Its role was to visit the American Air Force bases and supply doughnuts, coffee, candy and cigarettes to the personnel on the bases – free of charge, I might add. My connection with the Clubmobile was that one of these buses was based at Harleston where I was living during the war. I had a job on this after school hours. The job was to clean out the coffee urns and make the doughnuts so they would be ready for the next day's trip. Everything was contained in the bus for making and storing the doughnuts. There were coffee-making machines; the coffee was of the instant variety and was made on the bases as required. The milk was evaporated and tinned. This was easier than fresh milk. Since sugar was rationed, it was something else to see all the sugar that was used to 'dunk' the doughnuts. It took about three hours to make the doughnuts (hundreds of them) and clean up. All the doughnuts had to be put on racks and stored in built-in cupboards. The destination boards at the front and rear of the bus were made into speakers. Music was broadcast from these and played from a record player inside the bus. A small lounge was situated at the rear of the bus, which was used by the two ladies while traveling to and from the bases. The bus was stationed in the car park at the rear of the Swan Hotel in Harleston. The driver and the two young ladies lived in the hotel itself. The driver stayed with the bus, but the two young ladies were changed to other duties after about six months. Two of us boys were employed to do the above duties and were paid seven shillings (35p) a week. This was a lot of money in those days for schoolboys of 13–14 years of age. Not only that, but we could eat as many doughnuts as we wanted.

An added bonus for me, being mad on aircraft, was that on the weekends we could travel around the bases. Here was a chance to talk to my schoolboy heroes. I could get close to the aircraft: B-24s, B-17s, P-47s, P-51s and various other visiting aircraft and the odd British plane that had dropped in overnight, either damaged or low on

fuel returning from the previous night's raids. I don't think the general public knew a lot about Clubmobiles. Of all the books I have read about the American Air Force, very few even mention them, and even less show photos of them. Yet, to the GI, they were as popular as the NAAFI to the RAF. Today I don't think I can eat as many doughnuts as I could in those far-off days, but I still retain my liking for them.

Dick Wickham

Above and Right: *The long lunch tables, set for crowds of children, were decorated with foil-wrapped chocolate bars laid end to end down the centre. A GI scooped some up and put them in my lap. We were served with turkey and cranberry sauce ("They put jam on their meat," I told my mother that night). Then there was pumpkin pie – a marvellous new taste.'
Norwich girl, Ann K. Spredbury (via Pat Everson)*

'After the drab colours of the camouflaged RAF bombers, the Liberators with their different colours seemed fantastic to us. Being at a school that took boys from all over the city, we had quite an intelligence service. Hardly a plane took off, or crashed, without us knowing about it. If we knew they'd set off on a mission from St Faith's in the morning, we wouldn't go home after school. We'd cycle straight to the base to watch them come back. We were old enough to know what was going on, but not old enough to have to worry about it. It was all excitement as far as we were concerned.'

Tony North, Norwich schoolboy

'As a boy of eleven I walked the two miles from home to the runway, creeping through the hedges and climbing into one of the aircraft. I didn't like the olive-green ones, so I picked a silver bomber. I got in through the open bomb bays. The smell was incredible. I didn't know then that it was from the aviation fuel and cordite. All I could see were what I thought were bombs, but were actually oxygen bottles and I took it into my head that it was going to blow up, so I got out as fast as I could and ran. Later, that plane took off on a mission and never

came back. Only much later, did I find out that she crashed at a farm near Sidestrand, killing all ten on board.'

Fred Squires, Norfolk schoolboy. The Liberator was *Shoot, Fritz, You've Had It* of the 566th BS, 389th BG, which crashed and exploded at Northrepps, Norfolk, during assembly on D-Day 6 June 1944. The tail landed at Pond Farm, Sidestrand. Lieutenant Marcus V. Cowlney and all ten crew were killed.

'You people were brave and so very hospitable to us "Yanks".'

Al Steller, 709th BS, 447th BG

'Those boys used to come to our house at any time. They knew where my mother left her spare key and would let themselves into the house knowing that my parents would never mind. They called No.79 their Norwich home. I had a lovely twenty-first birthday party at home, which wouldn't have been possible without the little luxuries they sneaked from their bases.'

Muriel Lawrence

'Most prominent in my memories of your courageous people – your great aircrews, and their supports, your ATS, WLA and so many who inspired this Yank – is the family of Mr Tom Betts of Mergate Hall Farm near Hethel, who adopted me and in spite of my American strangeness, treated me as one of their own. And since I worked a night schedule on base I became a part-time daytime farmer, as the Betts' place was only five minutes' bike ride away. Although awkward at farm chores, believe me, I did try to earn my keep.'

Martin H. Schreck

'I had never seen an orange before and didn't know what to make of it.'
George Evans, on receiving an orange from WAAC Mary Frances Elder at Ketteringham Hall

The English people are amazing. They have been at war – total war – for two years. They all seem to be doing their part to keep the Germans away from their homeland. The youths are in the services if possible or in military production of some sort. With the men gone, many of the women are taking their place in the factories, fields, home guard, anywhere. They have had little food due to severe rationing, no autos, air raids and or alerts every night and some daytime, too. But never do I hear them complain. Cheerfulness and good humor is what I find. In my wandering on the buses, I have been approached many times by people who sincerely welcome me and thank me for the sacrifices that I was making for them. Truly heart-warming. I feel great compassion for them all, and indeed, feel happy to be serving on their side.

All Americans associate England with fog and rain, but so far we have had reasonably good weather. But of course, this is only September. What has impressed me most is the apparent timelessness of everything. The buildings appear to have been there forever, just like the hills and roads. The stone streets, curbs, narrow sidewalks, and buildings, shout age and history. 'We've been here for centuries and will be for many more.' The streets and lanes have been utilized for centuries and appear to have been made out of necessity, rather than having been pre-planned. Only those roads of Roman origin were designed for military use; leading from one defensive point to another, as straight as terrain permits. It seems the haphazard growth lent itself to the charm, character and beauty of the country.

To better acquaint us with our allied planes, the RAF brought in a few of their planes for us to see close up. The Spitfire is a splendid fighter, very pretty in flight and maneuverable. I even enjoyed the sound of her engine. The Halifax appears old,

'We would meet the local people in the pub and there were ladies who would do our laundry, and everyone was just as gracious as could be.'
Wilbur Clingan, 453rd BG Operations Officer, Old Buckenham

You can imagine the impact it had, around 3,000 men arriving in our small village, all with film-star accents and many with suntans. I am only glad I was a small child at the time! Our narrow roads were busy with convoys of supplies and there were many young and so-friendly Yanks who stopped to ask the way. They were very good to the children and we were invited to the camp on special occasions for a party. I can still picture what it was like when the trucks drew up to the school and lifted me over the tail-lift and into the truck. That was Thanksgiving, 1943. There were eighty-five children and two evacuees in the school at the time.

Pat Everson, a ten-year-old Norfolk schoolgirl at Seething and Mundham County Primary School when the 448th BG arrived at Seething airfield.

'Once we landed at RAF Ford in southern England, and as we got out of the aircraft a load of English WAAFs came up and said they would take us to the base service club. We were a mix of officers and non-coms but that made no difference. At the base club they had the best scotch whiskey I ever tasted and we had a good old time until the plane was serviced and ready.'

Technical Sergeant Forrest S. Clark, air gunner, 67th BS, 44th BG

boxy and slow. Her .30 caliber machine-guns seemed small and ineffective, but then it is a night bomber whose biggest danger is flak. I did like the machine-gun ammunition supply system, which had long continuous racks giving automatic feeding to all guns. The four-engine Lancaster bomber has a very thick wing that should provide tremendous lift. Maybe it appeared so thick when compared with our own Davis winged Liberator.

They gave us a flying exhibition, with the Lancaster being the most impressive in my estimation. They 'feathered' one outside engine and then proceeded to bank into the dead engine – always a no-no in my experience. No problem. Then they feathered both engines on one side and still flew and maneuvered with ease. Very impressive, but I still believe we have the better aircraft. All we need is a chance to prove it.

Diary entries, Will Lundy, 44th BG

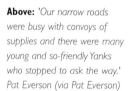

Above: *'Our narrow roads were busy with convoys of supplies and there were many young and so-friendly Yanks who stopped to ask the way.'*
Pat Everson (via Pat Everson)

Right: *A GI and his new friends, in Manchester. (Pat Ramm)*

The US chaplain from Horsham St Faith brought a group of incredibly handsome young men to sing at Silver Road Baptist Church. I still remember the face of the one who sang the solo, 'The Old Rugged Cross'. After the service, we had a cup of tea with the airmen and I learned one was called Spam. Because I didn't understand his accent, I never found out why! But Chappie told my mother, a young widow then, that he would arrange for me and my sister to spend Christmas Day at the airbase, while she relaxed at a friend's house. It was a very cold morning when the jeep arrived, and the ice crunched under our feet. How smart Chappie's uniform seemed, with its brilliant badges and bars. He took us to his office on camp and let us play

with the typewriter and the kittens which slept in a box under his desk. Later, we saw a Disney film and walked along endless corridors of glittering Christmas cards and lifesaver sweets that hung as trimmings over our heads. Chappie cut strings of them down to give to us. The long lunch tables, set for crowds of children, were decorated with foil-wrapped chocolate bars laid end to end down the centre. A GI scooped some up and put them in my lap. We were served with turkey and cranberry sauce ('They put jam on their meat,' I told my mother that night). Then there was pumpkin pie – a marvellous new taste.

Ann K. Spredbury,
Norwich girl

Above: *'We were a little suspicious of them at first, but they seemed to take to children ... they gave me a set of sergeant's stripes, (which I wore on the arm of my raincoat) and a flying helmet ...' Pat Ramm, Old Buckenham schoolboy. Pat is the boy in the middle of this photograph displaying his sergeant's stripes. The group of schoolchildren are listening to two 453rd crewmen recounting their mission experiences at Old Buckenham in 1944. (USAF)*

'YOU CAN'T MISS IT'

'Straight ahead, you can't miss it' ... this simple direction, when given in the British Isles, is easy to follow once you learn how to translate it. When received, take a coin from your pocket, any coin, and flip it. Heads, turn right; tails, turn left; if the coin stands on edge, go straight ahead.

You'll soon learn, however, that you can never go straight ahead in Britain. Streets aren't made that way. Matter of fact they always show every indication of a bend, something like an outside curve in a world-series baseball game. Streets in England are about as straight as Hitler's intuition.

When you come to the inevitable fork, turn right or left, you'll find it really makes little difference in the long run. Then ask the next pedestrian for further directions. If he says, 'Take the second turning to your left, then first right and second left, round the roundabout,' thank him politely and proceed as directed.

You'll soon find a wee doubt creeping across your mind, so inquire once more. If this pedestrian tells you to 'Go straight ahead to the bottom, turn right, then left at the first turning,' keep right on following directions; but also keep your fingers crossed, for you'll soon discover there is no bottom, there is no top, there is no hill, only a T ending; so at this point you can either go right or left.

We embarked by lighter to the dock in Scotland where we were put on the train about 1530. The engines vary in size from little playthings to big ones about three-quarters the size of ours. The English coaches are built much the same as ours except that the steps are about four feet high and all the stations have raised platforms. The undercarriage is light with four wheels at each end and very light springs as well as wheels. The insides of the coaches aren't unlike ours but are narrower and can be cut in two by a door in the middle. Capacity: forty-eight men. Some coaches we saw were divided into separate compartments with access only from the outside. Certain ones were designated as 'smoking' or 'non-smoking'. The freight cars are a different story. They're only about one-fourth the size of ours – twelve feet long and four feet high – and remind me of little mining cars except for their high carriage and springs. They have very small capacity, and the trains don't seem very long although some of the engines are fairly large. The boxcars are round-roofed and look like a portable hog-house with straight sides – a crude analogy but an apt one.

It got dark soon after we loaded on the train and we experienced our first blackout conditions in England. Since we had to pull all the curtains and the windows were closed, the coaches got pretty smoky and stale. A large percentage of the men smoked and we didn't think much about it – and couldn't have done anything about it if we had. Non-smoking sections were unheard of. I didn't smoke, but I always brought my cigarette rations since they made good trading material for candy bars, especially toward the end of the ration period when the smokers were getting low on tobacco. We didn't get fed that evening but had Cracker Jack boxes of 'K' rations to eat on the train which contained canned ham and cheese, crackers, hard candy, and a small pack of about five cigarettes – usually Camels or Lucky Strike. The later 'C' rations were an improvement, but not by much, and to this day I can't eat Spam. It was a pretty uncomfortable ride and it must have been nearly daylight by the time we got to bed.

We found the English customs strange and not particularly to our liking. Add to that a 'strange' language and the makings of friction were there, as later incidents confirmed.

Captain Ralph H. Elliott, pilot, 467th BG

Experience has taught most GIs at this point to use the old system of Einey-Meany-Mieny-Moe, and to move right or left, whichever way it comes out. The law of average helps a little, and you stand a good chance of being right fifty percent of the time.

If you're wrong, ask again, and if the helpful British citizen tells you to 'Go straight ahead, you can't miss it,' then you'll know you're back where you started from. At this point we advise you to call a taxi.

***Stars and Stripes,* newspaper for US servicemen**

Left: *British ATC (Air Training Corps) cadets and a ground mechanic at Snetterton Heath, 1944. (via Pat Everson)*

'I had just arrived in England and was unused to the blackout. The sun was shining when I left the base and walked into Norwich to visit the Lido ballroom. When I left it was pitch black and I did not know the way back to my base at Horsham St Faith. I asked someone the way and he said:

"Just keep walking straight up the road outside. You cawn't miss it."

I did as he said, one foot on the pavement and one in the gutter up the street in the dark. I hadn't gone more than a hundred yards when I walked into a lamppost and knocked myself out.'

458th BG ground crewman at Horsham St Faith, near Norwich

We all know the name of Lindbergh,
and we've read of his flight to fame ...
But think, if you can, of his maintenance man,
can you remember his name?
And think of our wartime heroes,
Billy Bishop, Buck McNair and Hampton Gray ...
Can you tell me the names of their crew chiefs?
A thousand to one – you can't say ...

Now pilots are highly trained people,
and wings are not easily won ...
But without the work of the maintenance man
our pilots would march with a gun ...
So when you see mighty aircraft
as they mark their way through the air ...
The grease-stained man with the wrench in his hand
is the man who put them there.

'Remembering the Forgotten Mechanic', Anonymous

I was an airplane engine mechanic for B-17s, but our crew did everything: engine changes, fixed gun turrets, installed armor plate, even changed damaged skin. We took care of planes that needed more extensive work than they could do at Bomb Group airfields. For example, there was a period of time when the B-17s were having trouble getting the landing gear down. They were coming in on their bellies, one after another. I also did modifications to

the life rafts; the hatches wouldn't open.

When a pilot came to pick up his aircraft, he wouldn't go up with it unless I came along on a test flight. That was his insurance policy. Many times I was up there with my fingers crossed, after having worked all night to change a bullet-riddled engine and all that came with it.

Harold Belkin, 5th Service Air Depot at Little Staughton

'Major Saltsman returned with two bullet holes. One went through the tailwheel so he landed with a flat tyre. Also, the navigator was hit and lost quite a bit of blood. The sight of this turned the stomachs of the other crewmembers, but as I was raised on a farm where we did our own butchering, this never bothered me. Consequently, for the rest of the war it was always my job to clean out the ship whenever we had wounded on board.'

94th BG ground crewman

I knew most of the 332nd Squadron ground crews. I lived at the railway level crossing only a stone's throw away. I was twelve years old when they first arrived. I visited the airfield most days for two-and-a-half years. I did their shopping for things they wanted from Bury St Edmunds. My mother was a seamstress and she did alterations on their uniforms. We had a lot of chickens and they were always glad to get fresh eggs. After a few months, a lot of the guys moved out of the billets and made their own accommodations. I went to see them sometimes when they were working on the B-17s and they allowed me to go inside the planes on occasion. I remember well that I was not to touch the two red destruction switches up near the windscreen or the landing-gear switch. I travelled the line almost as I liked but quite often the MPs would chase me off. I thought they had caught me one day. I was sitting in the cockpit of *Brennan's Circus* when an MP drove up in his jeep right under the nose. I was very still and they did not see me. I had many such close calls.

Cliff Hall, Suffolk schoolboy who lived at Culford, near the 94th BG base at Bury St Edmunds (Rougham). *Brennan's Circus* was ditched in the North Sea returning from Munster on 14 October 1943. Lieutenant Joseph X. Brennan and all ten crew were rescued.

l.s.d.

'British money is pounds, shillings and pence. The British are used to this system and they like it, and all your arguments that the American decimal system is better won't convince them. They won't be pleased to hear you call it 'funny money', either. They sweat hard to get it (wages are much lower in Britain than America) and they won't think you smart or funny for mocking at it.'

A Short Guide To Great Britain, War and Navy Departments Washington, DC, issued to every GI arriving in Britain in 1942

It's always a problem for servicemen. In the first place a private like myself with ten months' service got a gross monthly pay of $30.00, and considerably less with insurance deducts, etc. Secondly, English money is chaos! 4 dollars to the pound conversion, then 20 shillings to the pound. So about 20 cents to a shilling, 50 cents to a half-crown. However, beyond that, I couldn't understand the language. 2 and 6? Two and six what? Threp 'n bit? Hay penny? Florin? It might as well have been a foreign language. The answer for me was to dig down in my pocket and drag out my total fortune of coins. Then I'd hold it out for examination and selection for the payment of my purchase. I let them have their pick, hoping I had enough, and thanking heaven for the completely honest English.

Will Lundy, 44th BG

My Darling Wife:
… a few of the impressions I've had of England… The money system is our first obstacle and, while we'd tried to work it out ahead of time, it's different when you come to use it. All the things we buy, even at the P.X., require English money and we're even paid that way. To outline it briefly as to coins: a half penny or a ha'pny equals 1 cent. 1 penny = 2 cents. Three'pence, or thru'p'ney bit = 5 cents. The penny is about the size of a 50 cent piece but copper. Sixpence, 10 cents, a shilling or a 'bob' = 20 cents, and a florin, or 2 shilling piece = 40 cents. A half a crown is 50 cents and is called half a dollar, half a crown, or two and six, meaning 2 shillings and sixpence. There are other coins but they aren't common. As for bills, the main one is the one pound note worth $4.035 at the present exchange rate. The only catch is that the pound note is about one-fourth again as wide as a dollar bill and won't fit in our billfolds. They also use a 10-shilling note ($2.00), the same size as our bills. The biggest bill is the 5-pound note worth $20.16. It's really not so bad and we're getting the hang of it.

The towns remind me of nothing I've ever seen. They seem to be made up entirely of two-storey brick apartment houses from 1 to 5 blocks long and in rows back-to-back. No houses are of wood and in the city few stand singly. When looking over the top of them, all one sees is a sea of chimneys. I've counted twelve to a single apartment building, each one of which has up to five separate pipes or flues sticking out the top. I can see now why they have chimney sweeps. With all those flues and everybody burning soft coal it must be a profitable business.

The country is quite beautiful and green. The land is rolling and pastures and woodlands are extensive. The soil is yellow to brown and black with a brown loam predominating. The streams suggest good fishing although I suppose dodging the game wardens might present problems. One almost forgets this isn't a pleasure trip except when it comes time for blackout or something like that. Miss you … Goodnight, R'

… The countryside is quite beautiful with the leaves all turning color. We saw several holly trees with their bright red berries, but on the way home couldn't find the patch we'd seen so didn't bring any home. The leaves are bright green and with the red berries make an unusual picture. We stopped in town and got some apples and a sack of chestnuts, so this afternoon we've been sitting around listening to the radio and roasting the nuts... The insides are white and when roasted are about like the inside of a baked potato ... taste like baked sweet potato ... I've been chopping wood this afternoon – just to try out my new ax and also to get a little exercise. I think I'll go over and take a shower after I finish this – won't know how to get along when I can take a shower without going two blocks. The Limeys are doing better on the hot water lately, and we've been having hot water to shave with. Believe it or not, long woollies are a necessity over here to keep from freezing – don't mind them after I get used to wearing them. It stays dark till 0800 and cold too, getting dark again at 1700. It almost snowed this afternoon … The English are at least twenty-five years behind in home conveniences, plumbing, and most everything else, and this base isn't even up to that – which isn't out of the ordinary for the army. The stove we have isn't worth a thrup'ney bit for heating purposes …

Captain Ralph H. Elliott, pilot, 467th BG, letters home to his wife Vonny (Yvonne)

The formations let down into the darkening east. He leaned forward waiting for England.

England. He said it in his mind, and then slow in his mouth, without moving his lips.

When he was eight years old he read Robin Hood the first time. And after that he must have read it twenty more times. Sherwood Forest and Nottingham town, in the days of Richard the Lion-Heart. He'd dreamed of it then, waiting for the day when he would stand at the rail of a ship watching for England to come out of the sea, out of the haze.

Almost like now.

But it wasn't the same. Because now, for a little while, England was home, more home than Colorado, more home than the house on York Street could ever be.

It slipped in gently, as always, clean and friendly and far off. That would be Land's End, Cornwall, and Devon. The names rang. He could sit with a map and say the names out loud, and never get tired of the sound of them. Torquay and Nutts Corner, and Coventry and Charing Cross.

The Fortresses hit the coast at 6,000 feet. A flight of Spitfires was playing in the clouds at three o'clock low.

A guy named Mitchell lay on a cliff above the sea and watched the gulls and dreamed the Spitfire. And a guy named Leslie Howard, who was Mitchell for a couple of hours' worth of movie, crashed back there somewhere, coming home from Lisbon, probably leaning forward, watching for England to show through the haze.

Strange how any land could be so many shades of green, with the lazy netting of the lanes that wandered everywhere to nowhere.

Looking down there, War was just a word without meaning. It looked so peacefully lovely, yet the people who lived there had fought since the beginning of time, since long before the Romans. And they were still fighting.

He flew his turn for a while, taking it easy, not trying to squeeze the lead ship any. He was glad when the pilot took over again. It was better just to look.

He tried to remember it as it must have been once long before William the Conqueror, when King Lear was wandering mad on the heath. He couldn't bring it though. He couldn't believe it had ever been wild. Everything looked permanent, steady 'til the end of time.

Nissen huts, barracks, gun emplacements, airfields, Public houses, crossroads, bomb dumps, more airfields.

He was so tired of sitting he wanted to bail out. Yet he would have liked to fly on for hours, up to the lands of the Scotsmen. Stornaway, Inverness and the Isle of Skye.

Two Lancasters were landing on an east–west runway. A flight of P-51s came over the top from nine o'clock.

Night was slipping over the world from the east, but there was still day back at six o'clock.

Though it was not his land, and though he had only lived there a little while, he thought he knew why these quiet Englishmen raised so much hell with anyone who tried to take over.

He was tired; saggy tired, starting at the knees on up to the eyes. But he felt good, just so glad to be there, there were no words to tell it, not as good as after Berlin or Munich, but almost.

It was almost dark then, and the stars were coming through.

'This Is England', Bert Stiles, 1944 London paper clipping. Stiles was co-pilot on First Lieutenant Samuel Newton's crew, then Second Lieutenant John W. Green's in the 401st BS, 91st BG at Bassingbourn. While he was flying a 35-mission tour, 19 April–20 July 1944, Stiles wrote the classic, *Serenade to the Big Bird*.

Above: *Pin-up at Thurleigh. (MWB)*

Overpaid, Oversexed and Over Here

'During the war the music hall joke was that "Yanks" were "overpaid, oversexed and over here".
I'm still here and I'm overpaid ... two out of three ain't bad.'

Anglophile Lieutenant Colonel James A. 'Goody' Goodson

Dear old England's not the same,
We dreaded invasion, well it came,
But it's not the beastly Hun,
The G.D. Yankee Army's come.
We see them in the train and bus,
There isn't any room for us,
We walk and let them have our seats,
Then get run over by their jeeps.

'The GIs', by a WAAF at Shipdham

Above: *'I remember the Americans arriving in this country. They came in no uncertain fashion, with their jeeps, their superior uniforms, their big mouths, their big hearts. Here they were, in Suffolk.' George Greengrass (MWB)*

We got as far as Luton-Dunstable, our first stopover in the UK. This was a small rural market-town area in the Midlands not too familiar with GIs, much less airmen. The first place we went was to a pub in the middle of the town. This was a very popular pub with the locals and they had not seen many Americans before. A group of us enlisted men and officers crowded up to the bar. We had been there only a short time when someone suggested a party and asked the barkeep what the entire stock of liquor and beer in the pub was worth. Taken quite aback by this request, the barkeep went behind the bar and into the back office to talk to the owners.

Left: 'It seemed to me that our enlisted men could not hold onto money from one payday to the next. I gathered from what I heard that within a few days of being paid, all their money was lost in crap games or gambling of some sort. I often would loan them just enough money to get the necessities they needed from the PX; anything more would soon be gone.' 1/Lt. John W. McClane, navigator, 44th BG (Bill Cameron Coll)

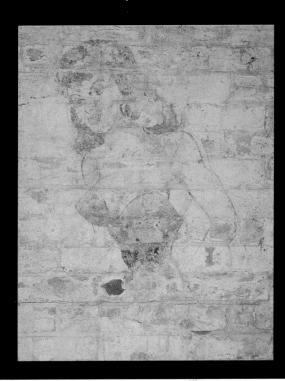

Right: Pin-up at Mendlesham in March 1973. (Steve Gotts)

She came back in a matter of minutes with the owner in tow. The owner was as much surprised as she was and asked us why we had made this request. We said we had just that day arrived in Merry Old England from the United States and were heading for combat duty.

We wanted to have a party and in order to do so we needed a goodly supply of hard spirits. The pub owner got out his pencil and paper and figured out that the liquor and spirits in the pub were worth so much. He handed a piece of paper to one of the officers. The officer looked at it and immediately dug into his pockets and took off his hat and passed it around to the others in our group. We all put something in the hat and lucky for us it was all in English pounds.

'That'll do it lads,' said the pub owner as he counted out the money on the bar. 'The place is yours for the party', he added. For the rest of that day and well into the night we had one huge party staying in the pub until closing time. I remember that there was a hedgerow outside not far away from the pub and by closing time there was an American airman and an English girl spaced about every five or ten feet behind that hedgerow. Some of the airmen had passed out from too much scotch

whiskey. There was considerable lovemaking.

I ran to catch the tailboard of the last convoy truck out of town back to the base and just managed to grab it in the darkness of the blackout. We left the next day for the base at Shipdham and I never saw that town or that pub again but I always remember that party. It was a memorable way to be welcomed in England for an American airman about to encounter the hazards of flying missions.

**Technical Sergeant Forrest S. Clark, air gunner,
67th BS, 44th BG**

'If the weather was bad or our group was stood down, a lot of cards were played in the officers' club: bridge, poker and a game I never learned, called 'Red Dog'. The stakes must have been high, for both our bombardier, Jerry, and navigator, John, approached me for loans about the middle of each month because they had lost all their money playing 'Red Dog'. I saw crap games being played in a barracks when there were literally hundreds of pounds awaiting the outcome of the roll of the dice.'
**Robert L. Miller, pilot, *Son Of A Blitz*,
863rd BS, 493rd BG**

Above: *'Buxom Beauty' – inspired by the September 1944 Varga calendar girl – on a wall of the hospital block at Kimbolton in the late 1980s. (Bill Espie)*

One of the most dangerous activities while stationed at Shipdham had nothing to do with flying combat missions. This perilous event was forced upon us by necessity to catch a ride to town. Transportation was courtesy of a 22-ton GI truck and drivers with nerves of steel. The vehicle had a Wild West covered-wagon tarpaulin stretched over hoops. There were canvas end flaps that secreted what little view there was from the hapless passengers … The fifteen-mile ride seemed like an eternity. I wanted to get on my knees and pray for deliverance but there was not room. All an airman could do was close his eyes and hope for the best. Somehow or other we always managed to arrive safely, even if our nerves were in a state of shock. Jumping off the tailgate was like being born again … The pleasures of leave in town were always overshadowed by the thought in the back of our minds that we had to get back to base via the same means …

First Lieutenant John W. McClane, navigator, 44th BG

A liberty run of trucks went in to Norwich every night, parked at the Cattle Market, and brought home those who had visited the flicks, the Norwich pubs, or their girls. The Red Cross clubs in Norwich were excellent, the Maddermarket players gave good theater, the Lido, Blackfriars, or Samson and Hercules had dances. We fell easily into English ways, or at least, we got about on the wrong side of streets and with the odd money, and suffered not too much with pubs for drugstores. You almost got used to British accents but you kept your own. In fact we bent English ways to ours and had the girls talking American slang and dancing jitterbug ways.

The 467th Bombardment Group, Allan Healy

Above: *Liberty Run! (Rackheath Memories)*

On Saturday 6 November 1943, a liberty run of eight 6 x 6 trucks left 3rd SAD for Norwich. Americans of the 46th Air Depot Group had been paid five days before, and their pockets were loaded with pound notes as they gleefully headed for the city. The trucks arrived in Haymarket Square and airmen scattered in every direction into the blackout. One airman stopped off in a pub and was greeted by one of the local 'commercial ladies', who offered her services for the sum of £10. Realizing that £10 was the equivalent of $41.50 in American currency, he declined because of that, and her looks. After a series of negotiations and urging by her, they agreed upon a sum of £5 and she led him to a suitable air raid shelter with benches. They had been there for about twenty minutes when the air raid warning sounded. This was Raid 44 and the

Below: *A GI truck. (MWB)*

last one ever to strike Norwich, and two enemy bombers were approaching. One dropped phosphorous bombs, causing ten fires throughout the city. The second aircraft dropped HE bombs but most fell on a golf course.

When the All Clear had sounded, it was well past departure hour for the Liberty Run back to Watton, so the airman and female companion decided to spend the remainder of the night sleeping on the benches. After napping for a short time, he woke and tried to see the time. His wristwatch was missing; his wallet was gone and so was his expensive fountain pen. The 'commercial lady' was sleeping soundly and her purse was on the ground alongside the bench. Opening her purse he found his watch, his wallet and his pen, which he removed. He then retrieved the £5 note given her for 'services' and took off for the Red Cross club in the Bishop's Palace for the remainder of the night. What a clever way to celebrate Norwich's last air raid with a freebie.

3rd SAD newsletter March 1994. The city was one of five medieval cities in England that Hermann Goering vowed he would destroy. The first raid was on 9 July 1940. Norwich suffered thirteen raids in 1940 and in 1941 fourteen more raids followed. They had eight months of respite from attack until the night of 27/28 April 1942 and another heavy raid the following night. The Baedeker Blitz of Norwich began as the city was attacked twelve more times by the Luftwaffe during the rest of the war. Raid 44 was the last by the Luftwaffe on Norwich in WWII. The raids caused extensive damage and major loss of life.

'Overpaid, oversexed, and over here' was such a neat phrase that unfortunately it gained much credence as a general complaint from the English people. I personally attest that from my vantage point Anglo-American relations were excellent. Despite the great inundation of men and machines, the extremely civilized English took it all in their stride with great good nature. I was quite at home with these people. They were friendly, literate, and had beautiful manners – true even of the poorest

folk. Everywhere I went I was treated with unflagging courtesy and respect. Over 25,000 English girls took American husbands during the war … The villagers near the airbases quickly adopted the American flyers as their own. The Yanks visited in their homes, shops, and churches and became a part of village life. Each day the villagers anxiously awaited the return of the mission in the afternoons, counting the planes in the formation just as we did.

Chick's Crew, 'The Ties That Bind', Ben C. Smith

Above: *'Over 25,000 English girls took American husbands during the war …'* Chick's Crew, Ben C. Smith (MWB)

Barrage balloon cables are always fun to dodge … The British are good with anti-aircraft guns and balloons, but I wonder sometimes if they don't get more of us than they do of Jerry. Makes life interesting to say the least. We didn't endear ourselves to the British by telling them they ought to cut the barrage-balloon cables and let the bloody island sink. In return they replied, 'There's nothing wrong with you Yanks except you're overpaid, oversexed, and over here.'

Captain Ralph H. Elliott, pilot, 467th BG

'I asked one of the young Americans on the base at Polebrook, "Could I look round the Forts?" He said, "Sure son". Then he paused and said, "Have you got a sister mister?" I thought it strange. Why would my sister be interested in looking around aircraft?'

Aircraft-mad Northamptonshire schoolboy

Right and below: *'They wanted to know where the cinemas and dance halls were, where were the girls, what did we do in our spare time?'* Connie Richards (Richards Coll)

The village was all agog. People were standing around talking, hands up to their mouths. 'The Yanks are coming here, have you heard?'

Men in the two old pubs were a bit despondent, also cautious.

'I suppose you've heard the rumour, the bloody yanks are coming here,' they chatted between a game of skittles, a pint of beer and a game of darts. 'They'll be after our women – they are all oversexed.'

That was my first recollection of hearing about the Americans coming to my village. I had my own thoughts, so did a lot of my friends. We could always get some gum or sweets or perhaps a pair of nylons, and we could always say we were older than what we were, then they would take notice. Anyway no good thinking these things, perhaps they wouldn't come.

The war was on although I didn't know much about it, only that we didn't get much food and clothes were rationed. At night my parents had to put a blackout at the window so that no light showed outside, and we had to have evacuees from London to live with us away from the bombs up

there. We were quite happy, we had to be. As the weeks passed I began to notice a great change in the sleepy country village of Milton Ernest. The big house, Milton Ernest Hall, where I used to play and ride my bicycle around the courtyard with my friends Betsy and John Starey, whose grandparents owned the place, was now barbed-wired off. 'No admittance' signs were put up and two big guard posts were put up at the gates. American lorries and jeeps were coming and going and then the Yanks appeared. Good-looking men in uniforms.

My mother had warned me not to talk to them as she said I was too young, but when you are young you do lots of things which are not always right, and you have a mind of your own. After school, I used to go home and get changed and walk down to the gate with a friend to speak to a couple of MPs that were on the gate. Taking with me two hard-boiled eggs, which I used to cook. We kept hens in the back garden, and eggs, fresh ones you couldn't get during the war. They used to eat them on duty and give me a packet of gum. The usual chat took place. They wanted to know where the cinemas and the dance halls were, where were the girls, what did we do in our spare time? We said we didn't have much spare time as we were at work (that was a lie, we were still at school) and could they take us out? Well the older girls got to them before we did. I had a sneaking suspicion they knew I was still at school.

The months went by, I got to know a lot of them and the village settled down to accepting them. They were good to us then, as we were the 'Chewing Gum Kids'. They learned to play skittles, darts, etc. There were weddings at the parish church and film shows at the school. The first one I remember going to was called 'Stage Door Canteen'. Afterwards we had real ice cream. They took part in a lot of village functions and gave so much to us. One in particular was a James E. McPhail, 'Scotty,' who was a photographer. He used to come to my home and have his English dinner: roast meat, Yorkshire pudding and real home-grown vegetables. We became very friendly, my parents and him. They called him their adopted Yankee son. I think he was 19–20 years old. My dad liked him. My mother did washing for him.

One day he told me that Glenn Miller was playing at a dance to be held in the Club Castle. I wanted to go so badly but my mum, bless her heart, said 'No'. I had heard of Glenn Miller and liked his music in those days and having a great bandleader in my village, I had to go, and that was that. So I arranged with my girlfriend who was going out with Staff Sergeant Max Calker, that they would get me in. That was justly done and that night I remember with pride seeing the band and I actually spoke to Glenn Miller. Broderick Crawford was there too and a few words were exchanged.

They were happy years, some tinged with sadness. The guys from the 306th BG at Thurleigh, about two miles from Milton Ernest, also came to the pubs in the village. Sometimes you asked, 'Where is Joe?' and the answer you received was, 'Sorry honey, he didn't make it back from today's mission.'

As a girl I used to watch them go out in their B-17s in the mornings and count them when they came back to their base later in the day. Around the Milton Ernest and Bedford areas their memories still live. But eventually the war ended, and for me no Yankee boyfriend. My photographer friend married an Irish nurse. A lot of my girlfriends were GI brides and it was to be that I stayed on in that village to marry an English boy at the same parish church many years later.

Where are you now you MPs who ate my boiled eggs? James McPhail and the hundreds of guys who chatted us up on the corner of Thurleigh Road?

'Selinas' the Mexican, who bought me my first shandy in the pub?

'Lubkee', who gave me my first Chesterfield cigarette and said to take the package home for my pop?

**Connie Richards,
Bedfordshire teenager**

Above: *Maj. Glenn Miller pictured here at a 'Music for the Wehrmacht Hour' broadcast by ABSIE (American Broadcasting System in Europe) from London in November 1943 with singer and movie actress, Irene Manning. Miller was posted as 'missing' on a flight in a UC-64 Norseman from Twinwoods Farm, Bedford, to France on 15 December 1944 when he failed to arrive in Paris for a Christmas concert. He was never seen again. Both he and entertainers like Bing Crosby and Manning, who starred alongside Jimmy Cagney in the classic Yankee Doodle Dandy and featured in several musicals, were a big morale boost at USO shows on the air bases during the war. (Richards Coll)*

Below: *Lover's lament on a wall at Thurleigh in 1994. (MWB)*

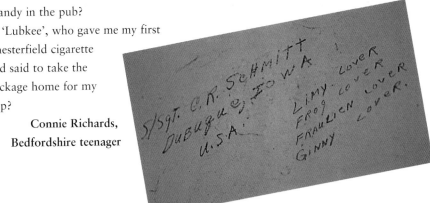

Over the months, the regular boys who came into the Red Cross club in Bethel Street, Norwich, became familiar faces.

'Hi, Pete. Hello, Joe. See you, Carl.'

'Morning, Chef. Morning, Jean.'

I came to know many of them only by their Christian names. On the evening of 6 June, there were only about three or four officers in the Club. The quietness and the strange emptiness of the building seemed to echo the atmosphere that had been gathering ever since the morning flight of the bombers. The eerie quiet continued all the next day, and in the evening three young officers, who had always been four, came in. I passed them in the corridor. I said, 'Hello, Steve, Harry, where's Pete?'

Steve looked straight through me. He stopped to say to the empty air above my head, 'Peter won't be in to dinner.'

The three of them walked on, tall and straight and smart in their pinks.

And Over There, Jean Lancaster-Rennie

Above: *Joe Micksch, a sergeant armourer in the 392nd BG at Wendling, by an English haystack. (Joe Micksch via Ben Jones)*

We had two uniform colors – pink and green. Both were of wool gabardine; the 'pinks' were gray with a pinkish cast while the 'greens' were a forest green. The blouses were usually green but could be worn with either the green or pink trousers. The pinks made the snappier uniform combination with the green blouse and were usually worn on pass. Later on we started wearing 'Ike' jackets which were blouses cut down to waist length. They were more comfortable than the regular blouse and we wore them everywhere.

Captain Ralph H. Elliott, pilot, 467th BG

Below:
'Yankee officers cause us to smile,
With their light pants, you see them for miles,
We wonder if they're mice or men
Decided they're wolves, we avoid the den.'
'The GIs', by a WAAF at Shipdham (MWB)

INTRODUCING ENGLAND

You are going to Great Britain as part of an allied offensive – to meet Hitler and beat him on his own ground. For the time being you will be Britain's guest. The purpose of this guide is to start getting you acquainted with the British, their country, and their ways. America and Britain are allies. Hitler knows that they are both powerful countries, tough and resourceful. He knows that they, with the other United Nations, mean his crushing defeat in the end. So it is only common sense to understand that the first and major duty Hitler has given his propaganda chiefs is to separate Britain and America and spread distrust between them. If he can do that, his chance of winning might return.

If you come from an Irish-American family, you may think of the English as persecutors of the Irish, or you may think of them as enemy Redcoats who fought against us in the American Revolution and the war of 1812. But there is no time today to fight old wars over again or bring up old grievances. We don't worry about which side our grandfather fought on in the Civil War, because it doesn't mean anything now. We can defeat Hitler's propaganda with a weapon of our own. Plain, common horse sense; understanding of evident truths. The most evident truth of all is that in their major ways of life the British and American people are much alike. They speak the same language. They both believe in representative government, in freedom of worship, in freedom of speech. But each country has minor national characteristics which differ. It is by causing misunderstanding over these minor differences that Hitler hopes to make his propaganda effective.

TWO GREAT NATIONS DIVIDED BY A COMMON LANGUAGE

'We'd become used to seeing strange-looking servicemen in Norwich from the early days of the war. When the "Yanks" first appeared in the city in 1942, they were very noticeable in their different style uniforms, with their different language, which was English and yet it wasn't! For example, we'd never heard of a drawingpin described as a "thumbtack", a torch as a "flashlight", nor petrol as "gasoline". Completely foreign!'

Nora Norgate, eighteen-year-old Norwich girl

'We arrived at Liverpool Street Station without mishap and decided to take the tube downtown. This was a mistake, as none of us had learned to speak the language and it was practically impossible to communicate with the natives. We lost Junior on the tube and didn't see him till we returned to the base.'

Bill Carleton, 351st BS Engineering Officer, 100th BG

'Landing at an RAF base after a mission, they always fed us fresh farm eggs and french-fried potatoes after we had had a dram or two of spirits. I always wondered where they got the eggs; we did not have them on our base. This base, being a photo reconnaissance base, had a great number of women photo interpreters with whom we were billeted. Interesting to say the least, I learned that it was vulgar to use the term fanny in mixed company, but all right to use ass.'

Robert H. Tays, Liberator pilot

'Another difference. The British have phrases and colloquialisms of their own that may sound funny to you. You can make just as many boners in their eyes. It isn't a good idea, for instance, to say 'bloody' in mixed company in Britain – it is one of their worst swear words, To say: 'I look like a bum', is offensive to their ears, for to the British this means that you look like your own backside. It isn't important – just a tip if you are trying to shine in polite society ...'

A Short Guide To Great Britain

48

You defeat enemy propaganda not by denying that these differences exist, but by admitting them openly and then trying to understand them. For instance: the British are often more reserved in conduct than we. On a small, crowded island where forty-five million people live, each man learns to guard his privacy carefully – and is equally careful not to invade another man's privacy.

So, if Britons sit in trains or buses without striking up conversation with you, it doesn't mean they are being haughty and unfriendly. Probably they are paying more attention to you than you think. But they don't speak to you because they don't want to appear intrusive or rude.

The British dislike bragging and showing off. American wages and American soldiers' pay are the highest in the world. When payday comes, it would be sound practice to learn to spend your money according to British standards. They consider you highly paid. They won't think any better of you for throwing money around; they are more likely to feel that you haven't learned the common-sense virtues of thrift. The British 'Tommy' is apt to be especially touchy about the difference between his wages and yours. Keep this in mind. Use common sense and don't rub him the wrong way.

You will find many things in Britain physically different from similar things in America. But there are also important similarities – our common speech, our common law, and our ideals of religious freedom were all brought from Britain when the Pilgrims landed at Plymouth Rock. Our ideas about political liberties are also British and parts of our own Bill of Rights were borrowed from the great charters of British liberty.

> 'My British buddy,
> We're as different as can be,
> He thinks he's winning the war –
> And I think it's me.
> But we're in there pitching ...'
> **Anonymous**

Remember that in America you like people to conduct themselves as we do and to respect the same things. Try to do the same for the British and respect the things they treasure.

Don't be misled by the British tendency to be soft-spoken and polite. If they need to be, they can be plenty tough. The English language didn't spread across the oceans and over the mountains and jungles and swamps of the world because these people were panty-waists. Sixty thousand British civilians – men, women and children – have died under bombs and yet the morale of the British is unbreakable and high. A nation doesn't come through that, if it doesn't have plain, common guts. The British are tough, strong people, and good allies. You won't be able to tell the British much about 'taking it.' They are not particularly interested in taking it any more. They are far more interested in getting together in solid friendship with us, so that we can all start dishing it out to Hitler.

McAdams, our flight engineer, who was about five-foot-four, was what we called a 'little Napoleon'. Once he went to a bar in Norwich and met a British line sergeant, who must have weighed about 300 lbs, standing alone at the bar. McAdams knocked into him and said, 'Who the hell are you? Do you need the whole damn bar?' (The bar was 50-foot long). The sergeant had just returned from two years in North Africa. He didn't even use his fist. He just swiped McAdams with his hand and knocked him 20 feet through the air. McAdams broke his arm in the fall and flew for four weeks with his arm in a cast.

John A. Holden, navigator, 452nd BG

Right: *93rd BG personnel at Hardwick in March 1943. (USAF)*

BRITAIN'S WARTIME APPEARANCE

You will find out right away that England is a small country, smaller than North Carolina. Britain – that is England and Scotland and Wales together – is hardly bigger than Minnesota. England's largest river, the Thames (pronounced 'Tems') is not even as big as the Mississippi when it leaves Minnesota. No part of England is more than one hundred miles from the sea. If you are from Boston or Seattle, the weather may remind you of home. If you are from Arizona or North Dakota, you will find it a little hard to get used to. At first you will probably not like the almost continual rains and mists and the absence of snow and crisp cold. Actually, the city of London has less rain for the whole year than many places in the United States, but the rain falls in frequent drizzles. Most people get used to the English climate eventually …

On furlough you will probably go to the cities, where you will meet the Briton's pride in age, and tradition. You will find that the British care little about size, not having the 'biggest' of many things as we do. For instance, London has no skyscrapers. Not because English architects couldn't design one, but because London is built on swampy ground, not on a rock like New York, and skyscrapers need something to rest their foundations on. In London they will point out to you buildings like Westminster Abbey, where England's kings and greatest men are

Below: *American football game at Bedford Rugby Club ground. (via Richards)*

buried, and St. Paul's Cathedral with its famous dome, and the Tower of London, which was built almost a thousand years ago. All of these buildings have played an important part in England's history. They mean just as much to the British as Mount Vernon or Lincoln's birthplace do to us.

The largest English cities are all located in the lowlands near the various sea coasts. In the southeast, on the Thames, is London, which is the combined New York, Washington, and Chicago not only of England but of the far-flung British Empire. Greater London's huge population of twelve million people is the size of Greater New York City and all its suburbs with the near-by New Jersey cities thrown in. It is also more than a quarter of the total population of the British Isles. The great midland manufacturing cities of Birmingham, Sheffield and Coventry (sometimes called the Detroit of Britain) are located in the central part of England. Near-by on the west coast are the textile and shipping centres of Manchester and Liverpool. Further north, in Scotland, is the world's leading ship-building centre of Glasgow. On the east side of Scotland is the historic Scottish capital, Edinburgh, scene of the tales of Scott and Robert Louis Stevenson, which many of you read in school. In southwest England in the broad mouth of the Severn is the great port of Bristol.

Britain may look a little shop-worn and grimy to you. The British people are anxious to have you know that you are not seeing the country at its best. There's been a war on since 1939. The houses haven't been painted because factories are not making paint – they're making planes. The famous English parks and gardens are either unkempt because there are no men to take care of them, or they are being used to grow needed vegetables. British taxicabs look antique because Britain makes tanks for herself and Russia and hasn't time to make new cars. British trains are cold because power is needed for industry, not for heating. There are no luxury dining cars on trains because total war effort has no place for such frills. The trains are un-washed and grimy because men and women are needed for more important work than car washing. The British people are anxious for you to know that in normal times Britain looks much prettier, cleaner, neater.

Some of the boys, it seemed, had not been reading their '*Britain*'. Especially the bit about not wasting food. The food at the club was very good. There was always apple pie on the menu. Apple pie, strawberry shortcake, lemon meringue pie, doughnuts – these seemed to be their staple diet! There was always custard, and if a man didn't want custard, all he had to do was to pick up a plate of apple pie that had no custard on it. One day, a big, tough looking officer picked up a plate of apple pie with custard and put it on his tray. He and his friend took their lunches to a table. I was there just as this big officer had lit his enormous cigar. He had finished his first course, and had pulled over his apple pie. He smoked for a few minutes, until there was a long tube of ash on his cigar. Then, very deliberately, he stubbed out the cigar, ash and all, on the plate of pie and custard. I felt sick, sick. I could say nothing, do nothing. Nobody took any notice; apparently they had seen it before. I never had, nor do I ever want to see it again. If he thought to show his superiority, and/or his contempt for our efforts and our food, in fact he only showed his abysmal ignorance. He may have been an officer – he was never, nor will he ever be, a gentleman. They were not all angels.

And Over There, **Jean Lancaster-Rennie**

THE PEOPLE – THEIR CUSTOMS AND MANNERS

The best way to get on in Britain is very much the same as the best way to get on in America. The same sort of courtesy and decency and friendliness that go over big in America will go over big in Britain. The British have seen a good many Americans and they like Americans. They will like your frankness as long as it is friendly. They will expect you to be generous. They are not given to backslapping and they are shy about showing their affections. But once they get to like you they make the best friends in the world.

In 'getting along' the first important thing to remember is that the British are like the Americans in many ways – but not in all ways. You will quickly discover differences that seem confusing and even wrong. Like driving on the left side of the road, and having money based on an impossible accounting system, and drinking warm beer. But once you get used to things like that, you will realize that they belong to England just as baseball and jazz and Coca-Cola belong to us.

The British of all classes are enthusiastic about sports, both as amateurs and as spectators of professional sports. They love to shoot, they love to play games, they ride horses and bet on horse races, they fish. But be careful where you hunt or fish. Fishing and hunting rights are often private property. The great 'spectator' sports are football in the autumn and winter and cricket in the spring and summer. See a 'match' in either of these sports whenever you get a chance. You will get a kick out

Below: *Playing baseball at Thurleigh. (via Richards)*

Above: *Playing baseball at Bedford Rugby Club ground. (via Richards)*

of it – if only for the differences from American sports.

Cricket will strike you as slow compared with American baseball, but it isn't easy to play well. You will probably get more fun out of 'village cricket' (which corresponds to sandlot baseball) than you would out of the big three-day professional matches. The big professional matches are often nothing but a private contest between the bowler (who corresponds to our pitcher) and the batsman (batter) and you have to know the line points of the game to understand what is going on.

Football in Britain takes two forms. They play soccer, which is known in America; and they also play 'rugger,' which is a rougher game and closer to American football, but is played without the padded suits and head-guards we use. Rugger requires fifteen on a side, uses a ball slightly bigger than our football, and allows lateral but not forward passing. The English do not handle the ball as cleanly as we do, but they are more expert with their feet. As in all English games, no substitutes are allowed. If a

man is injured, his side continues with fourteen players and so on ....

The British have theaters and movies (which they call 'cinemas') as we do. But the great place of recreation is the 'pub'. A pub, or public house, is what we would call a bar or tavern. The usual drink is beer, which is not an imitation of German beer as our beer is, but ale. (But they usually call it beer or 'bitter'). Not much whiskey is now being drunk. Wartime taxes have shot the price of a bottle up to about $4.50. The British are beer-drinkers – and can hold it. The beer is now below peacetime strength, but can still make a man's tongue wag at both ends.

You will be welcome in the British pubs as long as you remember one thing. The pub is 'the poor man's club,' the neighborhood or village gathering place, where the men have come to see their friends, not strangers. If you want to join a darts game, let them ask you first (as they probably will). And if you are beaten, it is the custom to stand aside and let someone else play.

They were wonderful boys. At first we weren't sure what to expect. But in a few weeks it was like having one big family. They didn't like our bitter to start with, but they soon got used to it. It was the same with darts. Most had never played before so we had to teach them. Then it became their game. Our pub is in the path of what they called Bomber Alley. All the planes used to fly overhead to get to the airfield after bombing the Germans. But not one of our regular boys got killed. One plane went down in Switzerland, but they all got back later. The nearest we came was Scottie. We were all sitting around with long faces when we heard that he hadn't got back to the airfield. Nobody had a drink … nobody. It was like a funeral. Then the door burst open and in walked Scottie with a huge bunch of carnations. All he said was 'I'm back'. I'll never forget that moment.

Some of the boys married the local girls they were going out with, and most of the evenings we spent round the piano singing all the old songs like 'Roll Out the Barrel' and 'Daisy, Daisy'.

Publican, the late Mrs Daisy Elmar, who, with her late husband, Jimmy, ran 'The Three Nags' at Fritton, Norfolk. Mr and Mrs Elmar became as well known to the men at the local airfield as their commanding officer. Their centuries-old thatched pub became a second home to the Americans.

Below: *306th BG personnel helping with the harvest near Thurleigh in 1943. (via Richards)*

The British make much of Sunday. All the shops are closed, most of the restaurants are closed, and in the small towns there is not much to do. You had better follow the example of the British and try to spend Sunday afternoon in the country.

British churches, particularly the little village churches, are often very beautiful inside and out. Most of them are always open and if you feel like it, do not hesitate to walk in. But do not walk around if a service is going on.

You will naturally be interested in getting to know your opposite number, the British soldier, the 'Tommy' you have heard and read about. You can understand that two actions on your part will slow up the friendship – swiping his girl, and not appreciating what his army has been up against. Yes, and rubbing it in that you are better paid than he is.

Children the world over are easy to get along with. British children are much like our own. The British have reserved much of the food that gets through solely for their children. To the British children you, as an American, will be 'something special.' For they have been fed at their schools and impressed with the fact that the food they ate was sent to them by Uncle Sam. You don't have to tell the British about lend-lease food. They know about it and appreciate it.

Above: *365th BS, 305th BG personnel helping with wheat shockers in a field near Chelveston in August 1943. (via Bill Donald)*

Below: *'Many of them also learned to ride bicycles, and we thought it awfully funny to see some of them learning. They mostly landed on their knees with the bike on top of them.' A Suffolk girl who lived on a farm at Framlingham airbase, home of the 390th BG (USAF)*

We called those boys 'our boys', and their ships 'our ships'.

The 571st Squadron was just across the road from our farm, and we got to know almost everyone in it. Soon after the boys arrived, names began to appear on the doors of their huts. There was 'The Sleepy Lagoon', 'Ye Olde Pig Sty', 'Consumption Center 3rd,' 'The Dog House', and several names of nightclubs. At harvest time the boys used to ride on our empty wagons, and some of them came and helped us in the fields. They were interested in our farm and our work, and the neat way we made our stacks. We exchanged ideas about American and English farming.

The train from Framlingham to Wickham Market was always packed. They made jokes about our train, as it is only a small branch-line train, with three coaches and a small engine. It amused us to see the boys get on when they first came. They clambered on from both sides and some even rode in the engine – they just seemed to swarm onto it like a bunch of ants, but they soon learned the right way. Many of them also learned to ride bicycles, and we thought it awfully funny to see some of them learning. They mostly landed on their knees with the bike on top of them. When they could ride quite well they carried others on the crossbars, and one often saw two or three on one bike. They found it difficult to remember to cycle on the left side of the road.

The boys liked to tease us. There was always something being said about our 'limey' weather, and they teased us about the way we talked, and tried to copy us. It sounded funny to hear them say, 'I cawn't'. I expect we were just as funny when we tried to talk through our noses like them … we shall never forget the 390th, the boys who had come so far from their homes in America, many of them never to return. For more than two years they lived in and were a part of our countryside, and we missed them sincerely when they were gone.'

A Suffolk girl who lived on a farm at Framlingham airbase, home of the 390th BG

You can rub a Britisher the wrong way by telling him 'we came over and won the last one.' Each nation did its share. But Britain remembers that nearly a million of her best manhood died in the last war. America lost 60,000 in action. Such arguments and the war debts along with them are dead issues.

Nazi propaganda now is pounding away day and night asking the British people why they should fight to save 'Uncle Shylock and his silver dollar.' Don't play into Hitler's hands by mentioning war debts. Neither do the British need to be told that their armies lost the first couple of rounds in the present war. We've lost a couple, ourselves, so do not start off by being critical of them and saying what the Yanks are going to do. Use your head before you sound off, and remember how long the British alone held Hitler off without any help from anyone.

In the pubs you will hear a lot of Britons openly criticizing their government and the conduct of the war. That isn't an occasion for you to put in your two cents worth. It's their business, not yours. You sometimes criticize members of your own family – but just let an outsider start doing the same, and you know how you feel!

The Briton is just as outspoken and independent as we are. But don't get him wrong. He is also the most law-abiding citizen in the world, because the British system of justice is just about the best there is. There are fewer murders, robberies, and burglaries in the whole of Great Britain in a year than in a single large American city.

... The stores are much the same as ours but named differently. A drugstore is a chemist, a theater a cinema, a hardware store an ironmonger, and a tavern a pub. Beer is bitters and whiskey is spirits, although too scarce to mention almost. A single girl can't get a room, as people are narrow-minded in that respect ... There's a funny racial problem here, Honey, and especially the southern boys don't like it. As far as the English are concerned, it doesn't matter whether a fellow is white or black, and the English girls go out with Negro soldiers as well as white soldiers. You can imagine what happens when a colored boy walks past with a better-looking girl than the white soldier has. Of course, many of the English are beginning to size up the situation and racial prejudice is developing just as in the States. Girls are beginning to realize the difference and the better ones avoid the Negroes just to avoid the social ostracism of the white soldiers. How it will end I couldn't say, but I suppose if the war lasts long enough a racial problem may well develop.

Captain Ralph H. Elliott, 467th BG pilot, letter home to his wife Vonny

Above: Black American personnel in the 'local' near Debach air base in 1944. Although Anglo-American fraternization was popular and, indeed, encouraged, racial segregation was exercised at all levels and mixed-race relationships with English girls were not tolerated in the US forces. Outbreaks of fighting between whites and blacks led to each race having their own 'liberty towns' allocated near bases so as to avoid potentially damaging outbreaks of racial violence. (via Truett Woodall)

56

Once again, look, listen, and learn before you start telling the British how much better we do things. They will be interested to hear about life in America and you have a great chance to overcome the picture many of them have gotten from the movies of an America made up of wild Indians and gangsters. When you find differences between British and American ways of doing things, there is usually a good reason for them.

British railways have dinky freight cars (which they call 'goods wagons') not because they don't know any better. Small cars allow quicker handling of freight at the thousands and thousands of small stations.

British automobiles are little and low-powered. That's because all the gasoline has to be imported over thousands of miles of ocean.

British taxicabs have comic-looking front wheel structures. Watch them turn around in a twelve-foot street and you'll understand why.

The British don't know how to make a good cup of coffee. You don't know how to make a good cup of tea. It's an even swap.

The British are leisurely, but not really slow. Their crack trains held world speed records. A British ship held the Trans-atlantic record. A British car and a British driver set world speed records in America.

Do not be offended if Britishers do not pay as full respects to national or regimental colours as Americans do. The British do not treat the flag as such an important symbol as we do. But they pay more frequent respect to their national anthem. In peace or war 'God save the King' (to the same tune of our 'America') is played at the conclusion of all public gatherings such as theater performances. The British consider it bad form not to stand at attention even if it means missing the last bus. If you are in a hurry, leave before the national anthem is played. That's considered all right.

At home in America you were in a country at war. Since your ship left port, however, you have been in a war zone. You will find that all Britain is a war zone and has been since September 1939. All this has meant great changes in the British way of life.

Every light in England is blacked out every night and all night. Every highway signpost has come down and barrage balloons have gone up. Grazing land is now ploughed for wheat and flowerbeds turned into vegetable gardens. Britain's peacetime army of a couple of hundred thousand has been expanded to over two million men. Everything from the biggest factory to the smallest village workshop is turning out something for the war, so that Britain can supply arms for herself, for Libya, Russia, and every front. Hundreds of thousands of women have gone to work in factories or joined the many military auxiliary forces. Old-time social distinctions are being forgotten as the sons of

factory workers rise to be officers in the forces and the daughters of noblemen get jobs in munitions factories.

But more important than this is the effect of the war itself. The British have been bombed, night after night, and month after month. Thousands of them have lost their houses, their possessions, their families. Gasoline, clothes, and railroad travel are hard to come by and incomes are cut by taxes to an extent we Americans have not even approached. One of the things the English always had enough of in the past was soap. Now it is so scarce that girls working in the factories often cannot get the grease off their hands or out of their hair. And food is more strictly rationed than anything else.

From *A Short Guide To Great Britain*, War and Navy Departments Washington DC, issued to every GI arriving in Britain in 1942

Above: *'British automobiles are little and low-powered. That's because all the gasoline has to be imported over thousands of miles of ocean.'* A Short Guide to Great Britain *(via Pat Everson)*

NUMBER PLEASE!

[Two GIs, Chester and Dick, on their first pass to Norwich, missed the last Liberty Run trucks back to Flixton. Here is what happened.]

'Maybe if we get out to the Bungay highway we can catch a ride', Chester suggested, undaunted.

They walked and walked some more. After a while Dick stopped suddenly, clutched Chester's arm and pointed. There was one of those bright red telephone booths, which are so familiar a sight in England. Dick entered the booth and picked up the receiver. 'Operator', said a soft feminine voice.

'Listen, operator,' Dick said urgently, 'a buddy of mine and I are trying to get to Bungay. Are we on the right road?'

'Yes,' the operator said, 'you are on the Norwich–Bungay road. If the phone booth is on the right side of the road you are heading in the right direction. Bungay is eleven miles away. Ring me up at the next booth you come to, and I'll tell you if you are still on the right road.'

After what seemed like another twenty miles of walking, they came to another phone booth. Lifting the receiver, Dick again heard that voice of sweetness and light. 'Yes, you are still on the right road. Bungay is eight miles away.' The boys kept walking.

They kept on and at each telephone booth they paused to receive their reassurance. As the first grey suggestion of dawn appeared on the eastern sky, the voice said, 'When you turn the corner, you will be in the town of Bungay. On the main road, two miles further on, you will find a junction. Choose the left road and you will soon be at your airfield. Good morning and happy walking.'

An hour and a half later, the tired, worn-out bodies of Dick and Chester were stretched out in their respective beds.

John Archer, English schoolboy and 8th Air Force historian

These English telephones beat me. The receiver and dial is like ours but not the operation. You pick up the receiver and dial the number and the operator says 'two and six' or whatever the charge is, which you put in the slot. Then you push the button 'A' and it rings up the money. If there's no answer, you push button 'B' and get your money back. Main trouble is understanding the operator, and darned if I can tell when the call is through and when it isn't.

Captain Ralph H. Elliott, pilot, 467th BG

Above: *Capt. Richard Graves, flight surgeon (left) and Lt. Jay Brekkon, 848th BS, 490th BG, making a call from a telephone box. (Arnold Delmonico)*

ANGELS?

Above: *Cherubic young B-17 ball turret gunner, S/Sgt. John B. Palmquist, awarded the Purple Heart for shrapnel wounds received on 28 April 1944. Palmquist was still hospitalized on 7 May when five of his 100th BG crew were lost when their B-17 was set on fire after flares carried in the top turret compartment exploded. (John A. Miller Coll)*

squadrons were just off the base. As we approached the barrack area, we noticed a sign which some wag had hung on the first billet, 'GIRLS WHO VISIT ON A WEEKEND MUST BE OFF THE BASE BY TUESDAY.'

Second Lieutenant Richard 'Dick' Johnson

Above: *Purple Heart and Legion of Merit medals. The Purple Heart is awarded to anyone wounded in action while serving in the US Armed Forces. Some 6,845 awards (and 188 Oak Leaf Clusters) were made to 8th AF combat crews 17 August 1942–15 May 1945. (MWB)*

'When the Americans arrived, they became my heroes ... I decided that GIs were the closest thing to angels I'd ever met.'

Ann K. Spredbury, Norwich schoolgirl

The last week of April found us on a bus headed for the famous 303rd BG known as 'Hell's Angels' to which we had been assigned. As we drove past the little village of Molesworth and turned onto the base, which was a little over a mile from the village, we were greeted with some strange sights. There were so many B-17s that they couldn't be easily counted. The 427th Squadron to which we had been assigned was on the base, while the other three

In January 1942 the first American servicemen landed in this country. Their coming – two million were to follow between 1942 and 1945 – had a profound effect on East Anglian village and town life. When the first American servicemen since World War I arrived in England in 1942, many East Anglians found, to their surprise, that a good many of these Americans had our names and that some had better connections with the Puritan 'family' of

John Winthrop, of Groton, Suffolk, who voyaged with other local men and women to the New World in 1629, than many native claimants.

For my part I had an American cousin on my father's side in the 8th Air Force, a native of Ohio and, later in the war, a cousin on my mother's side, a native of Ipswich, married a Wattisham-based American from Pennsylvania. Allan A. Michie, the well-known American journalist and commentator of the war years, who had friends in West Suffolk, told me after the war that some 50,000 Americans, mostly 8th and 9th Air Force men, married local girls. Indeed, the marriage rate in some areas was extremely high.

As a guest of my American cousin [I went to] the famous American Red Cross Rainbow Corner, now demolished, at the corner of Shaftesbury Avenue and Windmill Street, Piccadilly, where there was a notice over the main entrance which said 'Through These Portals Pass America's Finest'. An American, seeing me reading this, said: 'Son, that may be true. It all depends on who's the judge, but I reckon that it would be true to say that we are no better and no worse than our fathers and your fathers who served in World War I. We certainly ain't angels.'

Christopher R. Elliott, newspaper article

Below: *'Target for tonight' was a favourite expression used by RAF Bomber Command crews. It's American derivation, where the 'target for tonite' was a 'hot date', is a double meaning used to adorn the Fortress flown by Lt. Verle's crew in the 305th BG at Chelveston in March 1944. (USAF via Bill Donald)*

MEMORIES OF A YOUNG BOY IN WARTIME ENGLAND

I was born in 1936 so by 1942 I was at an impressionable age. My first inkling that something big was going to happen was when lorry after lorry came passing through the small town where I lived loaded with sand and ballast. They were building the 'dromes' as we called them. My father came home one day and said, 'the Yanks are coming today', so he rigged up a seat on

Above: *The Lone-Star Ranger: this bandy-legged cowboy, now no more, at Deopham Green in the 1970s. (MWB)*

the crossbar of his bicycle and rode me down to a place called Snetterton Heath about one-and-a-half miles down the road. We waited and in 'they' came – the planes all painted khaki. Within a matter of months we had five different airbases within a radius of five to six miles around the town of Attleborough (where I lived). It was the

same all over my region of England, airfield after airfield, because our region was nearest to Germany.

Anyway, after a couple of days the Americans were let out for the first time. They came by our house in 'hundreds'. One man came by in Texan cowboy boots and shouted to me that he was The Lone-Star Ranger. At which I ran indoors to tell my parents (I really believed him).

In no time we kids were chewing gum and eating candy. Real luxury to us because we had been on food rationing for years by then and although we did not starve, food was very basic, to say the least.

Lots of airmen used to ask if I had a sister. 'Yes', I would say. 'How old?' 'Well she's 8 (or 9 or 10)', depending on what period of the war I was asked. I could not understand at the time why their enthusiasm waned when I told them.

We boys soon had our own 'Yank friend'. Mine was a man called George who came from New Jersey. He was a waist gunner in a Flying Fortress (B-17s – we called them 'Forts'). I would come out of school and go straight into the camp, right past the MPs who waved me through; go into his hut or wait for his plane to land and he would take me to the PX. I was given coffee and doughnuts (with a hole in the middle). Both of these were welcome to me. I was also given razor blades, chewing gum, candies, etc. When I arrived back home my father was most angry and would say, 'no more scrounging!' I kept saying I did not ask for anything but from then on the PX was out of bounds for me. However, my visits to the airfield continued until the end of the war. I was allowed rides in the aircraft when they were ground tested around the perimeter track. My pal did not come back one day; all his kit had been moved out. I found out later that his plane was shot down over Brunswick. To this day I do not know whether he survived. He was a very kind man. Of course I made other American pals, but it was never quite the same.

Anyway, other memories which spring to mind are big thick comics ('Superman', even in those days), O'Henry candy bars and, of course, Lucky

Strike cigarettes. But most of all – the aircraft. I would see them go up in the morning, round and round, forming a special formation and then off they would go; coming back about tea time. Some were on fire. Some had engines stopped. Several times I saw men parachute out. Crashes happened all the time. There was a large hospital at a place called Morley and after each raid streams of Red Cross vans would go by to the hospital.

It was quite a sight to see all those aircraft in the air on their way to Germany – not dozens but hundreds, yes, I mean hundreds. Of course we boys said our Lancaster and Mosquito planes were best, but then you would expect us to! We had to admit that the rest of your equipment was better. Our bombers went out by night. I can hear my father saying, 'Here go our boys again'. The roar would be continuous for about an hour. They would come back again at about four o'clock in the morning. However, it was not so exciting as you could not see them.

We also had visits in turn from the Germans. The ones I did not like were the V1 'buzz bombs'. We called them 'pilotless' aircraft. On Sunday nights in the underground shelters there was great excitement (at least for we children), what with the smell of the oil lamps and sand filtering down each time there was a fresh explosion.

One day when I came home from school my sister kept telling me to be quiet. She was trying to listen to the wireless (by that time my mother had died – late in 1944). My sister kept saying 'I think the war is over in Europe'. My thoughts were, well, what will happen now? How will it be different? I had never known peacetime. All it meant to me was, no aircraft, tanks, soldiers, barrage balloons or nights under the table or down in the shelter.

As I grew older I realized just what had happened. All those ambulances going to the air force hospital, all the names on the village war memorials and the stupidity of it all. Lastly, all the men like a waist gunner called George from America, who never came back.

Michael R. Downes

KINDNESS WE WON'T FORGET

I have been one hundred per cent pro-American since 1944 when I visited Flixton airfield as a humble sixteen-year-old naval cadet with two friends – an ATC cadet and another naval cadet. We had cycled from Lowestoft and, after a casual word with the Snowdrop at the guard post, we proceeded to the control tower and were assigned to a flight on B-24 *Little King* (pilot F. G. Drake). After several hours, we returned in the late evening, too late to return home having no lights. We were shown to the mess where food such as we had never seen before was on offer. We were then driven in a jeep to a hut with ten empty beds (a missing crew). Next day, after eggs, bacon and hash browns, we took off again in *Hustling Hussy* (pilot M. O. Reid), for another long flight. Memorable days, great guys! The courtesy and generosity the three of us received will never be forgotten.

Les Skitterall

Below: 'We were shown to the mess where food such as we had never seen was on offer.' Les Skitterall (MWB)

When the truck came to deliver coal, it was always driven by a crew of GIs who were in the guardhouse for committing various offences, mostly for staying out when their passes were over. They would maybe be free for a day or two and would come into the Red Cross club in their best uniforms, go off to Norwich for the evening and promptly be back in the guardhouse the next day. The MPs (Military Police) always patrolled the city in twos and had the nickname of 'Snowdrops'.

Phyllis Smales, teenager, American Red Cross club, Rackheath

Below: *GI artists were masters of the double entendre. (via Richards)*

World War II airmen will remember the refrain of a lusty song, 'He took out his tally-whacker'. The object of this song was to see how quickly the airman could consummate the love act with his girl. So they invented many ways. One was that he could do it before she could say, 'Merry old England'. I recall one drunken flight sergeant singing over thirty verses of this song each with a different line. The airmen I knew could sing such a song the night before a mission yet on the mission they could pray and think of home and their mothers.

I have seen men drunken, making lusty remarks, and falling down and crying one night and the next day they are bright, assured, and youth shines in all its glory from their eyes. It is the contrasts of wartime that makes all events and persons noble and in some way or another immortal.

My waist gunner, Sergeant Jack Harmon, used to remark that while we were so busy pursuing girls and pub jumping we were, 'walking on some very historic soil.' Returning from leave in London, Harmon would say, 'They tell me I had a good time.'

He could walk into a dance and in five minutes have dates with several girls. After the leave when we got back to base, he couldn't remember any of them.

'I've got a Yank. Have you?' the girls would say. Sometimes we could get the girls to take cigarettes or silk but it didn't always work. There used to be a saying among the American airmen in Britain that if you got caught in bed with a British girl during an air raid, 'What better way was there to go (die) if you had to.'

It was the custom for American airmen to have rendezvous with English girls in the fields about the base, and one of the most convenient places was in some haystack. Quite often an airman would be missing from his barracks late at night and we would all know where he was. 'Mississippi's got his gal in one of the haystacks.' One night there was a rather brilliant moon. An airman from our base and his English girl were making passionate love in one of these haystacks. A single Jerry plane made it over the coast and through the defenses to drop one bomb that struck a haystack setting it on fire within sight of the base. The airman and his girl came running out of the haystack adjoining and ran for

Left: *GI's dream of American Beauty! (Rackheath Memories)*

cover. The next day an order was posted that no airmen were to leave the base after dark unless they were on an authorized leave convoy bound for town. There was to be no more haystack lovemaking and no more haystack dates. Many times one would know an airman was in a haystack because of his bike propped against the side. One of our gunners told me that it was much more comfortable making love in a soft bed of hay than in one of the GI cots or on the floor.

Some may wonder where the redeeming social values or spiritual qualities lie in these stories. They are replete with spiritual values and the human qualities of life and living. In wartime the desire for reaching out, for union with others, whether in love, lust or sex, was underlaid by the spirit of compassion of one human being for another. While sex and lust may have been present, the overriding aspect of these unions and communions was that human beings joined together in the face of the overwhelming fears, devastation, death, hatred, cruelty, and disregard for human life that accompany all wars. In one way or another, these coming together incidents sought to reaffirm the essential humanity of all the victims, the combatants, and the bystanders, the exploited and the exploiters. In this manner they are all testimonials to the redeeming quality of the human condition.

Technical Sergeant Forrest S. Clark, air gunner, 67th BS, 44th BG

Left: *T/Sgt. Forrest S. Clark, gunner, 44th BG. (Forrest S. Clark)*

A 'Rosie's Riveter' cleans the Plexiglas nose of a B-17F just off the production line at the Lockheed-Vega plant in California in 1943. 'Rosie the Riveter', the title of a song which was first released in February 1943, and sung by The Four Vagabonds, soon became the catchphrase that represented all women war workers in the US. In 1944 the movie of the same name appeared. (Lockheed)

While other girls attend a favorite cocktail bar,
Sipping dry martinis, munching caviar;
There's a girl who's really putting them to shame –
Rosie is her name.
All the day long, whether rain or shine,
She's part of the assembly line,
She's making history working for victory,
Rosie, Rosie, Rosie, Rosie, Rosie, Rosie the riveter.

'Rosie the Riveter'
by Redd Evans and John Jacob Loeb, 1942

Left: *Essential supplies distributed to the GIs by the American Red Cross girls. (MWB via Gordon Richards)*

Above: 'Large Nissens made up the Aero Club where enlisted men could enjoy a library, game tables, a snack bar, and the attentions of the Red Cross girls.' Allan Healy (USAF)

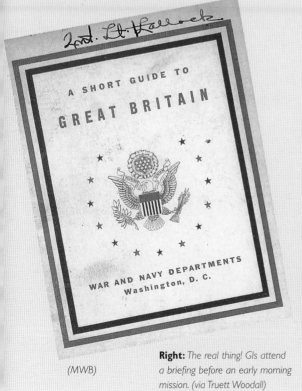

(MWB)

(MWB)

Above: GI issue prophylactic kit and a packet of Trojans for the weekend pass. (MWB via Gordon Richards)

Right: Patriotic make-up compacts and cosmetic mirror and special size Armed Service Editions of well known novels designed to fit easily in the pockets of service-issue tunics and coveralls. (MWB via Gordon Richards)

Right: The real thing! GIs attend a briefing before an early morning mission. (via Truett Woodall)

Above: *'After painting the chapel-part of the building a more pleasing shade of light green, it was decided I should paint a crucifix on the wall behind the altar. This I did in February/March 1944. When I finished the painting I asked Father Beck if it was OK. He said it was fine except I didn't put the feet together as they should be, but not to worry about it because nobody would notice. Boy, was he wrong about that. However, it was well received even though it gave the chapel a definite Catholic appearance.'* Charles 'Bud' Doyle, 389th BG. *During restoration, the restorers found another religious figure under a coat of white paint. (MWB)*

Religion

'We were called out to a very early briefing. When we entered the briefing room the chaplains were very visible. This made us uneasy and we thought it must be something big.'

Staff Sergeant Laurence S. 'Goldie' Goldstein, radio operator, 388th BG

'The crews begin to gather and soon the Catholic chaplain is giving the prayer to all of us Protestants.'
Lieutenant Robert L. Ferrell, twenty-year-old lead navigator, 458th BG

REFLECTIONS

Combat crews, ground crews, and all those men associated with the behind the scenes planning were usually a very close group, and the only thing on our minds was survival and the end of the war. 'When do we go home?' was the key phrase passed among us. In the Air Corps to my knowledge, religion never entered into our thoughts. What a man believed in was of little concern to each of us. If you did your job and were a nice guy, that was all

Above left: *Larry Nelson of the 82nd FS, 78th FG, in the cockpit of his Mustang,* Heavenly Body. *(USAF)*

'jesusgodpleasenojesusgod pleasenojesusgodpleaseno'
What you said when he was dying in your arms, *Yank* magazine, 1945

that mattered. As far as combat aircrews were concerned, a man's religious beliefs mattered even less. The most important thing to each of us was whether he'd do his job for the survival of the crew.

The religious background of my crewmates was not important to me. We worked together for our survival, each man learning and perfecting his skills. The thoughts of survival and going home were always in our minds.

Our crew met each other at the beginning of phase training, and the first thing our pilot said to us was, 'We are a crew and nothing else is as important as helping your crewmates survive.' He also stressed flying safety as a major component for our coming through combat safely. When we flew, our minds were focussed on our job as part of a ten-man crew. The six enlisted men lived together

Left: *S/Sgt. Larry S. Goldstein of the 388th BG at his radio in a B-17 in 1943. (Larry Goldstein)*

Right: *Larry Goldstein in the radio room of a Fortress at Duxford in 1992. (MWB)*

and the four officers also lived together. This did much to mold us into one unit.

On our crew, two of us were of the Jewish faith, myself and the navigator Lieutenant Phil Brejensky. As we were both from Brooklyn we were the butt of many jokes, all taken lightly. Our stateside training was both a happy and serious time. We had many laughs but we all knew what we were training for, and there was always a time for humor and good-natured ribbing. When we went overseas we were ready, and each of us was truly concerned with the survival of the 'Worry Wart' crew, and putting forth our best individual effort in the airplane. Flying combat was both exhilarating and at the same time frightening. The rigors of combat flying, equipment failure, the extreme cold, and the ever present danger of flak or enemy aircraft did not give a man much time to think of religion except to pray in his own way. As a flyer I never gave much thought to being shot down and never thought much of my Jewish background and how I would be treated if captured. I guess that is the way a 21-year-old man thought at that time. I know that many of the combat crewmen I met after the war thought the same way; that is until they were floating to earth in the parachute. There was some

brutality by German civilians and soldiers, and in some cases I believe that Jewish airmen were probably treated a little more harshly.

Prior to my being drafted in 1942, my childhood was spent as part of a middle-class Jewish home. My parents were religious, and my sister and two brothers and I respected our parents and their beliefs. We all gave considerable thought to our Jewish heritage.

One of our neighbors was a very religious Catholic lady whom I considered to be my second mother. I was a part of her family, and when I was drafted she had a St Christopher medal blessed by the parish priest and asked me to wear it around my neck. My mother had given me a Star of David medal to wear also, so I went forth to war well armed against all that might harm me. On several occasions I was asked if I was Jewish or Christian since I was wearing both medals. My answer was always the same – we can't take chances in these aircraft.

Overall, our mix of religions and regional backgrounds probably brought us closer together. We were friends and comrades working for the same thing.

Staff Sergeant Laurence S. 'Goldie' Goldstein, radio operator, 388th BG

'As briefings break up I have seen groups of crewmen off in a corner kneeling while the rest of us head for the flight line. Once I inquired and was told that the Catholics flying the mission were going to confession and receiving communion. We have no Catholics on our crew. Ken and I passed this scene once and I paused to watch.

"What's going on there?" I asked him.

"They are getting the last rites," he said.'

Technical Sergeant Robert T. Marshall, radio operator, 385th BG, 15 October 1944

'While going over the maps, perhaps talking to the bombardier, I became cognisant of someone trying to get my attention. Just as I looked up, I caught a full slash of water in my face. It was the group chaplain asking God to look after us as we began our combat tour. Later, I was to know why there are no atheists in combat. On many missions, I had good reason myself to pray for God to spare us just this one more time. I will never understand why God answered this prayer for some and so many others were required to give their all.'

First Lieutenant John W. McClane Jr., navigator, 44th BG

To further acquaint him with flying, one of our chaplains requested permission to go along on one of the test flights. This was granted but unfortunately, engine trouble developed. Emergency procedure was immediately utilised which included the opening of the bomb bay doors for emergency bail out. The Chaplain, who was in the cockpit, asked how his parachute worked. He was told to put his hand on the red handle, jump, count three and pull the handle. With that, the crew went back to the emergency at hand. Suddenly, the co-pilot said: 'My God, there's a 'chute!' A quick check indicated that, sure enough, they were short one man. The Chaplain had gone. The crew radioed the tower for a jeep to pick up the errant cleric and returned to base to report on the Chaplain lost on a flight over England.

Bill Carleton, engineering officer, 100th BG

Out over the North Sea we were flying the tightest and the best formation anyone ever saw, and this was just the beginning! Then, up near the border of Denmark, we were led into a great cloud mass. Really pea soup! There was a great flash ahead of us as the lead element of our squadron collided. We were leading the second element. Our left wingman came sliding over the top of us, just missing us. The pilot said, 'I don't know what to do!' A second or two later he said, 'I'm going to stay on this heading in a slow climb.' We came out on top just under 30,000 feet! Suddenly, the ball gunner called out: 'A Ju 88 just popped out right below us!' Then he cried, 'My GOD! My guns are frozen up!'

I was right waist gunner and I gritted my teeth, expecting the slugs from that Ju 88 to come right up my rear end! Maybe he was having his problems too; whatever, the '88 leveled off and flew away.

'Thanks GOD!'

John A. Miller, 100th BG, 3 March 1944, Berlin

After the mission briefing, Father Gerald Beck, our Catholic group chaplain at Hethel, would distribute communion to the combat crews. It was not uncommon to see a Protestant boy also receive it, to enhance his spiritual insurance. Many, many times, did I see Father Beck driving his jeep at top speed from B-24 to B-24, making sure that no one was denied communion before takeoff. One time in North Africa, he was inside the Liberator administering the sacrament at takeoff time and was an observer for that mission. He loved it. Father Beck was probably the most influential driving force behind the men of the 389th BG. He defended his boys, regardless of their guilt. He played poker with his boys; officers and enlisted men alike. (Win it from the officers and loan it to the enlisted men.) Shooting craps was his meat. He would shout as he threw the dice, 'For the chaplain!' He played baseball with GIs twenty years his junior. He would drink beer with them in town (removing his chaplain's cross and replacing it with a Field Artillery insignia to get the full benefit of a night with the boys).

Saviour of many. Enemy of none.

Russ D. Hayes, gunner, 389th BG

Above: 'After the mission briefing, Father Gerald Beck, our Catholic group chaplain at Hethel, would distribute communion to the combat crews.' Russ D. Hayes, gunner, 389th BG (USAF)

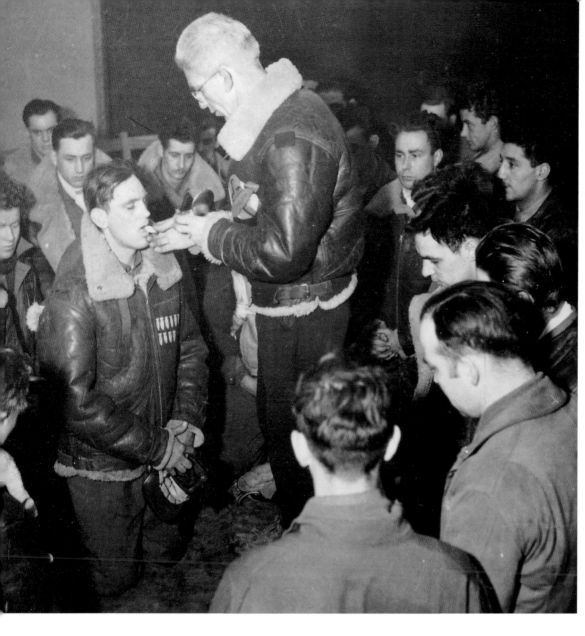

Below: *The chapel at Hethel in the early 1980s. It is now completely restored. (MWB)*

When we arrived at Hethel, Chaplain Widen, the Protestant chaplain, was already there having come over from the USA with the 389th ground echelon. He and Father Beck really hit it off good and told Pappy we could do anything we liked to make the place more like a church. Father Beck immediately turned this little chore over to me. I have always been pretty good at scrounging up stuff and I had an excellent partner in Rocco Moreo, a radio operator on one of the crews. All I had to do was ask and he delivered everything from extra blue blackout curtains, to paint, to a services board that I painted in blue, black and gold.

We even talked Lieutenant Zuna at the motor pool out of a jeep that we never returned. After painting the chapel-part of the building a more pleasing shade of light green, it was decided I should paint a crucifix on the wall behind the altar.

Above: *'The chaplain's office became more like a club than anything else … I painted the map of Europe on the office wall so we could discuss the various missions as they came up.' Charles 'Bud' Doyle, 389th BG (MWB)*

'An almost hopeless feeling welled up inside of me. It occurred to me that only God could see me through it safely. In desperation I silently bargained with God: "Lord, if you'll bring me through this alive, I'll serve you for the rest of my life." This hasty communication brought much relief from the almost unbearable anxiety.'

Second Lieutenant Robert W. Browne, pilot, 487th BG

This I did in February/March 1944. When I finished the painting I asked Father Beck if it was OK. He said it was fine except I didn't put the feet together as they should be, but not to worry about it because nobody would notice. Boy, was he wrong about that. However, it was well received even though it gave the chapel a definite Catholic appearance.

The chaplain's office became more like a club than anything else. The place was full most of the time with men from the various combat crews that treated it like a second home. I painted the map of Europe on the office wall so we could discuss the various missions as they came up. The combat mess was just in back of the chapel, so coffee and occasional steaks were to be had courtesy of Tiny, the Mess Sergeant.

Charles 'Bud' Doyle, 389th BG

Above: *John W. McClane, navigator, 44th BG. (McClane)*

'This mission was the first time I can remember praying out loud for God to let me live through the battle. I asked him to let me survive the day. I promised I'd do anything he asked of me if only he would spare me.'

Lieutenant John W. McClane Jr., navigator, 44th BG, describing his third mission, to Berlin on 29 April 1944

Something strange happened on 26 September 1944. A bible prophecy, uncannily accurate, foretold the safe return of seven crewmen of the Flying Fortress, *Heavenly Body*, after ditching in the English Channel. Before the Fortress took off from Horham early that morning to bomb Bremen, the radio operator, Staff Sergeant Gilbert Woerner, inserted a £1 note at random between the pages of his pocket bible for safe keeping. When he returned, he saw that the book had been opened at Revelations viii. 1–4, an allegorical description of the experience the seven crewmates had just undergone.

Heavenly Body left its formation over Germany with one engine out. Over the Channel two other engines failed and the bomber crashed on the water, breaking into three. The pilot and co-pilot were trapped in one section, which sank quickly beneath 20-foot waves. The other seven crewmen either huddled in their rubber dinghy or clung to its sides. Chapter viii of Revelations reads: 'And I saw the seven angels that stood before God.'

While the airmen were buffeted by waves and drenched by spray, they looked up to see a British Air Sea Rescue plane circling overhead, radioing their position to rescue craft … Revelations: 'and another angel came.' The crewmen waited anxiously for help. Some 30 minutes passed.

'There was silence in heaven about the space of half an hour.'

Finally, they saw a rescue launch speeding towards them. As it approached, the circling aircraft dropped smoke flares to direct it to the survivors …

'And the smoke of the incense, which came with the prayers of the saints, ascended up before God out of the angel's hand ...'

Newspaper report

'Believe me, I am not ashamed to say that I was scared today and never prayed harder to come through.'

Larry Goldstein, radio operator, 388th BG

Chaplain Duhl and Father Sharbaugh were always at the briefings. On every mission the crews had the opportunity, which many took, to have a word with their Chaplain and the comfort of prayer. This, more than anything else, gave those of us who didn't fly but who watched the men go out, a truer realization of the fact that death rode with them. And it gave us a conviction that everything we could do to protect the fliers in careful preparation and training would be done to prevent every loss that work and care could make possible. To the fliers, and to their people at home, this devout ministration was a strengthening thing.

The 467th Bombardment Group,
Allan Healy

'George Triantifillous (The Greek) was in his ball turret, no doubt praying as the flak was doing everything but flying the airplane. Planes were falling and burning all over the sky and the worst was yet to come. The airplane commander was having a problem with a ship that cut across his formation causing him to curse the wayward pilot with every known cuss word he could shout on the intercom.

Suddenly, a voice on the radio from the ball turret, hardly audible, said: 'Don't listen to him Lord, he don't mean it.'

Russ D. Hayes, gunner, 389th BG

Long missions, eight hours or longer, were extremely tiring and mentally fatiguing. I recall a long, deep mission into southern Germany with flak most of the way, some bad weather and the loss of several aircraft and crews. This was somewhere between my 25th and 30th mission. We came home exhausted, and something happened to me after landing. War, death, and destruction just didn't make any sense to me anymore. That evening, instead of singing and whooping it up at the bar as was my custom, I chose a table off in the corner to be by myself. My friend, Father McDonough, came over with a drink, having noticed the change. I told him my problem and asked for help. He was silent for some time, contemplating the drinks and my problem.

Then he looked me square in the eye and said: 'Tays, all of the major religions of the world have as their primary mission to teach man to live in peace and harmony with his fellow man. When I do not do my job as a man of the cloth, then you will have to do your job as a soldier.'

His wisdom shocked me into reality and has held me on a meaningful course ever since. Thanks, Father McDonough, wherever you are.

Colonel Robert H. Tays, pilot, 392nd BG

A fine young man lived in our barracks. He was tall, nice-looking, very modest and unassuming. He never used profanity, nor did he drink. Nightly he sat on his bunk, took out his bible and read it for perhaps an hour or more. Despite our normal irreverence, we did not ridicule him. Rather we stood in awe of him, so much so that we never cursed nor misbehaved in his presence. To us he was saintly. On his twentieth mission we saw his plane go down in flames. There were no parachutes. This sad event finally and irrevocably extinguished any thirst for religion that might have been growing in my young heart. I could not believe in a God that rewarded devoutness in such a manner. It was not until many years later that I came to have a spiritual life.

Chick's Crew, **Ben C. Smith**

Above: P-51Bs and Ds of the 374th FS, 361st FG from Bottisham, Cambridgeshire, sporting D-Day invasion stripes and fuselage drop tanks. Nearest Mustang is Bald Eagle. (USAF via Tom Cushing)

Right: On 5 July 1944 Lt. Col. Francis S. 'Gabby' Gabreski, CO, 61st FS, 56th FG, scored his twenty-eighth fighter victory of the war. Gabby was shot down on 20 July by flak at Bassinheim airfield and was captured. (USAF)

Pursuits

If ever I mount up to heaven
And enter those high 'pearly gates',
My first word of thanks
To the Lord from us 'Yanks'
Will be for the P-38s.
High in the blue, little angels,
Winging their way to the aid
Of the bombers that soar,
To settle a score,
And lessen the price to be paid.
In the very next sentence I utter
Before I have scarcely begun
With awe in my voice
I shall humbly rejoice
For the gift of the P-51.
Ask the lad who goes up in a Fortress;
If he must he will swap off his gun,
For a dear 'little friend'

To protect him no end.
He will trade for a P-51.
Though now I should be rather breathless
As I give out with thanks up in heaven,
'Tis a fool I would be
If I didn't agree
To give thanks for the P-47.
Up where the con trails linger,
Five miles up and more,
He's a demon from hell
The 'Huns' know well
And a sight the 'Forts' adore.
Say, here's to our gallant fighters;
A toast to their crews of one.
And a word of thanks
From a crew of 'Yanks'
Who make the bomber run.

A toast to 'Little Friends' by Clement L. Lockwood

Above: Develess 3rd *and* Heat Wave *of the 369th FS, 359th FG, 67th Fighter Wing at East Wretham in 1944. On 21 November 1944 near Merseberg, 1/Lt. Claude J. Crenshaw, flying* Heat Wave, *shot down four Focke-Wulf 190s and claimed a probable to take his score to seven confirmed kills. This tally is even more impressive considering that only three of his guns were working and he was also forced to open fire at deflection angles of up to 90° plus!* (Tony Chardella)

Above: *P-51D in the colours of Captain Donald R. Emerson's 336th FS, 4th FG Mustang off the starboard wing of* Fuddy Duddy *in 1995. Emerson was killed by flak on Christmas Day 1944.* (MWB)

Right: *Don Allen, a chief mechanic, painted Emerson's distinctive Donald Duck, 'dukes up and fighting mad', on the cowling.* (MWB)

... I was so very anxious to fly. When the RAF airman told me it would be 7/6d a day (seven shillings and sixpence, or about 37p) I told him I couldn't afford it. You see, I thought I had to pay them. I had always heard that to be a member of the British armed forces you had to have a bit of money.

The airman laughed at me and said: 'No, we pay you 7/6d a day.' I said: 'You loveable fool. You could've had me for nothing.'

I really thought they were crazy to pay me to fly.

Anglophile Lieutenant Colonel James A. 'Goody' Goodson, who in 1940 joined the RCAF and gained his wings before joining No. 133, one of the three RAF 'Eagle' Squadrons formed in the UK from October 1940 to August 1941 (the other two were Nos. 71 and 121). Late in 1942 he joined the 336th FS, 4th Fighter Group, USAAC, finishing the war with fourteen victories in the air and fifteen on the ground.

The 356th Fighter Group was forming at Westover Field in 1943, and we became the first pilots to join the new group, flying P-47 Thunderbolts. Our aircraft were delivered by sea to the UK while we

Above: *Fading memories. A Thunderbolt on a wall at Wendling in 1981.* (MWB)

traveled in the troopship *Orion*, arriving at Glasgow in August 1943. From there we continued to Goxhill near Hull, where our fighters were awaiting collection and delivery to our operating base at Martlesham Heath in Suffolk. I was allocated P-47D, 42-74702 with the 361st Squadron letters QI:F. Mine was named after the girl I left behind in the States, Doris Clark ... and so it was that Clarkie came with me and brought me luck. Before I left for England, Doris had given

Above: *361st FG insignia on a wall at Bottisham in May 1981. (MWB)*

Below: *P-38 Lightning being prepared for take-off. (USAF)*

one engine caught fire. Dave also had a go at him. No chutes were seen, but we saw the aircraft crash into the ground. Camera-gun films confirmed our success and we were both credited with half a Ju 88.

Three weeks later, on 13 February, on a sweep into France led by Lieutenant Colonel Coen, we were bounced by a mixed group of 109s and 190s near Chartres. In the fight that followed, we claimed five enemy aircraft destroyed, without loss. It was like a rat race, with fighters milling about all around. One 190 appeared in front, long enough for me to fire off a burst. My hits were sufficient to destroy it although I was too busy to watch it go down. I was also credited with two more 190s damaged in this scrap.

During a bombing attack by B-17s on Berlin on 6 March, I added another 109 to my score. A month later the 356th FG escorted bombers to Brunswick but no enemy fighters were encountered. We went down to search for ground targets and arrived over Gifhorn airfield, where we found aircraft lined up in rows, just asking for trouble. The whole of the 361st joined in the attack; coming in low, one behind the other, each making three passes. We could see the Germans running everywhere, trying to escape. By the time we were through, it seemed that every enemy aircraft on that airfield had been destroyed. I was credited with the destruction of two Ju 88s plus a shared 190 and a

me a tiny check shirt on a hanger, as a momento. This was always hung in the cockpit whenever I flew.

The first time I engaged an enemy aircraft was in January 1944, with Lieutenant David Thwaites as my wingman, returning from an escort mission. We saw a Ju 88 away down below, somewhere near Cambrai. With permission to break formation, we dived on the bomber at something like 250 to 300 knots. Of course I opened fire much too early in my eagerness, but closing in, a long burst hit the '88 and

Above: *Captain Sidney Hewett of the 361st FS, 356th FG, in the cockpit of his Thunderbolt. (via Theo Boiten)*

Ju 52. My friend Ernie Parham was brought down by ground flak.

My luck eventually ran out on 4 May 1944, after 166 hours of combat flying. It was about 10.30 to 11.00 a.m., on the way back, near to Steinhuder Lake ... we were bounced from above and behind. There were about fifteen of them, long-nosed 190s with yellow noses, and our group numbered about the same. They opened fire on the way down and one shell exploded on my canopy, showering me with perspex fragments. A second hit the wing root on the right side sending splinters across the fuselage and injuring my left leg. I guessed that others had probably entered the engine cowling through the gills. We were at 18,000 feet and although the Pratt & Whitney continued to run, oil pressure was rapidly falling. The explosion had jammed my canopy and it looked impossible to get out through the small breakout panel while wearing a parachute. The engine soon stopped but the aircraft continued to fly reasonably under control, despite the steep dive. A small wood of pine trees appeared ahead with open ground beyond. This was one time when the big, bulky P-47 was definitely to be preferred rather than the lighter P-51 with its underslung radiator.

Braced for the impact, I felt the first contact with the treetops as we cut a swathe through them,

cushioning the descent. Emerging from the wood, the aircraft slithered to a halt in a small wheat field. The wings stayed on and there was no fire. Without a parachute, it was possible to vacate the cockpit, but in my haste, I forgot to release my oxygen tube and radio connection. This prevented me from reaching the ground and left me hanging upside down from the cockpit.

Two victorious 190s made a low pass but fortunately did not open fire – no doubt thinking that I was a goner. Although my leg was quite badly injured, four times I went back to my aircraft, after the crash. First to switch off the fuel, second to try to set it on fire, third to acquire the escape-pack from the parachute and finally, to retrieve my lucky mascot, the little check shirt.

Captain Sidney Hewett, 356th Fighter Group, in conversation with the late Charles 'Holly' Hall. A kind, elderly German lady wrapped his leg in a sheet and later he was taken to the town jail at Diepholz, to the west of Hanover. On 29 April 1945, he was released from prison camp, flown back to France in a C-47, and then shipped back to New York, without returning to Martlesham Heath.

Many a pilot who flew the pursuits
Has winged his way into heaven
But I know that the boy who was leading the flight
Was a kid in a P-47

As missions grew long through death laden skies
Our bombers had little to fear
We had the best escort acclaimed by us all
'Twas a squadron of Thunderbolts near

Many a bomber knocked out of the fight
Forever their praises will sing
For while limping home through treacherous sky
They had 'white noses' under each wing

How well I remember that beautiful sight
Wispy contrails high in the heavens
And how we all welcomed the tail gunner's words
'Here come the P-47s'

Anonymous

Above: Lt. Walter Konantz of the 338th FS, 55th FG, at Wormingford with his dog Scotty, which had a 'wheel', fitted to its broken leg, sustained in an accident with a jeep! Konantz was the first pilot in the 55th FG to destroy an Me 262 jet fighter, on 13 January 1945. (Konantz Coll)

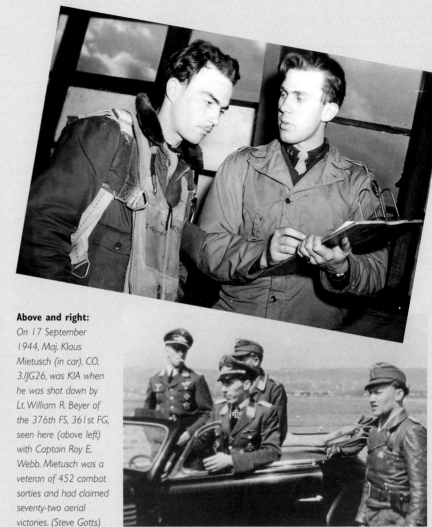

Above and right: On 17 September 1944, Maj. Klaus Mietusch (in car), CO, 3./JG26, was KIA when he was shot down by Lt. William R. Beyer of the 376th FS, 361st FG, seen here (above left) with Captain Roy E. Webb. Mietusch was a veteran of 452 combat sorties and had claimed seventy-two aerial victories. (Steve Gotts)

Left: John 'Wild Bill' Crump and 'Jeep', the coyote who flew five fighter missions with him in a P-47 Thunderbolt fighter. Jeep was the mascot of the 360th FS, 356th FG at Martlesham Heath, near Ipswich, Suffolk. Jeep was only two weeks old when Crump acquired him from a Nebraska farmer. He accompanied his master to Baton Rouge, La., where Crump qualified as a fighter pilot and Jeep was given his GI immunisations and military papers. To bypass Britain's strict rabies laws Jeep travelled in a gas mask case aboard the Queen Elizabeth. Crump recalls: 'Halfway across, a colonel came to my quarters to inquire if I actually had a coyote aboard. I couldn't deny it since Jeep was snoozing on my bunk. He came from Oklahoma and knew about coyotes, but he saw how tame Jeep was and didn't show any concern – maybe because there were no live chickens on the ship. Jeep became a favourite of the squadron and became especially friendly with the squadron cooks.' Jeep flew his five combat missions in September 1944 during Operation Market Garden, in which approximately 350 US AAC fighters bombed and strafed targets in the Netherlands in support of Allied airborne landings. On one mission Crump came under attack and when he threw his Thunderbolt around the sky in a successful evasive action, the negative G-force kept a frightened, wide-eyed Jeep floating around the cockpit until Crump anchored him to a convenient handle. On 24 November 1944 Jeep was killed when ironically, he was run over by a four-wheeled jeep. Jeep was buried with full military honours at Playford Hall, an impressive Elizabethan mansion and an Eagle Squadron billet four miles from Ipswich. A bugler sounded taps, and a 'missing man formation' thundered overhead with a low-altitude victory roll by Crump. Jeep is the only member of the species canis latrans known to have served in combat in WWII. After his death, Crump flew with no other mascot. (Bill Crump)

Left: Jeep's grave in the grounds of Playford Hall. (MWB)

Right: *Victory score. (MWB)*

Below: *No Guts No Glory! taking off amid smoke at North Weald. (MWB)*

Above: *Lt. Col. John C. Meyer, CO, 487th FS, 352nd FG in the cockpit of Petie 2nd at Bodney. Meyer destroyed twenty-four enemy aircraft in the air (and two half shares) 1943–45, as well as thirteen on the ground. (via Bill Espie)*

Below: *Another Petie 2nd at Lakeland, Florida in 1987. (MWB)*

Above: Sizzling Liz *in close.*
(MWB)

Below: Spitfire II *in tight. The*
RAF escorts were always a
welcome sight in WWII.
(MWB)

I broke into the first attack but a deflection shot from one enemy aircraft hit me (20mm) and my airducts were punctured enabling me to pull only thirty-five inches boost at 20,000 feet. The same hit also caused my guns to become inoperative and blew away my elevator and trim tab controls. Several attacks were made in rapid succession upon me, causing me to break several times more – always into the attacks which this time were coming from all directions. I finally half rolled to the deck, with one Fw 190 right behind me. He fired all the way down and because of insufficient manifold pressure in my aircraft, kept with me easily. I evaded by violent sliding and supping. I hedge-hopped from the point where I hit the deck (approximately ten miles south-east of Ghent) to just north of Dunkirk with the 190 about 100 yards behind me all the way. I managed to evade his 20mm until his supply was exhausted. He then

continued to fire the .30 cals, which did no serious damage when they did hit. The enemy aircraft broke off the engagement and I crossed the French coast. Some fragments from one of his 20mms embedded themselves in my leg, but were removed at a hospital near Eastchurch airdrome where I finally set down. Landing was made after sunset (approx 2005 hours) with no flaps (hydraulic system shot out) and with wheels down. The ship nosed up at the end of the field.

Combat report, Lieutenant John W. Voght, P-47 Thunderbolt pilot, 56th FG, 2 September 1943. His pursuer was Leutnant Dietrich Kehl of II.Stab/JG26, who followed Voght from Lille to the coast before exhausting all his ammunition on the P-47. (Kehl was later KIA, on 25 February 1944 in combat with a 4th FG P-47 near Metz). Hauptmann Johannes 'Hans' Naumann, II./JG26 CO, and his fighters, flying at 25,000 feet in thick but broken cloud, spotted two flights of 56th FG Thunderbolts led by Colonel Hubert Zemke, in a clear layer below. Zemke, who had led three twelve-plane formations off from Halesworth that evening, had decided to make one final turn and sweep behind the Fortresses, which because of the thick cloud, had aborted their raids on airfields in north-west France. Naumann got behind the Thunderbolts, dived, and pulled up in their blind spot beneath. The first burst from Naumann's cannon caused Lieutenants Wilfred Van Abel and Walter Hannigan in Zemke's second element to fall away and crash. Van Abel baled out and was made POW. Hannigan was killed. Zemke had his instrument panel shattered and took a 30mm strike in the wing root, which severed a trim control cable. Worse, his engine quit. Zemke dived away to a safer altitude but just as he was preparing to bale out, his engine started again. (A 20mm shell had hit the turbo-supercharger under the rear fuselage, which starved his engine of air at the higher altitude). Zemke got back to England without incident. Victory claims by Naumann, and Feldwebels Karl Ehret and Wilhelm Mayer of 6./JG26, were sent to Berlin but only Ehret received confirmation of a victory over the Thunderbolts because the other crashes had not been witnessed.

The mission I remember clearly is the last one, on 12 July 1944, to Munich. We were hit on the outskirts and barely made it to the target. We dropped our bombs and tried to keep up with the squadron, but on three engines this proved futile. We had lost a lot of gas and found we had only enough to get us to the beachhead in France. About this time a P-51 Mustang came alongside. Across the nose was *Hurry Home Honey* from the 357th FG. The pilot suggested we try for Italy but was informed by our navigator, Lieutenant Ginn, that we would not make it over the mountains. Captain Wilson, our pilot, asked the navigator to lay course for Switzerland. The pilot of the P-51 wished us luck. (I found out later he was Major Richard A. Peterson of the 357th FG based at Leiston). We met

Above: *Leutnant Karl 'Charlie' Willius, Staffel Kapitan, 2./JG26 climbs into the cockpit of his Fw190A-8 at Florennes, Belgium in 1943. The national flags painted beneath his cockpit denote the countries over which Willius had seen action (Holland, Belgium, France, England and Russia). After claiming a 44th BG B-24 on 8 April 1944 on his 371st combat mission (his fiftieth combat victory), 'Charlie' was hit by a Thunderbolt of the 357th FS, 361st FG, flown by 1/Lt. Alton B. Snyder, and was killed when his Fw190A-8 'Black 5' exploded near Genemuiden, Holland. His widow Lisette received a posthumous Ritterkreuz on 9 June 1944. (Lisette Arend-Willius)*

Right: *1/Lt. Alton B Snyder Jr., 357th FS, 361st FG, who on 8 April 1944 shot down Lt. Karl 'Charlie' Willius. (Steve Gotts)*

ENCOUNTER REPORT

A. COMBAT
B. APRIL 8, 1944
C. 375TH FIGHTER SQUADRON, 361ST FIGHTER GROUP
D. 1545 HOURS
E. 7 MILES NORTH OF ZWOLLE
F. CU AND HAZE
G. FW 190
H. 1 FW 190 DESTROYED
I. I WAS FLYING WABASH YELLOW LEADER. WE WERE ESCORTING B-24S ON WITHDRAWAL OVER THE ZUIDER ZEE. I SAW TWO FW 190S MAKE A HEAD-ON ATTACK AT THE BOMBERS. WE IMMEDIATELY BOUNCED THE TWO E/A. JUST AFTER COMING THROUGH THE MAIN BOX OF BOMBERS THE TWO E/A BOUNCED A STRAGGLER FLYING AT 10,000 FT AND BEHIND THE MAIN BOX. I OBSERVED STRIKES ON THE B-24 BUT HE DIDN'T GO DOWN. THE E/AS IMMEDIATELY SPLIT ESSED AND WE FOLLOWED THEM DOWN TO 3,000 FT OPENING FIRE AT 300 YDS. I OBSERVED MANY HITS ON FUSELAGE AND WING ROOTS. THE E/A STAGGERED MOMENTARILY AND SPUN INTO THE GROUND, BURSTING INTO FLAMES. I CLAIM THIS FW 190 DESTROYED.
J. 750 ROUNDS E2-N 42-75558
(SIGNED)
ALTON B. SNYDER JR., 1ST LT., AIR CORPS.
Encounter Report, First Lieutenant Alton B. Snyder Jr., 8 April 1944, via Steve Gotts

a few Me 109s and Focke-Wulfs but they were either out of ammo or nearly out, so they made a few half-hearted passes and left.

As we neared the Swiss border, the Germans had laid out a large red cross and were firing red flares for us to land. We were losing altitude. The fighters had damaged another engine but our pilot decided to fly inland as far as possible. We finally landed at Altenrheim/SG near Lake Constance. We were told it was the shortest landing a B-24 ever made. We landed in a swamp and the wheels were half hidden by mud ...

Rocky Starek, *Fat Stuff II,* **B-24 gunner, 712th BS, 448th BG**

Above: *Beer is served at the reconstructed 8th Air Force bar at Wright-Patteson AFB. (MWB)*

Left: *Fields of Little America. (MWB)*

Fields of Little America

'Whether the British will keep all of these airfields after the war is a question, but there are so many I'd guess not. There are literally hundreds of fields of all kinds and actually some of the boys get in the wrong traffic pattern and land in the wrong field or in the right pattern and still land at the wrong field.'

Captain Ralph H. Elliott, pilot, 467th BG

The first thing I recall on arrival was checking into our squadron living site and the hut, which was to be home for the next year or more. I noticed that someone was cutting off a piece of the beams in the hut to make firewood ... The quarters did receive a ration of coal for the fires. We all, or most of us, including myself, wore warm socks even in bed and were seldom without them. The floor was always wet. Yet the dampness seeped into the beds and into the quarters and the wind across the Norfolk Broads and the Fens rattled against the huts. The cold was the same damp chill that invades the English cathedrals and in a country without central heating in the 1940s, it was most difficult to avoid.

**Technical Sergeant Forrest S. Clark,
air gunner, 67th BS, 44th BG**

Above: *Robin Hood in the former library at Deopham Green. (MWB)*

The combat crews were kept separate from the rest of the base personnel and we lived primarily in the north-east corner of the Molesworth base in small Nissen huts with twelve men to a hut, making two crews. Right next door lived eight officers who formed the rest of the two crews. We had a little coke stove, but toilet facilities were a little lacking. We had a couple of flush toilets but no facilities to take a shower, so we rigged up a couple of barrels with a charcoal stove underneath to get a little warm water. A dirty body at high altitude was so much harder to keep warm and it always surprised me that better washing facilities for the combat crews were never provided.

**Howard F. Hernan, gunner,
303rd BG**

Above: *Nissen hut at Framlingham in the early Seventies. (MWB)*

Right: *Progress threatens to envelop the Bovingdon control tower in 1994. (MWB)*

Where you get watered scotch at four bits a snort
And those limey cabbies don't stand short
Where the prices are high and the queues are long
And the Yankee GIs are always wrong

And these pitch black nights when you stay out late
It's so bloody dark you can hardly navigate
There's no transportation so you have to hike
And you get your can knocked off by a GI bike

The isle ain't worth saving I don't think
Cut the balloons and let the damned thing sink
I ain't complaining I'll have you know
But life's rough as a cob in the ETO.

Anonymous

Left: *Pin-up, one of several painted on walls at the 14th Combat Wing HQ at Shipdham during the war by Jack Loman using paint bought at Jarrolds department store in Norwich in 1943. This photo was taken in 1981! (MWB)*

Where the heavy dew whips through the breeze
And you wade through mud up to your knees
Where the sun don't shine and the rain flows free
And the fog's so thick you could hardly see

Where we live on Brussels sprouts and spam
And the powdered eggs which aren't worth a damn
In town you can eat the fish and spuds
And down the taste with a mug of suds

You hold your nose when you gulp it down
It hits your stomach and then you frown
It burns your tongue, makes your throat feel queer
It's rightly named bitter, it sure ain't beer

Our barracks were Nissen huts made of corrugated steel, half-round in cross section, about 40 feet long and 16 feet wide with concrete floors. There were doors in each end and a big window on each side of the door, but the front end had an attached alcove with an outside door so you could come in at night without showing any light. We always had to keep the heavy blackout curtains in place if any lights were

Below: *706th BS insignia on a wall at Bungay (Flixton) in 1991. (MWB)*

Above: *Overgrown entrance to a Nissen hut at Great Ashfield in 1997. (MWB)*

on, and no one could smoke outside without shielding the end of their cigarette – usually in the palm of their hand. When the CQ (charge of quarters) woke us for a mission, he always checked to see that the curtains were closed before he turned on the light. The huts were lined but not insulated so were pretty cold in the wintertime. Rats would get in between the lining, and when things got dull we'd chase them out to shoot at with our .45s – never hit any. We had a coke burner in the middle of the room, and when it was going the ones near it cooked while the ones at the ends froze – when we had fuel, that is. We got a coal-bucket full once a week. It was never enough but we were usually able to steal some from the locked storage bins to get by. The bins were about 10 feet square with brick about 3 feet up and heavy wire mesh above that for another 4 feet. When they filled the bins, the coke usually came up above the brick and we could get it out a piece at a time through the gap between the brick and the wire. Later on I bought an axe and a saw, and we burned wood from Sir Stracey's trees just over the fence behind the barracks. That was illegal but we never got caught …

I had a Mormon bombardier by the name of Jim Andrews for a few missions. His crew had finished ahead of him and he had three or four to go before he could go home so he flew them with us. Jim was a tremendous bombardier but a personal slob. He couldn't get enough blankets so he rigged a 200-watt light bulb on an extension cord and took it to bed with him, after dressing for bed in a set of long underwear, wool socks, shirt and pants, heavy flying pants, and a heavy winter parka, plus his three or four wool blankets. About 3 p.m. he smelled smoke, said he didn't see any fire, and went back to sleep. Next time he woke his parka was on fire so he put out the fire, turned off his light, and went back to bed. For the rest of the time he was with us, he wore the parka with a great big hole burned in it. The blankets all had holes in them too …

There were normally two crews in a hut, and this could be from eight to twelve men depending on the crew makeup … When a crew finished it's tour or didn't return, another crew would be assigned to their beds. The replacements were usually new to the base. By mixing new and old crews, the new ones could benefit from the older crew's experience. Because of very high losses, one group (492nd) was broken up and we got one of the squadrons, which made things crowded until transfers and combat losses got the numbers down again …

Captain Ralph H. Elliott, pilot, 467th BG

Morituri te salutamos. 'We who are about to die salute you!' These haunting words from the Roman Circus have come down through the centuries and, more than any others ever spoken, portray the loneliness of young men chosen for sacrifice. There was a time when the melancholy greeting seemed not inappropriate to my own generation.

Our day-to-day existence was not unlike that of the ancient gladiators. They lived life one day at a time, looked after their equipment, sharpened their weapons, practiced constantly for the fray, laughed, wept, caroused, ate, and made love at every opportunity. So did we. There was no escape; they were imprisoned until their moment of truth came. So were we. Our prison was of our own making – fashioned of loyalty, honor, and love for our friends. In our time those things counted for something. But it was no less a prison. We would not have thought of trying to escape, for to do so would have been letting down our friends. We lived as men who were earmarked for destruction just as the gladiators did. One could see it in the eyes of the men who flew the missions. The overlay of fatalism and pervasive dread was always there, subliminally.

A visitor could see it immediately. There was something wrong with these boys. They were not incapable of laughter, but for the most part they tended to be quiet, morose, and edgy. They drank too much and did not involve themselves in any enterprise that projected too much into the future. The new crews coming in were ebullient and enthusiastic, but this mood did not last. After a few missions they began to have that 'look.' When I first came to the squadron, I had an odd experience. One day about dusk I joined a volleyball game already in progress. It was so weird – no one shouted, laughed, or made a sound. The entire game was played in silence. There was a different dimension there. I have never forgotten how strange it was.

The early morning hours before a mission were a bad time for all. It was horrible to be in a warm sack, safe and secure, knowing that it was a cruel illusion which would soon be exchanged for the reality of a shrieking, sub-zero honor. It was much like death row on the morning of execution. We listened for the steps to come down the walk and scrooched a little farther down into our sacks. Everyone was awake already, adrenaline was flowing in profusion, and every fiber of our beings was alert and vibrating with apprehension. The CQ would open the door, switch on the light, and begin to call off the names of the crews who were to fly the mission. What a blessed reprieve when he did not call our names. What an utterly devastating, soul searing blow when he did! Some thought of the CQ as sadistic. In reality it was probably a painful chore for him. His way of handling it was unfortunate. He chose to be breezy and jocular, and it was just not that kind of scenario.

Equally traumatic was the sight of empty cots. A new crew would quickly be sent out to fill the vacant spaces left by our friends who had not returned from the mission the day before. At first

Above: *Barrack hut window at Bungay (Flixton). (MWB)*

the new people would seem strange and alien – totally inexperienced and unready for the perils that awaited them, like lambs for the slaughter. We tried to keep our distance from them, because getting involved meant that we would be replaying the scene in a few days or weeks. I am afraid that we resented the new people because they seemed like usurpers, taking the spaces which had been occupied by treasured friends. Of course, the poor, uncomprehending lambs did not understand our apparent indifference. The snobbish treatment was not really directed at them. It was our way of protecting ourselves against hurt. However, there was no way to prevent becoming involved with them; we were in too close quarters. Eventually they would become our friends, and we would be set up for heartbreak again. Four crews in our barracks had finished combat tours before I left England: Brinkley's, Brown's, Bayer's, and ours. The rest were lost. It would have been unnatural had we not experienced some self-pity. Most of us were quite vocal in the expression of it, and bitching was the leaven of our existence.

At a time when our losses had been particularly heavy, and morale was not so good, this particular colonel decided that what we needed was a good bracing. All of the combat crews were herded into some place, and he went on to say that we were acting like 'cry babies,' that killing and being killed was our business over there, that heavy losses came with the territory. He got this bad scene right out of a B movie. It was a brutal, sadistic piece of business and totally uncalled for. No one was mutinying; no one was refusing to fly. These men were specialists, they knew their jobs, and they had always performed well. What they would not do for anyone was submit to abuse. I can still see the hurt and anger on their faces as they listened unbelieving. There was a lot of muttering. These men were there not as slaves but as free men. Not a one of them would have stopped flying even if given the opportunity to do so. The flight crews never had any use for the colonel after this piece of gratuitous arrogance.

Life was a fast lottery, and the players changed on a daily basis. There was constant speculation in the barracks about one's chance of finishing a tour. Can you imagine making a book on your own life? We were preoccupied with the macabre business. Sometimes a crew would start getting close to the finish. This was the worst time of all for them. They began to assume a haunted look and clammed up completely. Two of our crews were lost on their

final missions, unusual, to be sure, but these tragedies had the effect of making us all extremely apprehensive when we began to get close.

When I first got there, only a few crews had ever completed a combat tour. Some crews started finishing after I was there for a while, and, then, loss percentages improved considerably when replacements began to pour in with a consequent improvement in morale.

Chick's Crew, 'The Gladiators', Ben C. Smith, radio operator, 303rd BG, Molesworth

Seething was a very small village located about ten miles south-east of Norwich. It was made up of one pub, one small store, a church and maybe a half dozen houses – not very large but very picturesque. The pub became a very popular gathering place for many of the ground personnel and flight crews. Most of the English pubs were alike, plain but clean and dimly lit. The Americans took to the English mild and bitter beer, ale and stout very well. Since it was all they could get, it was either adjust to it or do without. Since I didn't see any of them doing without, it must have been easy for them to adjust. At 10.00 p.m. sharp, the barkeeper called time and the last round was bought. When that was gone, the pub closed for the night.

The airbase station # 146 was a typical RAF base with its buildings set apart in small groups. Each group of buildings was called a site. Each squadron was assigned to separate sites as were the enlisted crewmembers and officers. The purpose of the dispersal was in case of an air raid where a couple of well placed bombs wouldn't put the whole group out of action. Numerous farms were scattered around the airfield, making it easier to camouflage. These farms were typical English, right out of the history book. The barns were built adjoining the houses for convenience in tending the animals. Many of the buildings still used thatched roofs and stone walls. Much of the equipment used to till the soil and mow the hay was long since outdated. Some of the farms were manned by groups of women belonging to the 'Women's Land Army.' They kept many of the farms producing while the able men were away in the service.

Crew 64, Staff Sergeant Gene Gaskins, air gunner, 448th BG, Seething

Life around the base now was beginning to be a bit move livable and to some degree, like home. The Aero Club lounge had been decorated by Corporal Ferris C. Parsons. It had deep sea murals to add a restful atmosphere. Mrs Holman Hunt added the interest in the library and Corporal Gerald E. Brown had painted Robin Hood scenes on the wall ... The game room provided two pool tables, three ping-pong tables and three dart boards. The room was decorated with Corporal Parsons' version of Donald Duck and Mickey Mouse, which was quite cute ... All these things served to make life a bit more interesting and add to the joy of being in Merry Old England.

Merry Old England, 452nd BG history

Above: *Sunset at Thorpe Abbotts. (Jim Gintner)*

Left: *Robin Hood's merry men in the former library at Deopham Green, still there today. (MWB)*

All about Norwich were the bases of the Second Division – the Liberator groups of the Eighth Air Force. Division headquarters was at Ketteringham Hall west of Norwich. The 96th Wing – our Wing – had its three groups to the north of the city, the 466th at Attlebridge to the northwest, the 458th at Horsham St Faith on Norwich's northern outskirts, and we, the 467th, seven miles northeast at Rackheath.

The Air Ministry had built our base. Its plan was far different from that of American bases. There were no serried rows of bleak buildings with grass and trees scraped from the ground and everything barren, efficient, and a scar on the landscape.

Rackheath had benefited from the necessities of camouflage. Nissen huts were grouped under tall trees at the edge of the woods, and in amongst them. Roads passed under rows of fruit trees. The farm croft and byre were left untouched. One site was far down by the rhododendron drive, another across the Jersey pasture where the ornamental sheep and tame deer grazed. You walked through a bluebell-carpeted wood in spring from Site 1 to the Operations block, and past straw-ricks from there to the briefing building. A hedgerow lined the lane of a civilian-traveled road right through the base, where, on Sundays, the children stood and asked, 'Any gum, chum?' Much of the farm-like quality of the countryside was preserved so that from the air only the slash of the runways showed.

We settled in. We were restricted the first month until we became operational. We learned to drink warm English beer and 'cider' at the officers' and NCO clubs. We sang around the piano about Pete the POM Inspector. We learned about English money – a little. It always seemed as if a pound note was a dollar and in poker and dice games pounds were flipped about like confetti ....

... The sixteen months of life at a bomber base in Norfolk had many aspects. Much of life was communal yet each man, by some sort of trial and error method, found for himself a manner of life that was distinct. Each had a pattern of work and recreation, English friends, places he went to on leave and furlough, pubs he drank in during the long spring evenings, dances, girls, movies, and all the ways of living that made it a fuller existence. There was much we did for ourselves. Much of America was imported for our comfort, though we could not have an American drugstore or see women dressed as American women are. We had a PX, of sorts, a place where you went for your weekly rations; five packs of cigarettes (once down to four), four candy bars, some gum or peppermints, an occasional bonus of fruit juice, cookies, soap, razor blades, and other oddments that meant much to one's personal living. It was little and meager compared to American Army posts. We had a gym, where basketball was played and the Special Service sports equipment was tried out. Some tennis was played on Sir Edward's court. Softball games were played in many places from the perimeter strip to the areas about the Nissen sites.

Of course, the most popular recreation at Rackheath was time in the 'sack.' But there was much to do outside it. Large Nissens made up the Aero Club where enlisted men could enjoy a library, game tables, a snack bar, and the attentions of the Red Cross girls. The officers had their club, under the sign of the sword and chain, where a bar provided for most, and papers and magazines, checkers, bridge, or chess gave recreation to some. Here John Gile and Dick Grey pounded the pianos and the tin-plated roof reverberated to 'It's a long, rough road from Rackheath to Berlin,' and 'Rackheath Aggies.' Many of us had radios in our huts. We could hear the BBC and its renderings of American jazz, nature talks, or the news of Monty and his men. Often we listened to Calais One or the Luxembourg station with its German propaganda. A soft, feminine voice would try to make us homesick and they would play 'Home on the Range' and then sweetly tell us that we would never see America again. We would hear their programs interrupted as Feindliche Flugzeugen flew over the Reichsgebiet and the stations went off the air as the RAF passed. The best was American Forces Network on the Road to Berlin, which was all that radio should be and no soap to be sold.

The 467th Bombardment Group, Allan Healy

Above: *Attlebridge airfield in 1997. (MWB)*

Above: *Horsham St Faith and its wartime runways now more familiar as Norwich Airport. (MWB)*

Above: *Daisies growing on a disused air raid shelter at Horsham St Faith. (MWB)*

Above: The YMCA Flying Service, *the first of three such-named Liberators, and a YMCA wagon at a dispersal at Wendling in 1944. (USAF via Mike Bailey)*

Below: *Eagle mural in the ground officers' mess at Wendling in 1986. (MWB)*

After our home at Unthank Road, Norwich, was destroyed in the heavy bombing raids in April 1942, my family and I were evacuated to an old cottage at Wendling, where my father worked on the construction of the airfield. Jack Scott lived and worked at Canister Farm on the airfield itself. The Air Ministry wanted to demolish Jack's farmhouse. However Jack firmly believed in the saying, 'An Englishman's home is his castle'. Officials tried to persuade and convince Jack with all sorts of arguments and dire warnings but Jack was adamant: 'I'm staying ... I was here long before you arrived and I'll be here long after you've gone. That's all I have to say. Good day, gentlemen.' (Or words to that effect). So Wendling airfield was actually constructed around Jack Scott's smallholding. In fact, the control tower was built only 250 yards from his farmhouse, which was surrounded by technical site buildings. He stayed on his farm all through the war, with his goats grazing contentedly on the grass around the control tower.

The American airmen however, quickly recognized the fact that here was an ideal source of fresh milk instead of the powdered variety served in the mess halls. Many a time Jack was up at the crack of dawn only to discover that his goats had already been milked.

'Those bloody Yanks have milked my goats again,' Jack grumbled to my father.

However, Jack got on very well with the American airmen. They looked after his food requirements as and when they could, as they did for our family and many other needy people in the surrounding villages.

My mother did the laundry for the Americans. One day my father had all the muddy shirts and uniforms of the GIs' baseball team for her. My mother had a sister in Manchester and the Americans told her that she deserved a break from all that washing and housework. They generously clubbed together and paid the return (round trip) train fares to Manchester for my mother, young brother David, Joy and myself. It was a very enjoyable holiday and something which we could never have afforded otherwise. When we returned to Wendling, Dad and several of the Americans were at the station to greet us. From there we went to the Rose Cottage pub for a 'welcome home' celebration.

One night at the Rose Cottage, after one or two drinks, several young American airmen were telling my father (who originally came from London), about the skyscrapers and how very high they were. My father retorted:

'That's nothing! Do you know that when we build council houses in London they're so high that we have to wear oxygen masks to live in 'em!'

My father was friendly with several Americans. On one occasion, at about 6 a.m., there was a knock at the door of our cottage. It was 'Butch', who was in quite a state. He'd been to Norwich for a night 'on the town', missed the last train back to Wendling and was very worried because he was absent without leave (AWOL).

'What you need to tell those in charge,' advised my father, 'is that you arrived at Norwich station last night, running towards your train, and there was a band on the station, which suddenly started playing our national anthem 'God Save the King'. You, being anxious not to offend, stopped running, stood to attention and saluted ... just as your train pulled out. That's how you missed your train.'

Reputedly the oldest American on the base, Butch was promoted and given a job in the cook house, which was what he'd always wanted. Towards the end of the war Butch kindly gave me a photograph album, the two covers and the spine of the album were cut and expertly shaped with aluminium from a B-24's bomb bay doors. We then went to several Nissen huts, taking the wartime pin-ups off the walls and placing them in my album, a souvenir of those dramatic days.

John Gilbert, Norfolk schoolboy

Above: *Some of the Elvegren pin-ups removed from Wendling airfield by John Gilbert in 1945.*

Left: *'Disturbing Elements'.*

Centre: *'A Hitch In Time'.*

Right: *'Cover-All Beauty'.*

Below: *'Look What I've Got'.*

Far left: *Forlorn fuel tanks at Mendlesham in 1997. (MWB)*
Left: *Barracks block in 1997. (MWB)*

Below left: *Overgrown air raid shelter. (Mike Fuenfer)*
Below: *Overgrown tower at Rackheath. (MWB)*
Below right: *'It was cold – the wet North Sea cold that was as nothing we had experienced before. It cut through six blankets at night and lay about the small coke stoves like wolves about a dying doe.'*
Allan Healy (MWB)

Above: *A wartime hut at Attlebridge in the winter of 2002. (M*

Right: *Umbriago, of the 467th BG at Rackheath. Original 859th BS, 492nd BG pilot, Ernie Haar, flew this Liberator overseas then went to Rackheath with the Squadron CO James J. Mahoney in the 'new' 788th BS. (James J. Mahoney via Brian H. Mahoney)*

Below: *Umbriago, of the 467th BG at Rackheath. (James J. Mahoney via Brian H. Mahoney)*

Left: *Crew 51's mission log painted on a Seco hut at Rackheath by Sgt. Jack Hallman, a gunner in Eugene Garrett's crew. (MWB)*

Above: *392nd BG target list at Wendling in 1981. (MWB)*

Above: *'We would try to spin the sails of the windmill at the end of the runway with propwash on take-off.' Vince Reed, 466th BG, Attlebridge, Norfolk (MWB)*

Above left: Witchcraft. *(James J. Mahoney via Brian H. Mahoney)*

Left: That's All Brother *of the 467th BG at Rackheath. (James J. Mahoney via Brian H. Mahoney)*

Above: That's All Brother *of the 467th BG at Rackheath with forty bombs painted below the cockpit. Originally, this B-24 was flown by Danny Wolf in the 859th BS, 492nd BG at North Pickenham before they transferred to the 467th BG when the 492nd BG was deactivated following high losses. (James J. Mahoney via Brian H. Mahoney)*

Above: Betty Jane of the 427th BS, 303rd BG, which went MIA with 2/Lt. C.W. Heleen's crew on the mission to Gera oil installation on 19 September 1944. One crewman was KIA and eight made POW. (USAF)

Left: Cliff Pyle pictured in 1986 beside Texas Raiders at the Confederate Air Show at Harlingen. (MWB)

Right: We The People of the 422nd BS, 305th BG, at Chelveston, 7 March 1943, with the pilot, Capt. Cliff Pyle, far right. In more than thirty missions it never carried exactly the same crew twice, and no crewman was ever wounded. On 8 September 1943 it led the first 8th Air Force night-bombing mission of the war, returning to the ZOI on 31 May 1945. (Cliff Pyle)

Nudes, Names and Numbers

'We were flying somebody else's plane, the *Keystone Mama*.
I turned my flashlight on the brown lady with no brassiere, painted on the side,
and decided they were short of artists at this base.'

Serenade To The Big Bird, Bert Stiles. (*Keystone Mama* failed to return with Lieutenant Robert S. Wylie's
crew on 19 May 1944. Eight crew were KIA, one was made POW.)

Grim-faced Luftwaffe pilots, proud of the guts that take them within the suicide circle of a Fortress formation, determined to do or die for the Fatherland, must wonder what the hell kind of an air force they are up against. They come driving in, teeth clenched, hell-bent for Hitler, and along with a hail of lead they are greeted by the stupid grin of some absurd comic-book character, or the nude form of a Petty girl painted on the nose of the bomber they are attacking.

Most of the 8th Air Force bombers operating

from England have fantastic names scrawled across their elongated noses. Many of the names are illustrated by out-of-this-world characters, in brilliant colors, which could only originate in the minds of the men of one air force.

The Forts aren't named for any particular reason and no one in particular names them, it is a very American process.

A pilot from Maine is apt to come out any rainy morning and find that his plane has been named *Texas*. Or the quiet teetotaler who quit divinity

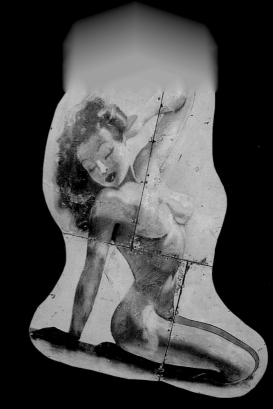

school to join the air force is apt to come out on the line and find a nude stretching from the plastic nose to the pilot's compartment, because his tail gunner (who did not quit divinity school to join the air force) knew a guy in Site Six who used to be a commercial artist in St Louis and could still draw a plenty sexy nude.

The names of many Forts and Libs are famous in America. Not all the exploits of the men and the bombers they fly are buried under their plane numbers in the files in Washington.

… The Fort, *We The People*, has been on at least thirty-two raids, and she has never had a single man aboard wounded. The most remarkable part of the ship's story is that the same ten men have never flown the bomber twice. Altogether *We The People* carried 114 men over enemy territory in her first thirty-two raids. Originally the ship was christened *Snafu*, and was considered a jinx plane, but the record is one of the best in the ETO.

Some of the bombers are dubbed with names the crews think are lucky. *The Bad Penny* was that kind of a name. The name, designed to bring to mind the old saw about it always turning up, seemed to work. It got such a reputation for always getting back that on one raid over Germany it was assigned

to what airmen refer to as the Purple Heart Corner. That is the last ship in the lowest element of the last formation. It ain't good. Anyway, on that raid First Lieutenant Elmer M. Richardson brought the plane back on one engine, looking like a high-altitude, precision bombing slice of Swiss cheese.

Many times the pilot, with a soft spot in the heart for his part of the country, names his plane after his hometown or some feature nearby – unless he's overruled by a corporal of the ground crew … *Maryland My Maryland*, *Brooklyn*, *Texas*, and the Fort named *Connecticut Yankee*, flown by First Lieutenant James Verinis, all reflect what someone on the crew thinks of when he thinks of home.

Above: *Colonel Robert Morgan and his crew pose for the camera as a ground crewman paints the 25th mission bomb symbol on the nose of Memphis Belle. (USAF)*

Above: *Robert Morgan at Duxford in 1999. (MWB)*

There are several *Boom Towns*. As far as anyone knows, no one comes from there. Captain Clyde B. Walker, one *Boom Town* pilot, comes from Tulsa, Oklahoma … *Mason's Morons* is named after a pilot of the same name, First Lieutenant Robert C. Mason … There are at least five Forts named *The Sad Sack*, and there are several variations of that. *The Sad Shack* and the *Shad Shack* are all tributes to the popularity of Baker's cartoon character.

There are several versions of the *Eight Ball*. Captain William R. Calhoun flew one *Eight Ball*, and First Lieutenant Walter T. Holmes won the DSC in the *Flying Eight Ball*.

The men in one group are known as the 'Ball Boys.' Every Fortress in the group bears the name of some 'ball' variation, and Captain Clinton F. Ball is their commanding officer. Back at their home station in El Paso, Texas, he named his Fort *Linda Ball* after his year-old daughter, and the rest of the squadron followed in the ball tradition.

… There are hundreds of nameless Forts here, and hundreds of Forts with names not mentioned here. Forts come in hundreds now. *The Black Swan*, *The Vulgar Virgin*, *Sweet Pea*, *Little Audrey*, *Unbearable* and *Piccadilly Commando* are random samples of Fort names.

Some of those have been shot down, some have been retired, and some are still going strong.

And a lot more, nameless, bearing only numbers, just go colorlessly out on their raids and lay it on the line.

Names usually don't make any difference to anyone, but just once in a while they are the cause of a fight, a drink or a friendship. *Mr. Cesspool* was the cause of a fight. 'Cesspool' was a character straight out of 'Li'l Abner' back when Daisy Mae was behind the eight ball in the hands of Carrimee Back, from Old Virginny.

One day some brass was making a tour of the field, and *Mr. Cesspool* was parked in a prominent place on the runway. The suggestion was made that the names on the planes should be ones that could be used in conversations – at tea in Claridge's.

Some colonel or lieutenant colonel picked up the suggestion and went overboard with it. For a few brief hours there were to be no more names on planes that couldn't be bantered about in mixed company. No more *Vulgar Virgins*, or *T.S.s*.

It would take a shipment of paint to cover the Fort names you wouldn't kick around in your living room, but the order fell flat and the names stand. If the brass had been up on their 'Li'l Abner', as they should have been, the whole episode might not have occurred …

***Stars and Stripes**, 'Nudes, Names and Numbers',*
Andrew A. Rooney, 5 August 1943

Above: *Sack Artists of the 67th BS, 44th BG at Shipdham. (USAF)*

Left: Becoming Back *of the 735th BS, 453rd BG at Old Buckenham in 1944. She did. Becoming Back ended her days at Kingman, Arizona late in 1945. (via Pat Ramm)*

Below: Yo-Yo 'It Always Comes Back' of the 305th BG at Chelveston did also. (USAF via Bill Donald)

Bottom: Geezil of the 369th BS, 306th BG at Thurleigh in 1943. (via Richards)

Mission 15 – February 14, 1945 – Departure Time 9.00 a.m. Target – Chemnitz, Marshalling Yards

The same target twice in a row. Again, it was a long and tiresome mission. We flew our new ship for the first time (44-6968). The weather was again against us. Contrails were dense and persistent, and we had to fly very tight formation in order to hold the squadron together. Flak over the target was ... [this sentence was not finished]. We flew No. 3 element lead today. We got quite a bit of flak on the way back from the Frankfort-Koblenz area. We bombed through a solid undercast.

First Lieutenant Donald J. Schmitt, pilot, *Son Of A Blitz*, 863rd BS, 493rd BG. His son, David, recalls: 'I was born on 27 March 1945 and Mother said that Dad named his plane as soon as he heard of my birth! Dad's thirty-fifth and last mission, to Roquefort, France – German Pocket, was on 16 April 1945. He wrote: "Easy mission, and our last. I'm so happy I can't even write anything on this mission."'

'Uncertain of the future, but fearing the worst, we read a prospectus about the 1941 calendar that Esquire is urging on its readers – a dozen pages of nepenthe, each illustrated by Varga, an artist who could make a girl look nude if she were rolled up in a rug. "Order it, look at it, feel it quiver; set it to the music of a slow drum ..."'

The New Yorker, 'Talk of the Town', 11 January 1941

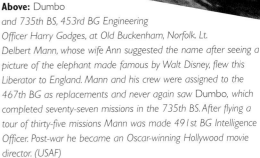

Above: Dumbo
*and 735th BS, 453rd BG Engineering
Officer Harry Godges, at Old Buckenham, Norfolk. Lt.
Delbert Mann, whose wife Ann suggested the name after seeing a
picture of the elephant made famous by Walt Disney, flew this
Liberator to England. Mann and his crew were assigned to the
467th BG as replacements and never again saw Dumbo, which
completed seventy-seven missions in the 735th BS. After flying a
tour of thirty-five missions Mann was made 491st BG Intelligence
Officer. Post-war he became an Oscar-winning Hollywood movie
director. (USAF)*

Above: Belle of the Blue *of the 423rd BS, 306th BG at Thurleigh on 20 July 1944 after a mission to
Frankfurt. Belle of the Blue failed to return with 2/Lt. Daniel W. Gates' crew on the 12 September 1944
mission to Ruhland. The ball turret gunner was killed by fighters. The rest of the crew managed to bail out
safely. (via Richards)*

Below: Nine-o-Nine, *which in
WWII was so-named because
of the last three digits of its
serial number. (MWB)*

When Sam and I first moved in, the pin-up girls
were a pretty lecherous lot. About one in five
owned a brassiere. Some of them blew down when

the windows were open, some of them we took
down when we showed the room to a couple of
nurses, so that after a while we had a pretty nice
bunch of girls, as nice as the ones in Fletch's room
across the hall.

... Above my sack, climbing, there was a picture
of Margaret Sullivan with bangs, a picture of Jane
Russell with legs, a picture of a little dream dame
called Doris Merrick ... and she came out in
Yank ... She had a sort of what-the-hell look on her
face, and I used to dream about going back to
Hollywood and meeting her in a drugstore on
Sunset after she had finished at the studio ... I said
goodnight to her the last thing every night.

... To the left of Miss Merrick was nothing but
the corner of the room, and to the right was a P-51.
Then came Ingrid Bergman with her hair grown out
from being Maria. Then came Ella Raines from
Yank, and some more P-51s put there by somebody
else, and some more dames, and down in the corner
a startling view of Maureen O'Hara ...

Left: Paper Doll *of the 423rd BS, 306th BG with flak damage in a sensitive spot. (Russell J. Zorn)*

Right: Methuselah 969 Years *(so-named for its last three numbers - 42-102969) of the 367th BS, 306th BG which failed to return with Lt. Earl R. Barr's crew on 12 September 1944. All except two of the crew bailed out before the veteran B-17 exploded but the only casualty was the navigator, who either fell out of his chute or did not have it on when the Fortress blew up. (via Richards)*

Below: *Names of famous Forts in the 487th BG on a wall at Lavenham in the early 1970s. (MWB)*

Around the top of the room, all the way around were all the Varga girls from a Varga calendar, put out by a plumbing concern, I think. There were also a good many pictures of girls in various stages of undress and discomfort, drawn by an artist with a mischievous mind, but a modest one … On top of the locker there was a picture of a girl Sam wanted to lure into marriage, maybe. Anyway, she was a dream, and some people didn't believe she was even Sam's girl. But I did …

The sacks were RAF sacks, because the whole rig used to belong to the RAF once, the whole station did. It was nice of them to let us live there, because it was probably the best room in England, even if that sergeant did take his radio back … On the wall above my sack was the map with all the places I've been in Europe. Some of the towns are left out on the map, so I have to draw in the bomb in the approximate place where our formation left a big hole …

We were lucky to live in such a place.

England was always out the window, and I often thought I'd like to live in that room again for a while after the war, and wander around and see what the country's like in peacetime.

Serenade To The Big Bird, 'Co-Pilots' House', Bert Stiles, 401st BS, 91st BG, Bassingbourn

girlfriend covered with pictures of a guy stepping out of a bathtub, draped only in a skimpy little towel, or see the walls covered with the pictures of a shorts advertisement or such pictures? None of you would. Then why keep a lot of junk hanging around and kid yourself about keeping up morale? ... I would much rather wake up in the morning and see a picture of a P-51 or 39 hanging above my bed or over the picture of my wife, whom I think is the best-looking girl in the world, than of some dame who has been kidded into or highly paid for posing for these pictures.

Private first class. Joseph H. Saling, Myrtle Beach AAF, South Carolina *Yank* magazine, 1943

Above: The Uncouth Bastard *of the 305th BG at Chelveston on 13 October 1943, the day before it failed to return with Robert W. Holt's crew on the Schweinfurt mission. Six crew were killed. Prior to joining the 305th BG this B-17 was Lucifer Jr in the 381st BG at Ridgewell. (via Bill Donald)*

Dear *Yank*:

I don't know who started this idea of pin-ups, but they say that it is supposed to help keep up the morale of the servicemen, or something like that. Here is my idea of the help it is. In the first place, I would say that 24 out of 25 of the men in the service are either married or have a girl at home whom they respect and intend to marry as soon as this war is over ... How many of you GIs would like to go home and find the room of your wife or

Our house was directly on the flight path as they took off each day on their bombing missions in Europe. I used to watch them go out – each one painted with a figure of a girl or other symbol and barely clearing our chimney pots as they flew out.

Neville Firman

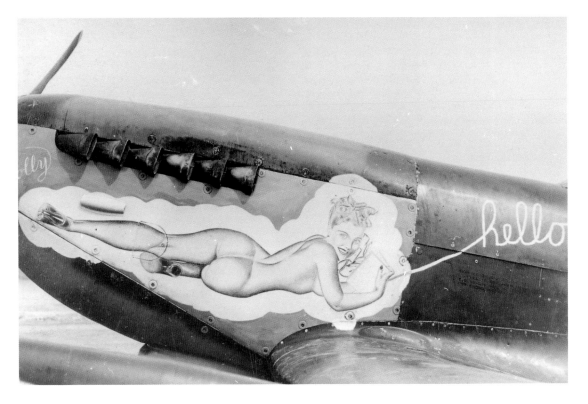

Left: *Spitfire IX, Hello Tolly, was flown to England via Goose Bay, Baffin Island, Greenland and Iceland by US test pilot Gustav 'Gus' Lundquist (he later married Tolly) to demonstrate the much modified Spitfire's long-range capability. An RAF officer looked at the wing-mounted drop tanks (a fuselage tank behind the cockpit and smaller tanks between the wing guns were also added) and enquired, 'Did you come far?' Gus replied, 'Dayton, Ohio.' The Spitfire was later scrapped, the cowling was removed and hung over the bar at RAF Boscombe Down. Lundquist joined the 352nd FG and was shot down on 29 July 1944 flying the CO's P-51, This Is It!. He became a POW. (Sam Sox via Bill Espie)*

Left: *Three nudes that once adorned the 350th FS, 353rd FG briefing hut at Raydon in WWII. (MWB)*

Below: *Delectable Doris, the name given to the original Liberator in WWII by Bill Graff (right) in honour of Doris his English fiancée, later his wife. (MWB)*

Returning to base, I was sent to Liverpool depot to ferry some replacement B-24s to Hethel. I got a Ford-built B-24J and signed for her. We checked her over, and took off. At Hethel, I discovered that she was assigned to me with a new crew chief, Sergeant Svec. He came to my barracks one evening with a roll of paper. 'Skipper, I've got a proposition, I've got a friend, Sergeant Michael Otis Harris, a painter who wants to paint a nose-art picture on our new ship to top them all,' and he unrolled the picture. A beautiful nude, artistically posed, but blonde. I said, 'OK Svec. Tell him it's a deal if the price is right – and if that blonde becomes a brunette.' 'Skipper, the price is right. He just wants to do it, for free.' 'OK Svec, the name is 'Delectable Doris' and I had to write it down for him to make sure.' The painting was done in record time.

Bill Graff, pilot, 389th BG, Hethel

'This is London'

'Have you ever sat in Trafalgar Square
Beneath the morning sun, in the morning air?
Have you looked at the lions 'neath Nelson's feet
And watched the traffic pass by in the street?
Have you seen the people taking their time
While Big Ben sounds out its hourly chime?
I'm sitting here now and it thrills me to see
A preview of peace. How good it will be!'

Stars and Stripes, **Private first class. Sidney Jrueger**

A two day pass or the seven day leave that came to most once, meant a trip farther away. Everyone went to London, saw Westminster, St Paul's, perhaps the Tower or art galleries, and all the sights an American tourist sees. One went to the theater at 6.30 and saw the Lunts or a musical comedy, or went to the Windmill. Most somehow found girls and sat in pubs or went to 'bottle clubs.' You saw the incredible gaiety and corruption that was Piccadilly in the wartime blackout. You were in a

Above: *392nd BG personnel feeding the pigeons in Trafalgar Square. (Art Crandell)*

large city again with lots of people and stores and something that passed for a carnival atmosphere.
The 467th Bombardment Group, **Allan Healy**

The lights (blacked out as they were) of London filled me with excitement. There was the allure of a totally different culture, not to mention the attraction of the many women (loose and otherwise), all older, to whom an American uniform

Above: *Trafalgar Square showing one of the famous fountains and Nelson's column. (MWB)*

Above: *Captain Chester 'George' Phillips of the 67th BS, 44th BG, on a pass in London with English girlfriends. For many, London was the last leave. Phillips, piloting B-24D Little Beaver, was killed leaving the target at Kiel on 14 May 1943. (Bill Cameron Coll)*

was exciting. So being single in London with money in my pocket was a blast. I thought I was sophisticated and grown up. Then one night I found myself lost at least ten miles from the centre of London with no buses running. I stopped in a pub in Islington and sought transportation of some sort. No results. I struck up a conversation with a fatherly gentleman who, after a beer, offered to take me home and let me sleep on the couch. Next morning it was, 'You must have breakfast and then we will put you on the bus.'

Next weekend I was back with a bag full of whatever goodies I could get my hands on, and thanks for the previous week's rescue. I was told, 'We will not let you go back to the Red Cross. You will stay for dinner and stay over with us. There is always enough for one more.' (These were people of little material wealth but a working class family with seven children aged four and up). After a few weeks and many good times I was told that I was not just another Yank, but a member of the family. I was given a key to the house so that I might come and go. I now had three sisters and two little brothers. Some of you know what it's like when a little boy sees his first orange. The air force provided many essentials to all its members – food,

clothing, and shelter – but I had found the missing ingredient, the love of a family. My own mother sent packages during the war with things I could not obtain for the girls, and correspondence carried on for years after the war was over.

Dan Jacobs, 96th BG, Snetterton Heath

… battered and dirty, worn and scarred, it swarmed with scores of different uniforms, and it spoke in a hundred different tongues. No matter where you were going in the United Kingdom, you had to go through London, and no matter how long you stayed you never saw it all. London was the babel, the metropolis, the Mecca. London was It. It had soldiers, sailors, and airmen in uniform, looking for fun. Some were in search of restaurants and theaters. Some were in search of bars and beer. Some were looking for girls. This is London at war, this is England – or a small part of it – with its hair down.

Here We Are Together, **Robert S. Arbib Jr.**

The crew all went on pass and decided to go to London despite the buzz bombs. We occasionally heard a V1 or V2 exploding, and we saw many

Above: *Painting the town red. (MWB)*

EDWARD R. MURROW (25 April 1908–22 April 1965) became well known for broadcasts during the London Blitz; broadcasts collected in *This Is London* (1941). He continued to report on war from Europe and North Africa throughout WWII.

Above: *The most famous of all Red Cross clubs was Rainbow Corner, which opened in London in November 1943 in what had been Del Monico's, and part of the adjoining Lyon's Corner House, on the corner of Piccadilly Circus and Shaftesbury Avenue. It remained open 24 hours a day every day throughout the war. There were two dining rooms, which could seat 2,000 people, and meals costing 25 cents were served. (USAF)*

Right: *'As we were coming back after supper the taxi driver took us round about and seeing a very large building I asked, "What's that?" He laughed and said it was Buckingham Palace. I couldn't see too much of it from the cab except to notice how immense it all was. It was built of gray stone with enough iron fences around it to make a battleship.'*

Captain Ralph H. Elliott, pilot, 467th BG (Bill Cameron)

areas where they had landed. We could identify them because of the distinctive damage pattern they made. If the V1 hit in the middle of a row of houses, there would be a big hole at the point of impact with the blast extending up and outward at a 45 degree angle so that the closest houses would be destroyed and the furthest ones at the end of the block might only have lost their roof. They were hard on the British morale and caused many casualties, but in no way affected the outcome of the war. Neither did they stop us from going to London on pass whenever we could. We took chances every day, and we didn't worry about the very unlikely possibility of getting hit by a V1 or a V2.

As it turned out, we didn't see or hear any this trip. Took the train from Norwich about 1400 and got into London about 1700. After being watch-officer and up most all night I slept most of the way. The fare is very reasonable – about $2 or £1 round trip ... We got a taxi and came up to this

hotel (Savoy), and honest, Honey, ... even with the war, this is a beautiful place and supposedly one of the finest in the world. It's near the center of town someplace. We take cabs when we go anywhere, as the roads seem to go in circles.

We went to a large Red Cross club for supper, as we were all hungry and didn't care to tackle a London restaurant yet. The boys say good meals are hard to get. We'll find out tomorrow. It's raining but we plan on going out later anyway. Getting around in the blackout may prove too difficult but we want to go to Piccadilly at least. As we were coming back after supper the taxi driver took us round about and seeing a very large building I asked, 'What's that?'

He laughed and said it was Buckingham Palace. I couldn't see too much of it from the cab except to notice how immense it all was. It was built of gray stone with enough iron fences around it to make a battleship.

Dear Folks:

London – the theaters here are built with a main floor called the 'stalls', a large balcony called 'dress circle' and three or less high balconies. Everyone smokes through the whole performance – either stage or cinema, and the smoke gets kinda thick after an hour or two. We ate mostly at the Red Cross, as it's impossible to eat well any other place ... I've stayed in some pretty nice hotels, but I've yet to get a good meal. It would seem strange to go into a restaurant where you could read a menu with something to eat on it. The potatoes are the only thing that even taste like the name. The meat is either mutton or ersatz sausage and the coffee tastes like chicory. The tea is usually OK so we drink that instead. In the middle of the morning, the sign 'morning coffee' or 'morning tea' is always put out ... same in the afternoon. I've never in my life eaten such unappetizing food. Their pastries are the flattest and the most tasteless I've ever eaten. The English have a way of eating I've never seen before. They hold their fork upside down, pile food on it with their knife, and mash it down so it stays until they get it in their mouths. Sure looks funny at first ...

...**R**

I spent hours exploring London: Westminster Abbey, the Tower, St Paul's Cathedral, Madame Tussaud's Wax Museum, and numerable military or historic museums. Piccadilly Circus, Leicester Square, Nelson's monument, Buckingham Palace, Selfridges, Harrods – all became familiar as I walked from one end of London to the other ...

Best of all, however, were the theaters. The first thing I'd do when I got to London was find out what plays were on and what tickets were available. I'd try to get tickets for one show in the afternoon and another in the evening, unless there was other sightseeing we wanted to do or no seats were available. Nat was from Boston and was well versed on the good plays and the best actors and I was never disappointed in his selection. *Hamlet* with John Gielgud at the Haymarket was the best theatre I ever saw. It was marvellous. I don't know when I'd enjoyed anything even half as much as I did that play. Gielgud was rated the best Shakespearean actor on the stage of the day, and in England that meant perfection – or very nearly so. Of course, *Hamlet* is a tragedy, but then I could enjoy that when it was so excellently done. Shakespeare's *Richard The Third* with Lawrence Olivier, and Emlyn Williams and *Yellow Sands* with Sir Cedric Hardwicke were wonderful as well. I occasionally hit a poor play, and some of the music hall stage shows weren't too good, but New York was probably the only place in

Above: *Earl Jake Lingle of the 306th BG in London. (via Richards)*

the world that could compare with London. It was said that if you went to a show every afternoon and evening, every day of the year, you could never see all that was offered. We occasionally went to a movie, but only if nothing else was available and, even then, it was often just a newsreel to fill in the time or to see the latest 'Movietone' war news. 'Newsreel Theatres' with news shows running about an hour were common in London and Chicago as well, and Lowell Thomas was usually one of the commentators.

Letters home to his wife Vonny, and friends, Captain Ralph H. Elliott, pilot, 467th BG

... Back in camp ... had a good time but not much rest. Went to see the *Memphis Belle* this evening after supper. It's the story of a B-17 and too realistic for comfort but quite good. There was a double feature with Benny Goodman, but I couldn't stand it and left. I'm sending you the two London programs as souvenirs. Gee, I wish you could have been with me and I know you do too so maybe I oughtn't to write it – but I do wish it anyway. We have a good fire going tonight – wood and coke both. We always run out of coke and before winter's over the field may be out too so I borrowed an ax and cut up some kindling. I think I'll buy an ax first chance I get. We get our coke ration twice a week, use it up, and swipe what extra we can ...

...R

'Listen Buddy!
Nothing bores me so terrific'ly
As being given so damned specific'ly
A wordy story – play by play
Of your latest visit down London way.
So Shaddup!'

Stars & Stripes

104

Life in London was very noisy as the V1 rockets were just starting. One dropped at the back of Selfridges and within minutes the dining room was cleared as officers piled into cabs to rush and see the damage. For many of them it was their first taste of being at the receiving end of what air warfare was all about. None of the bomber crews would sleep on the top floor – and who could blame them – I was not very keen myself ... We were based at Rattlesden, near the village of Stowmarket, in what was called 'Buzz Bomb Alley' as the V1s and later the V2s, cut out over London and came our way.

Mary Thompson

'I went to London and I was really down. All alone in a crowd, I met a good, decent, Irish girl working at Rainbow Corner and out of thousands of GIs, she liked me.

I would always see her when I made it to London. The first part of July 1944, she was killed by a 'buzz bomb'. All the damn luck!'

John A. Miller, gunner, 100th BG

The parents of an old pen pal have invited the American flyer to visit with them in the London suburbs. Their son, whom he has written to for several years, is in training at an RAF gunnery school in the Midlands. The middle-aged couple own their cottage, which is located in an area subject to a goodly amount of bombing by enemy V-type weapons. They proudly show the American their steel bed with an overhead frame designed to withstand a caved-in roof. At dinner that evening, the flyer realizes that the British couple have used up their entire meat ration for that week – a whole can of Spam!'

'... I was a quarter of a mile away from a V2 that exploded near Marble Arch in London. In my opinion this is the most sinister weapon yet invented. We stopped over in London for the night on the way back to Bury and were promptly greeted by a V1 at Waterloo station. The next day, 1 July,

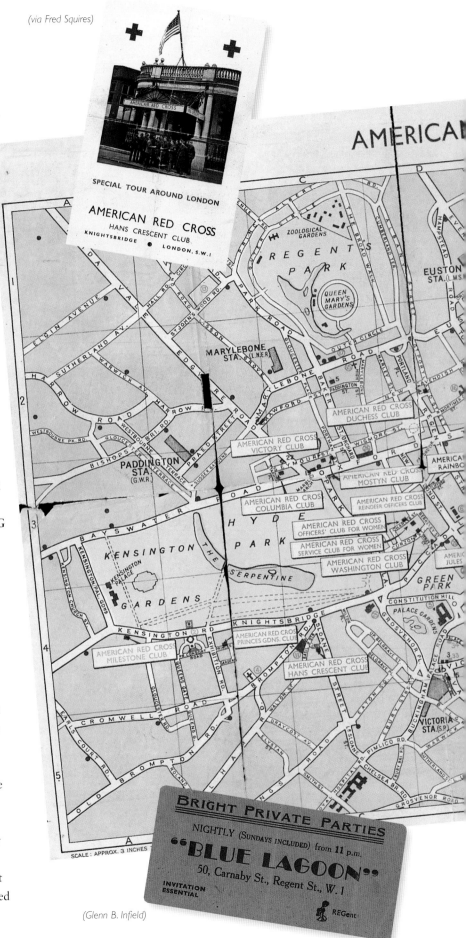

(via Fred Squires)

SPECIAL TOUR AROUND LONDON

AMERICAN RED CROSS
HANS CRESCENT CLUB
KNIGHTSBRIDGE • LONDON, S.W.1

(Glenn B. Infield)

RED CROSS MAP OF LONDON

Above: *Early American Red Cross map of London. (via Leslie G. Thibodeau)*

Left: *Two sergeants stop to admire two English girls outside Leicester Square tube station. (USAF)*

(Glenn B. Infield)

while we were on our way to Simpson's restaurant, a V1 flew over at about 400-foot altitude doing around 400 mph. Its noise was nerve-wracking (even more so than the London klaxons), reminding me somewhat of a pack of motorcycles racing by. It passed over us, its motor stopped and it began a 180 degree turning dive to the left, exploding a couple of blocks away. My admiration for the British people has increased a good deal since I arrived in Britain. They walk about as though the 'Vergeltungswaffen' do not exist.'

First Lieutenant Abe Dolim, navigator,
332nd BS, 94th BG

'Shortly before the V2 attack on London, there were about thirty-three missiles fired in the vicinity of Norfolk. We surmised that this target afforded a better opportunity for triangulation to determine the points of impact, since the Germans were pushed back up into Holland and Belgium at that time. In a period of seventy-two hours, three V2s came within a mile of the base. One was an underground burst, which blew out a hole about twenty feet deep. The other two burst at varying levels above the surface, one being at an altitude of about 1–2,000 feet, the parts being easily identifiable where they lay scattered on the ground. A day or two later, the missiles began falling in the vicinity of London.'

Colonel Albert J. Shower, CO 467th BG

I had just returned to England after escaping through France with the aid of American and French underground agents and was in what I thought was the relative safety of London. It was a few days after Christmas 1944, and despite the war and the intense bombing of the city, a gay holiday mood appeared to prevail. I had checked into a Red Cross club where British and American servicemen and women could find lodging and was catching up on many hours of lost sleep. London did show many scars of the German bombing and it was impossible not to be reminded of the damage done and lives lost in the Blitz.

People were going about their business as usual, taxis were running, stores were open, and everything was going according to routine.

However, I looked down the street and two or three buildings from where I was standing I could see that an entire block of houses had been leveled; smoke was rising from the rubble and rescue crews were pulling people out of the wreckage. Part of the buildings were still burning.

'We've been hit by one of those German V2 rockets,' said a British 'bobby' standing nearby when he saw my surprise and shock. 'They come over every day now, little gifts from Hitler.'

Technical Sergeant Forrest S. Clark,
air gunner, 67th BS, 44th BG

'They used to come up to London for leave and stay at the Reindeer Club for officers in Cork Street of which I was manageress. One day while in the dining room with the American Red Cross director, I saw an officer sitting at a table whose face was very familiar. I asked my director and she said, "Oh that's Jimmy Stewart, the film star".'

Mary Thompson

Things were not always so pleasant in London as the Nazis took great pleasure in dropping bombs on the inhabitants. Usually, the Nazi bombers would come only to the outskirts of London, drop their bombs on the suburbs, and hightail it for home before the AA got too heavy. Occasionally, however, they would bomb the heart of the city. Most of our crew was in London on this occasion when the Nazis mounted a large-scale attack against the centre. It was well after dark, between 9 and 10 p.m. on a moonless night. On such nights, blacked-out London was about as 'black' as any place could be. We actually had to use flashlights to see the sidewalks under our feet – small penlight flashlights at that! If we used our regular GI flashlights, a British 'bobby' would tell us in very stern tones, 'Put out the torch, Yank!'

When I realized that the bombs were getting close to my hotel (the Red Cross Reindeer Club), I went out into the street to get a better look at the action. Searchlights were lighting up the skies and picking up many Nazi bombers. They would hold a plane in their beams until one of the AA crews shot it down, then pick up another one. The British planes were also in the melee and their tracer bullets could be seen streaking across the sky. I have often wondered how those Limeys could fly their fighter planes at night, avoiding each other and their ground gunners, while very systematically shooting down the intruders.

Many of the bombers found their targets and dropped bombs all over downtown London. As I was viewing all this in awe and wonder, the people near me were running in various directions. Soon, a zone air raid warden happened upon me gawking up at the sky. He looked at me in exasperation and asked if I had never seen an air raid. Before I could answer 'No' he took me to the nearest air raid shelter and ushered me inside. There were so many people in the shelter, calm and collected, as if they took such refuge frequently. It was then that I realized where all those people I had seen earlier were hurrying to.

In less than an hour, the raid was over and we emerged to view the damage and be about our usual business. Several buildings in the area were damaged and a couple were burning slightly, but the London Fire Department was already busy putting out the blazes. My hotel was undamaged so I went back to the lobby where the others had gathered to exchange tales of their experiences. I was rather stunned to realize that I had been through an air raid, but thankful that I had suffered no injuries and very few inconveniences.

First Lieutenant (later Captain)
Alvin D. Skaggs, pilot, 448th BG

We three ended up at one of those bottle clubs called the 'Miami' club. We paid $45 for two bottles of whiskey (labeled 'Scotch') and the big fat owner of the club, who said that he had been to the United States, did us all the highly doubtful honor of joining our table and trying to drink up all of the whiskey he had sold us out of the bigness of his heart. We were sitting there drinking and talking about combat – the more we thought about combat the more we drank. From then on I don't remember

too much. I remember two WAAFs and after that it seems that Turnip got tangled up with the cigarette girl; and a faint memory of my getting involved with the oriental dancer in the floor show.

Bill Griswold, pilot, 100th BG

We were permitted a two-day pass every two or three weeks and found the Imperial Hotel at Russell Square to be very hospitable. We could usually get accommodations for the five of us enlisted men in a comfortable room and the Imperial had a steam bath facility that was great for revitalizing after a couple of weeks of sweating, working and splashing around with gun-cleaning solvents, etc. with no really satisfactory shower facilities. On this particular two-day pass I could not depart the base with my crew due to a duty assignment, so I requested they reserve a bed for my later arrival. When I got to the Imperial I found a single room adjoining my crew's room awaiting me. After a good night's rest I dressed and went next door to see what our plans would be for that day. To my

Above: *'From then on I don't remember too much. I remember two WAAFs and after that it seems that Turnip got tangled up with the cigarette girl; and a faint memory of my getting involved with the oriental dancer in the floor show.' Bill Griswold, pilot, 100th BG (MWB)*

surprise, I found their door ajar; clothing scattered about the floor and four gunners sound asleep! It became clear they had been burglarized. All their money and valuables had been expertly removed. Access had been gained by scaling a wall several floors above street level, entering an open window and exiting through the door and out via the fire escape. The Imperial management was notified. They expressed sympathy but fortunately I had enough money to get us back to base.

Technical Sergeant Frank M. Mead Jr., flight engineer/gunner, 837th BS, 487th BG

Above: *Piccadilly Circus.*
(Bill Cameron)

I finally got a three-day pass before going for check out in the left seat. A couple of us went to London to see the sights and took a bus to Trafalgar Square and then off to Piccadilly Circus. We went to a stage show just off the main square and afterward went into a small pub. There I met a nice looking young lady and struck up a conversation. Soon we were sitting at a table together and getting even more friendly. Suddenly she said,

'After talking to you for a while I would guess that you are still a virgin.'

I was startled, but managed to stammer, 'What makes you say that?'

'Well, at least half you Yanks are still inexperienced.'

'No, I wouldn't say that,' I said.

'Look, Yank, you keep flying missions and you may get shot down without ever experiencing the finer things in life. I can relieve you of this burden.'

'Really?' I asked

'Yes, and it will only cost you £3.'

After being hit by a two-by-four, it finally dawned on me that this gal was a mercenary. I wouldn't have believed it when we first started talking. I was tempted, but there flashed through my mind the movie I had seen in Nashville with the young actor, Glenn Ford. So I lied that I had to catch the next bus back to base. She seemed miffed that I had wasted her time.

… The couple of times I was in London, I didn't care for the attitude of some of the street people. While walking with a girl on Piccadilly Circus one evening, a newsboy hawking the London Times would yell, 'Hey, get your paper here.' Then *sotto voce* he would say to me, 'Rubbers, I got 'em for sale.'

If I didn't pay any attention to him he would yell, 'Give 'er a go, Yank, she's fourteen'.

Very embarrassing to me. And nearly every newsboy or street urchin would yell the same thing. I think that they meant that the age of consent in England was fourteen at that time.

Another thing that an American soldier would hear from the younger children was, 'Got any gum, chum?'

The thing that really caught my eye in London was the incredible number of bicycles. The streets would be full of them as far as the eye could see in the late afternoon. At times it was difficult to find a place to cross the street. It was necessary to go to an intersection and wait for a bobby to halt traffic before I could cross. It was equally as congested in Bedford and Cambridge. Gasoline was strictly rationed and cost the equivalent of about four dollars a gallon. I found it incredible that we were burning about two million gallons of gas per mission, and I suppose the British were doing the same thing on their night raids.

Lieutenant Richard 'Dick' Johnson

'We went on a two-day pass to London and we arrived in town late in the evening. When we woke up in the morning we read in the papers that American air forces had heavy losses on the raid the day before. It made us relieved that we were safe in London while our friends may have gone down, or are POWs.'
Staff Sergeant Laurence S. 'Goldie' Goldstein, radio operator, 388th BG

they seemed quite cheerful and I learned some of them had been there since the Blitz in 1940. I saw Green Park and a bit of Piccadilly, and of course uniforms and rank were all over the place. The taxis were beautifully polished and overhead were hundreds of balloons to discourage air attack.

Captain Franklin H. 'Pappy' Colby, 410th BS, 94th BG. At forty-one years of age, Colby was the oldest combat pilot in the 8th Air Force.

We got in at 18.30 in complete blackout. We tried several hotels but they were all full and finally we got a couple of beds in the King George Club for officers. Then it was on to the Park Lane Hotel where they had an 'American bar'. We met two pretty gals who took us to an underground restaurant called the 'Landsdown', some 50 feet below street level, so there was no worry from bombs. We had a wonderful dinner and dancing.

Above: *St Paul's from the River Thames. (via Jack Krausse)*

The bomb damage in London shocked me. At the back of St Paul's Cathedral there were whole blocks of houses that had been reduced to complete rubble. Almost every block of standing buildings had one or two gone where a bomb had hit and the marks of explosions and fires were everywhere. I was particularly astonished at the fact that the Underground and platforms had been converted into sleeping quarters for people who had been bombed out of their homes. They slept in three-decker beds along the back wall of the platform, with no privacy, and the noise from the continually passing trains. But

One might get a room in a four- or five-storey building half destroyed by a bombing. There would be running water and a bathroom down the hall. It was not the Waldorf Astoria but it was OK. Forget leg of lamb or roast beef. We would go into the city and scrounge up some newspaper-wrapped fish and chips. Base chow was much better, but this was all high adventure to us. Once we read a newspaper advertisement about the availability of horsemeat at a certain London restaurant. We made the trip to town just to try that horsemeat.

… Relations with the Britons saw an occasional difference of opinion and often comical differences in lifestyles. Once, members of the crew did witness that rare clash between the GI and the Tommy. While in a London pub, a British soldier made a crude ethnic joke that a Yank took exception to. It turned out a real riot. On another occasion in London, Lew, Jack and Gene were discussing the relative differences between the British and American peoples. Lew said that if one treated the British with kindness that they would reciprocate. Gene, however, said that he believed the American people to be much friendlier. Lew then saw a sweet little old lady coming up the street. Lew said that this was an opportunity to demonstrate English kindness. He approached the elderly lady and said, 'Good morning, madam, how are you this fine day?'

To this the lady replied: 'Mind your own business Yank!'

Gene was roaring with laughter. Lew was left wondering how he had been so lucky to have chosen this particular old lady from the crowd.

Technical Sergeant Norman R. Pickstone, engineer, *Peoria Belle*, 493rd BG

THE GIRLS OF LONDON

I was so shot when I got on the train I didn't look out the window until the train was half-way to London. Then I remembered I hadn't seen any of it. It was the same casually neat green England.

I thought about the towns I'd gone into on trains. Denver, Boise, Philly, the big town.

We came into King's Cross station and picked up a cab for Piccadilly.

'No Red Cross clubs,' Sam said, 'I'm sick of the army.'

We were sick of pilots and airplanes, and each other when we thought about it.

Against a background of London barrage balloons Sam looked okay to me again. I decided I could get along with him for a while.

The cab driver found us a hotel, lost in a court off St James's Street. We lay on the green silk bedspreads of the twin beds and drank three double scotches while we waited for the ceiling to lift.

'Nice sacks,' Sam said.

'Nice room,' I said.

Then we were ready to wander. I lost Sam in the first place. After a while I couldn't remember the places. I tied up with a RAF bomb-aimer, in the Ritz, and we had a Free Frenchman with us for a while after the Savoy, and a fairy tried to join in at the Dorchester.

We drank scotch till the scotch was gone, and gin and rum and Pimms and port until something happened.

When I came out into the clear I was tacking up a lonesome road in bright moonlight. Cool night, steady night, with no flak, and no 109s in the clouds, because there weren't any clouds, only the barrage balloons serene in the starlight.

The girl came out of the shadows, carrying a fur. Her voice was soft.

'A bit of love, Yank?'

She looked good with the moon in her hair, but I wasn't in the mood … not for a bit of love, I wanted all the love or none, and I knew she didn't have that much to give.

Serenade to the Big Bird,
First Lieutenant Bert Stiles

Above: *'The girl came out of the shadows, carrying a fur. Her voice was soft …'* Serenade to the Big Bird, *First Lieutenant Bert Stiles (MWB)*

London at night in the blackout was fantastic – and Piccadilly Circus was unbelievable. The statue of Eros, goddess of love, had been removed from the center of the circle, but her spirit was certainly still there. Piccadilly was busy by day, but by night it was a solid mass of humanity with the ghostly, blue light of the blackout lamps making it just light enough to get around – if it wasn't foggy, that is. The crowd was a mix of soldiers and sailors, of both sexes, a few locals and news-vendors, couples – both in and out of uniform – and a fair supply of prostitutes looking for a friend. I was accosted no less than nine times just walking from Piccadilly to the Mayfair Hotel one night. One dolly in a fur coat who stepped out of a doorway said invitingly, 'Six shillings tonight, Lieutenant'. It must have been just before payday. In addition to having a wife at home and the moral problem involved, there was also the considerable VD problem – which was the reason every crew going on pass had to sign off on the VD lecture before they left the base – and I wanted no part of it.

Captain Ralph H. Elliott, pilot, 467th BG

Thursday 21 December 1944: No mission today – cloudy, rain and fog. It is really terrible cold, raw weather. Gave three sex morality lectures this morning – 420 men. This is the last of the series, which has been going on this past week. Gave seven talks on Tuesday to over 1,100 men. All officers and men on the base must attend at least one a year. A regulation for all service men. It's a peculiar set-up. The doctor speaks first. He explains how to use a prophylactic to avoid VD. Then I explain the sex moral law, stressing obligations to God, church, country, self and others, especially the family, a wife, or a sweetheart. All this in order to avoid future regrets and remorse. One Squadron CO told me some of his men, after attending, cancelled their London passes. That's encouraging.

Father Joe Collins, Chaplain, 94th BG

'One lecture that stands out was the one on the evils of VD. This was a flight surgeon giving the talk who said, straight out "avoid all sex". He paused, then said, "Now after you've done it, here is how you use your prophylactics".'

John W. McClane Jr., navigator, 44th BG

Wartime London was not safe for a virgin Yank to be seen on the streets in uniform. We would start out in a group of six or seven of us to go from our Red Cross club near Marble Arch to Liverpool Street Station. As we went along the street, even in the blackout and in the Underground, Piccadilly Commandos were waiting for us. At one street corner two of our group would be grabbed as they passed by these prostitutes. By the time we reached the Underground station we were down to four. By the time we got to Liverpool Street station there were only two of us – myself and a buddy of mine.

'We're lucky,' he would say because we thought we would be the only two from the group to make it back to the base on time in case there was a mission. We were wrong. As we entered Liverpool Street station, two girls grabbed first him and then me and pinned us against the wall.

'You're going with us,' one said.

Above: *Sadly, the 6-foot-high dancing girls disappeared from Deopham Green in the late seventies. (MWB)*

But we explained we have to get the next train for Norwich or we'll be missing if there is a mission.

'Never you mind Norwich, you're with us in London now,' one girl said.

We never did get a train that night and we struggled back to Norwich by the early morning train and had to sneak into the base and miss roll call …

… I had many romances and many loves in wartime Britain but this is the strangest one of all. Americans made love to English girls in many bizarre places and situations. I had a crewmate who made love to his girlfriend in Hyde Park in the center of London after the All Clear; another made love in a shelter; another in the Underground; in the back of taxis; on the ground under barrage balloons; in the booths of pubs; in London buses; in trains, haystacks, farm fields; in hay wagons, in boats on the Thames, in the blackout without knowing who the girl was. The Blitz was still fresh in the minds of all Londoners. The air was filled with barrage balloons and sandbags were banked around all major public buildings including Westminster and the Houses of Parliament. On the streets men and women wearing

(Glenn B. Infield)

the uniforms of all Allied nations made the city look like an armed camp. Quick romance and lovemaking was taken as the order of the day among the forces …

My left waist gunner met an English girl at the railway station in London by chance one night. They formed a steadfast love relationship, so much so that she resolved to come to the US when the war was over. Jack always spoke so lovingly of her but years later when I mentioned her to him he shrugged off the question. I suspect that his case was indicative of thousands of American GIs who had passionate affairs with English women only to have to break them off in the post-war years.

Technical Sergeant Forrest S. Clark,
air gunner, 67th BS, 44th BG

'Once, returning from a three-day pass in London, I sat next to a lovely young lady from Ipswich. I was the only American in the train compartment. As I tried to get acquainted with the young lady the other passengers were acting very 'British' as if not noticing us. Just before reaching Ipswich station, I worked up enough courage to ask the young lady for her address and if I might call on her. She said yes, but I searched frantically and could not find a pen or pencil with which to write down her address. Without a word, but with just a trace of a smile, three passengers all at the same time, reached into pockets and purses and offered me a pen.'

Elvin O. Cross, tail gunner, 445th BG

I was in a dance hall somewhere around the Haymarket in London. World War II had taken its toll on the old city. There were many English girls at the dance, but one of them became quite friendly with me. She danced a lot of times with American GIs and I noticed that she seemed to be popular with them, but also that there was something sad about her. As the evening drew to a close and the girls began to depart, many of them accompanied by American airmen and others, she lingered behind. Suddenly, quite by surprise, she came over to me and said that she wanted me to accompany her. She had something or somewhere to show me. Of course, being a GI, I thought immediately that she was giving me the come-on and I got very

(Glenn B. Infield)

excited at this approach. I thought I had nothing to lose and maybe everything to gain by going with her. 'This is it', I thought. I could hardly wait. Off we went into the blackout and under the barrage balloons and hailed a taxi in the London night. Of course, being an American, I didn't know anything about London and let the girl give all the directions to the taxi driver.

We headed for the East End and crossed London Bridge, and then drove for what seemed like miles through the working-class sector of the city. I noted many bombed-out places visible still. Finally we got out of the taxi at a small park that was in the heart of the old section of the city. It was a clear night and I could see the outlines of the buildings quite clearly. We settled down on a park bench and she began to cuddle up to me. It was not long before we kissed. But I still did not know where and why she was here at this particular spot.

Suddenly, she stopped and pointing to a corner of the square she said, 'Look over there.'

As I did, I saw through the blackout that this section of buildings was bombed out leaving only a few walls standing. I could see them clearly against the night sky in the moonlight.

'I used to live there', she said. 'We got bombed in the Blitz. My parents were injured and died.' Then she began to sob and cry and I was completely taken by surprise and didn't know what to do or say to her.

This incident has stayed with me as a lesson about war and I shall never forget it. It as also a lesson in loneliness in wartime London. But above all, it was a lesson in the endurance of people, and the horror of war.

Technical Sergeant Forrest S. Clark

THE BULLDOG BREED

'I saw Winston Churchill, the great Prime Minister, drive by when I was on leave in London one weekend in 1944. His bulldog look was no sham. His defiant rhetoric and adamant stance rallied his people to do their part to help earn ultimate Allied victory when, early in the war, it looked like England was doomed to annihilation, as she faced the Nazi war-machine alone after the fall of France.'

Douglas D. Walker, armourer-gunner, B-24
'Carpetbagger' crew

I was sleeping in the early morning and all appeared peaceful and quiet. Suddenly, there was a shattering explosion followed by two or three more in quick succession. Plaster fell from the ceiling onto my bed and the entire building shook, swayed and appeared to crack. My roommate, a British airman, was standing before the mirror shaving when the explosion came.

'What was that?' I cried to him.

'Oh that, that's just one of those Jerry bombs. Don't pay any attention to them,' he replied as he continued to shave without missing a stroke.

Technical Sergeant Forrest S. Clark

I had a three-day pass to London, and was staying at the Reindeer Red Cross Club on Clifford Street. My accommodation was a cot set up in the hallway on the third floor. It was late in the evening and I had just gotten into bed when the air raid sirens sounded. As it happened, an elderly charwoman was mopping the floor near the stairway. I hurriedly got dressed and headed for the stairs. Now I could hear the buzz bomb (V1) coming – a sound never to be forgotten! I fully expected the cleaning lady to bolt down the stairs ahead of me, but she only leaned on her mop and listened. I made up my mind not to appear panicky in front of this brave lady, so I too stopped and listened. That devilish V1 sound came ever closer, until it appeared to be directly overhead. At this point the lady resumed her mopping. I kept listening and soon the pulsing

sound stopped and there was a terrific explosion in the distance. (I learned later that a bus had been struck and demolished at Kennington Oval). When the All Clear sounded I went back to bed, marveling at the savoir-faire of that calm old lady!

Second Lieutenant George M. Collar,
702nd BS, 445th BG

Above: *A V1 'buzz bomb'. (MWB)*

The next night the air raid sirens sounded. We were in the hotel bar at the time and should have stayed inside. However, we went out in front. The searchlights and guns over in St James Park were in action and had locked in on a low flying plane. I thought at the time that it was strange that the pilot was not taking evasive action. Then I realized that the ship did not have a pilot. It was a buzz bomb. Suddenly the engine stopped and then was a big explosion. The next morning we went to Mass in a church that was on the far side of St James Park. During Mass the drone of a buzz bomb was heard and then it stopped. That is when I hit the floor. There was an explosion. When I looked over the top of the pew, the priest was still saying Mass prayers. I don't think that he missed one word. A number of parishioners left to go see if they still had a home. A few weeks later I heard that the church was demolished by one of the bombs.

Norm Kiefer, 44th BG

About every two weeks we were given a three-day pass to do as we pleased and relieve the tension of combat. London town was our destination on almost every occasion. Good old London. Wartime London was a dark and forbidding place with little to cheer you up until you found the interesting places behind darkened doors and blackout curtains.

Staying at the Jules Club operated by the Red Cross for four shillings per night, we had a good base of operation to see London – one block from Piccadilly Circus and some of the best hotels and bars in town.

The day started with a continental breakfast in our hotel followed by a massage in the barber shop, then to the ticket desk for a stage performance for that evening. The Palladium was our favourite. Tickets were followed by an hour of reading the newspapers to see how the war was going. Lunch at the Brass Brasserie consisted of cold lobster tail, potato salad, and that good hard bread. The drinking for the day started here with a pint of something. Whitbread's dark ale was my favourite. Visiting famous places took up most of the afternoon. Piccadilly Hotel was a must for 'high tea' at 4 p.m., then to the evening theater performance starting at 6 p.m.. Intermissions between acts were drinking and snacking time. Interruptions by air raid alerts provided the same goodies, except we took them outside to watch the aerial combat show.

Most of the people went to the safe bomb shelters, but Fergie and I thrilled at the action of searchlights, flak, night fighters, bombs and all the reaction teams the brave British used to report the death and destruction.

Dinner at the private Exhibition Club came with drinking and dancing, and carousing until well into the night came after the show. Being a private club, it could stay open until 2 a.m. with continuous entertainment on three floors.

Robert H. Tays

I think we went on pass after our fifth mission. We had been decorated with air medals. The plumage of a warrior was just as important to us as it was to Caesar's legionnaires. We were inordinately proud of our silver wings, Presidential Unit Citations, and air medals. Men will endure much bizarre and varied punishment for the trinkets that declare them valorous. We were no different. Before we parted, there would not be one of us who was not tested to the limits of his endurance, but these trinkets were important to us as though they were the symbols of what we experienced.

We caught the train to London and bivouacked at the Strand Palace Hotel on the famous Strand, near Trafalgar Square. The edifice still endures. All of the combat crews stayed at the Strand Palace or the Regent's Palace in Piccadilly. The staid English management took the bawdy Yanks in stride, never lost their cool, and were totally hospitable, although I'm sure they were sorely provoked on occasion.

We dressed up in our ODs and ventured out into the night. Even in the blackout, throngs of people were surging up and down the street. Wartime London was a melting pot for the armed services of every nationality, and their uniforms were often picturesque. In the United Kingdom women were drafted into the services; so most decent girls were in uniform. Only prostitutes and elderly ladies were in street dress.

The conviviality of wartime is unimaginable if one hasn't actually experienced it. People who had not seen each other before five minutes ago became comrades. Romantic attachments were formed on

Below: *'We caught the train to London and bivouacked at the Strand Palace Hotel on the famous Strand, near Trafalgar Square. The edifice still endures. All of the combat crews stayed at the Strand Palace or the Regent's Palace in Piccadilly. The staid English management took the bawdy Yanks in stride, never lost their cool, and were totally hospitable, although I'm sure they were sorely provoked on occasion.'* Chick's Crew, *'London: Our First Pass'*, Ben C. Smith (MWB)

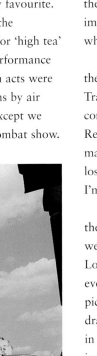

the spot, sometimes with no more than a searching look. Complete strangers drank out of the same bottle with no thought of disease. Virtuous girls (in another context) quickly availed themselves of the chance of dinner and dancing and a one-night stand with boys who would be dead within the week. Australians, Canadians, and Yanks prowled the city together, denigrating their English cousins and declaring their undying friendship. Language was no barrier. The bottle was the universal language bestowing upon Pole, Norwegian, Free French, and Yank alike perfect understanding and instant communication.

The great dance halls of London were fantastic fun palaces. My favorite two were Covent Garden and the Hammersmith Palace. They featured American-style swing bands; damn good ones, too. The peculiar Limeys had strange dance-hall behavior. There was no free-lance movement. All of the English danced in a circular direction, swooping and dipping with great sweeping strides – exactly like a giant carousel. I got dizzy just watching. It was insane to try to dance upstream. We got clobbered if we did. These orderly people would line up to go into the gates of hell. To them it made sense for all to dance in the same direction.

It was not unusual to see a sight like two desert rats from Monty's Eighth Army dancing with each other in full battle regalia, including tin hats on their backs, woolly-woolly uniforms, and leggings. The girls would not dance with these heroes; they had a very gamey smell about them. So they danced with each other.

The boys came stag, and the girls did too. Most often it was the girl who broke on the boy. Everyone was very polite about it; there were no scenes. If the girl wanted to dance with a boy, she came up and broke, and the other girl gracefully bowed out for a while, although she would be back in a short time if she liked him. I was much in demand as I could do the shuffling, graceful Lindy Hop of the southern negroes, and the girls loved it. The boys from Brooklyn and the Bronx did a frenetic hopping-about step that was also very popular, but they marvelled at my hang-loose southern version of the Jitterbug.

Above: *Five Americans in the 490th BG at Eye visiting London in January 1945. (via Don and Peggy Garnham)*

I remember vividly a slender English girl who let me take her home. She told me that I was nothing but a baby, which news took me aback. No matter she was very tender and sweet to the 'baby,' and I never forgot her.

We went from one pub to the other drinking gin and Guinness, a standard affectation of the English, but a pretty neat drink withal. One thing sure, it would get the job done. Imagine the improbable combination of gin and beer (Guinness stout) – boilermakers, English style.

I loved the uproarious good humor of the cockneys. These people were a breed apart, quite unlike the other English I had met. Hitler had not been able to break these people's spirit. They thrived on adversity. We had a grand time together, but inevitably time would run out on us. Of all sad words of tongue or pen, the saddest were these, 'Time, please, Lideys and Gentuhlmen!' Oh, how we dreaded to hear the familiar closing words.

To awake with splitting head and a full load of remorse – was it worth it? Hell, yes! We were soon at it again. In and out of bars, cafes, theaters, peep shows, and dance halls. Fish and chips, delicious

116

and served in a newspaper right on a street corner – I can taste them now!

Piccadilly was all of this. Nude girly shows the English had long before the US. My favorite was the Windmill, which never closed during the entire war, even during the bombings. The star of the revue was named Dixie. To be legal, there was one odd requirement. Once the girl had peeled down to the buff she had to remain completely motionless.

At least once or twice each night, the air raid siren would begin its mournful dirge, and the 'ack-ack' would start up. As searchlights plied the sky, we watched from the roof of the hotel, in our drunkenness scornful of shelter or succor. My companions were Australians or Canadians. The English always went dutifully to an air raid shelter. It was not that they were afraid; they were cool performers under fire. It was just that they always did what they were supposed to do, exactly as they were supposed to.

Something moralistic about my make-up made me eschew the favors of the army of prostitutes that thronged Piccadilly. I never liked the idea of buying sex; they didn't lack for customers, however, simply because I was squeamish. They were ignored by the bobbies who wisely knew that this had to go on in a war. These 'ladies of the night' were in every doorway with a cigarette lighted so you would know they were there. They never left the doorway. When they got a customer, the trick was turned on the spot – in a standing position. They could turn five tricks that way while turning one in a hotel room. Our lads called them Piccadilly Commandos, a name that stuck.

One night Jasper, the navigator, and I took some girls of dubious pedigree (non-commercial) to the ultra-swank Savoy restaurant proposing to have dinner with them there. The maitre d' politely but firmly told us that we would have to leave as he had no tables. There were plenty in plain sight, we protested. The girls laid him out in cockney, and we then told him about democracy in the United States and where he could shove his famous restaurant. He was completely unperturbed, merely saying, 'Mind you, sir, I shall have to call the police if you don't leave.'

Somehow I managed to disengage from riotous living for a brief season and went on a walking-riding tour to see the historic sights of London. Our hotel was only a few blocks away from the Nelson monument at Trafalgar Square. The National Gallery was nearby, but the museums were emptied of their treasures for the duration of the war, something I hadn't counted on. I began to encounter sights and places I had been hearing about all my life – Charing Cross station, Pall Mall, Leicester Square, Regent Street, Maiden Lane, Berkeley Square, Waterloo Bridge, the Tower of London. All of them were old friends. I had read about them in *Sherlock Holmes*, *Dr Jekyll and Mr Hyde*, *Oliver Twist*, and the other novels of my youthful reading.

I took a cab to Parliament and Westminster Abbey. The Abbey was the first Gothic architecture I had ever seen. I took my time and feasted my eyes on this sublime masterpiece of church architecture. I thought to myself: Can we really be descended from this race of master-builders and super-artisans? By comparison the best contemporary edifice is trite in the extreme. These people had caught a vision of beauty, which is not given to us to know.

Later, as I meandered through the streets, I heard a parade approaching. In the vanguard was a Scottish regimental band, their war drums throbbing. As the kilted veterans passed me, they began to skirl their pipes, the most stirring sound I had ever heard. It got my battle blood up, appealing to some antique strain in me that I was not aware of before. It is said the Scottish regiments marched into battle at El Alamein to the tune of their bagpipes and completely routed the Axis troops. I better understood this after hearing them that day.

After lunch I strolled through St James Park, a wonderful green place along the Mall in front of Buckingham Palace. I was unprepared for what I saw, a plethora of ruttish couples gamboling and lying about the greensward quite impervious to the passers-by. They simply spread newspapers over themselves to conceal their tender ministrations to each other. I noticed many of the males were Yanks who had taken to this primal English pastime like ducks to water.

Above: *GIs on a '48' pay a visit to Westminster Abbey. (Art Crandell)*

Scattered about the park were the traditional soapbox orators; indeed, they could be seen in Kensington Gardens, Hyde Park, and in any of the places where people congregated. I listened to them respectfully as did my British cousins. They could not be styled agitators; no one could agitate the British. Rather they were minor prophets polishing up their oratory. Many English politicians spent an apprenticeship on the soapbox.

I was bone-weary after my sightseeing tour, but not so much so that I was incapable of rejuvenation. I soaked in a tub of hot water, dressed and went back to the fleshpots of Piccadilly. It was our last night in London, and I didn't intend to spend it abed.

Next day it was time for the heroes to go back to the shooting war. For a while we had had a new

lease on life, and it was a welcome respite, to be replayed with great relish for days on end.

Chick's Crew, 'London: Our First Pass', Ben C. Smith, radio-operator, 303rd BG

Where most of the gals are blonde and bold
And they think every Yank's pocket is lined with gold
Then there's the Piccadilly Commandos with painted allure
Steer clear of them or you'll get burnt for sure

Anonymous

I didn't want to join the Air Force;
I didn't want my bollocks shot away.
I'd rather hang around
Piccadilly Underground
Living on the earnings of a high-born lady

Anonymous

Above: *American officers and lady friends sightseeing in London. (via Richards)*

claim there should have been a ribbon or a battle star for just surviving 'the Battle of Piccadilly.' One of my 553rd buddies claims he couldn't get through Piccadilly Circus any evening without being accosted at least seven or eight times by 'Piccadilly Commandos.' A typical blackout confrontation would go as follows: 'Hi, mate,' the girl would say, and while saying that, she would place her hand on your shoulder. Quickly, her hand would pass across your shoulder epaulet and down the sleeve. By this one quick move, she had determined a) this was an officer, and if so, the rank, or b) it was an enlisted man and the rank he held. She was now ready to set a price on her favors if she found an interested male.

Personally, I gave Piccadilly a wide berth. Once I went to Dirty Dick's in Soho. It was basically just another pub, but it was world famous. The benches and tables were hand hewn, and they sat in about two inches of sawdust. The overhead beams were full of cobwebs, dead cat's bones, etc. They told us the place hadn't been cleaned in two hundred years. That was a rough part of London, and probably still is.

Everyone remembers the barrage balloons all over London. It seemed to me that about every place they had to clear away a bomb-damaged building, the British would bring in a GI truck and park it. The truck would have a power winch and a balloon attached. At night, and sometimes in the daytime, too, a thousand or more feet of cable would be run out, putting the blimp-like balloon high over the city. They seemed to discourage the Luftwaffe from coming over the city at low altitudes.

The nightly air raids and the British 'almost nonchalant' attitude towards them puzzled me. Of course, they had had a long time to get used to them (if you ever do). We Yanks were sort of 'Johnny-come-latelys.'

The British attitude was well summed up by the man in his neighborhood pub who said, 'Well, first the bloody Jerry's got to find London in the blackout, then 'e's got to find Neasden, then 'e's got to find No. 12 Cheltham Court, and then I'll probably be down at the pub 'avin' me a pint.'

I remember everyone coming out of a London

Germany's air force had it somewhat battered, but it was unbowed. London was 'the place' to go on your 48-hour passes. I ought to know – I spent plenty of those two-day leaves there. In the winter of 1943, you could count on nightly air raids there, but the worst of the 'blitz' was over. It was business as usual all day long and with the famous English pubs, they observed their traditional hours. Pubs opened in the mornings, though not as early as American taverns, and then closed for a few hours around 'teatime'. In the evening they would open again until around 11 p.m. We Yanks didn't care much for the afternoon shutdown and we thought 11 p.m. was too early to shut down for the night.

Part of each visit to the 'City on the Thames' was spent in other pursuits. I always stayed in a private hotel near the tube stop at Tottenham Court Road. I got bed and breakfast there for nine and six (less than $2). It was from that location that I would plan my forays into the city. On a typical day, I would see something each morning that had tourist appeal. Included were such sights as the Tower of London, Houses of Parliament, Buckingham Palace, Madam Tussaud's Wax Museum, etc. Then, once I was convinced that I had done something cultural, I could get down to more serious matters such as girls, dances, and pub crawling.

Many of us who went to London often used to

I took a trip to London
To look around the town;
When I got to Piccadilly
The sun was going down.
I've never seen such darkness
The night was black as pitch
When suddenly in front of me,
I thought I saw a witch.

I could not see her figure,
I could not see her face,
But if I ever meet her
I'll know her any place
I couldn't tell if she was blonde
Or a dark brunette,
But gosh oh gee, did she give me
A thrill I won't forget

They sing of 'Dirty Gertie'
And Ma'moiselle in French,
But give me a Commando
In a foxhole or a trench
And in the thick of battle
You'll find me happy there,
But say chums, be sure she comes
From Piccadilly Square.

Now when my children ask me,
'Please tell us, daddy dear,
What did you do to win the war?'
I'll answer with a sneer:
'Your daddy was a hero;
His best he always fought.
With bravery he gave to
the Commandos his support.'

Oh it was Lilly from Piccadilly,
You know the one I mean.
I'll spend each pay day, that's my hey day
With Lilly, my blackout Queen.

Mickey Balsam

pub during an air raid one night and everywhere you looked you could see sparks flying off the cobblestones. The sparks were, of course, from the ack-ack shrapnel raining back to earth. It was a real war zone. One pub I was in that night had a sign in the bar that read as follows: 'WE REMAIN OPEN DURING AIR RAIDS, BUT IN THE EVENT OF A DIRECT HIT, WE CLOSE IMMEDIATELY.'

London Remembered, Roger Lovelace

London — To find a pub in a blackout, just get caught in pedestrian traffic on any corner and you will be pushed into one in straight order. The way you find the corner is to get off any bus and you'll be goosed up onto the sidewalk by a bicycle with a madman for a driver. The way you find a bus is to follow the first odor that reminds you of burning rags until you run into an exhaust pipe. That will be a bus. The odor will be gasoline. When you bump into a woman here at night, you don't say, 'Hya, babe.' You just take a deep sniff and if it's Yardley's you follow her. Were you ever in a blackout in a fog? We spent all one night crawling

Below: *The economic impact of much loose money in the hands of visitors from other shores caused a sharp decrease in morals, and the 'Piccadilly Commandos' and 'Hyde Park Rangers' did brisk business after dark. Their prices ranged from chocolate bars and nylons to 10 shillings in a doorway and £2.10s all night.' 8th AF crewman. 'Gwendolyn' and 'Penelope,' two Piccadilly Commandos, join in the VE Day 1945 celebrations in Piccadilly Circus. (via Robert Eberwein)*

Above: *Taxi cab outside the Dorchester Club. (Art Crandell)*

home on our hands and knees. Of course, we could have taken a taxi. In this town, if you put your name in a week in advance, you can get the one with two tires on it, if you're in a hurry, you take the one that burns kerosene. The decontamination service at the end of the run is free. There is also a mid-Victorian cab, but it is haunted. The other night we saw a poster advertising a Hedy Lamarr picture. We got in line and an hour later, when we reached the head of it, we were handed two links of strong sausage and a slice of Limburger cheese. That's what comes of having those ration lines too close to the cinema.

'Thoughts In a London Blackout:
Things Like This Make War Hell!',
Yank Magazine

The cabbies are the best of all the public servitors with whom the Yank does business. They are a shabby, sullen, but efficient brotherhood of specialists. To get a hacking license in London the cabby applicant must do months of tour by bicycle until each of the winding streets and mews of this sprawling city are mapped perfectly in memory. Then, from behind the wheel of his conventional black cab, he must demonstrate over and over again to exacting police inspectors exactly how to reach given addresses from varying starting points without a single wrong turning or yard of excess haul. The London cabby is a postgraduate who knows not only how to find his way around, but who is conscious of all his prerogatives and insists upon their fulfillment. His sixpence tip is part of the pay scale, an accepted formula. The Yank is a generous tipper, but he objects to being reminded, or having the recipient fix the amount. The feud brought together two positives, and the dispute was a long one, vigorously waged. Cabbies conditioned the unorthodox would-be passengers by passing them up on rainy nights. The feuding ended as soon as the Americans learned the sixpence tip was a part of the fare, though unregistered on the meter. Typically, they made their surrender generously.

Skyways to Berlin, 'The London Front', Major
John M. Redding & Captain Harold I. Leyshon

'All in all, it was a never-to-be-forgotten experience and most of all, it made me love London and England and it was where I made up my mind that theater was what I wanted to do with my life after the war, so I am grateful for the whole experience.'

Delbert Mann, Squadron Intelligence Officer, 491st BG and post-war film producer

'The Tower of London particularly impressed me as well as the place nearby where one of our Cameron ancestors, Dr A. Archibald Cameron, was beheaded because he supported Bonnie Prince Charlie during the rebellion.'

Colonel William Cameron, 44th BG, Shipdham

'The station clock with staggering hands and callous face, says twenty-five-to-nine. A cigarette, a cup of tea, a bun, and my train goes at ten.'

'Steel Cathedrals', D. Van Den Bogaerde

Sooner or later, American military had to get back to their bases and to do so they had to take railways. They will all recall the hot steaming tea in mugs and the soggy buns served up by volunteers at every railway station.

Every time one departed from Liverpool Street station, one never knew if it was the last time or not. Many an airman departing was killed in action before his next leave or pass. So for this reason and others, the station took on a highly charged significance to airmen. Trains departing that station served the East Anglia region of England, where the majority of the American airbases were located. Once, I shared a compartment with a young British soldier and his girl. They made love all the way to Cambridge where he got off. It was the custom in

those times to travel with curtains drawn on the compartments so as not to emit light in the blackout. It was unusual for the English to show so much affection in public.

Technical Sergeant Forrest S. Clark, air gunner, 67th BS, 44th BG

'A time in London and about Piccadilly, the best you could find in female companionship, and you caught the 8.00 p.m. train from Liverpool Street station to come back to complete your tour and really sweat the last ones out.'

Allan Healy

Below: *A GI forgot to post his key back to the Strand Hotel on Sherwood Street after his pass. It lay undiscovered at Shipdham until the 1980s. (MWB)*

The Tour

'Shorten your tour with a trip to the Ruhr'

Anonymous

After a period of orientation, we flew our first combat mission. The training was behind us; this was the real thing. We were not certain what was ahead of us, because in training we were never awakened at 3.30 a.m., never had to shave in cold water, or tried to eat breakfast on a nervous stomach. This was fun, I think. We flew under extreme conditions – the excessive cold, the use of oxygen for six-hour periods, the scene of fellow airmen being shot down, and lastly, the ever present enemy anti-aircraft fire and fighters waiting to knock us out of the sky. It was not until we returned to our home base and we began discussing the day's events that I realized how scared I was, but then again so was everyone else and not embarrassed to say so. This was only our first mission of a scheduled twenty-five called a combat tour before we could even consider a return to the States.

Above left: *Combat crews in the mess at Hardwick. (USAF)*

Top right: *After briefing, a combat crew in the 453rd BG at Old Buckenham pile on a jeep for the trip to the flight line. (USAF)*

Bottom right: *A Fortress crew prepare to board their B-17 for a mission. (USAF)*

Each flight became more dangerous as the air war was stepped up. If a crew survived eight to ten missions at this time they were considered lucky. Perhaps our darkest day was 30 December 1943, because on that day we lost a crew from our barracks. It was a crew that we had trained with and had become very close friends with. Living together as closely as we did made us feel almost like family. To lose a friend and to actually see it happen was devastating. Our morale was at its lowest point, especially when we returned to our barracks and saw their empty beds. We did not know whether they had survived the parachute jump, or had been killed. We did not have time to mourn their loss because we were called out for another mission the very next day and as was the case, our own survival was on our minds. It was about this time that I realized that this was a

dangerous game I was a part of. Was the glory of being a combat crewman worth it?

I never knew if I was a brave man, I had never been tested. Our crew never once discussed the possibility of our chances for survival, but I am sure that we all thought the same thing. When we first began flying together our goal was to not take chances and to put our faith in our pilots. 'BJ' kept repeating 'We will make it'. On one occasion, when we met our first ground crew chief when our own plane was assigned to us, BJ asked him how many crews he had. He said, 'You are my third – the other two went down'

BJ's answer to him was, 'We will make it – you can mark it down.'

We were not as sure as he was, but his self-confidence rubbed off on us. When I saw another plane get hit and go down, I watched for the parachutes to open. I immediately felt sorry for them but just as quickly I found myself saying, better them then us. Self-survival can play mean tricks with the mind.

Our twenty-five missions were not simple, each one worse than the last, but when, on 4 March 1944, returning from Berlin, we came out of the clouds over the English Channel and saw the White Cliffs of Dover, it was the most beautiful sight that I could ever hope to see. At this moment I did not realize the importance of my radio work. I had been too scared at that moment, but my training had paid off.

Staff Sergeant Laurence S. 'Goldie' Goldstein, B-17 radio operator, 388th BG, Knettishall

I'll never forget the people I met
Braving those angry skies,
I remember well, as the shadows fell,
The light of hope in their eyes;
And tho I'm far away,
I can still here them say,
Thumbs Up!
For when the dawn comes up:
There'll be bluebirds over, the white Cliffs of Dover,
Tomorrow, just you wait and see.
Anonymous

Above left: *91st BG Fortresses en route to their target. Nearest B-17G is Ack Ack Annie of the 322nd BS, which joined the group at Bassingbourn on 16 March 1944. (USAF via Tom Cushing)*

Above right: *A mightily relieved 305th BG crewman at Chelveston after his crew completed their twenty-fifth and final mission of their tour, on 29 May 1943. The B-17 they flew lasted only until 13 June when it failed to return with 2/Lt. Grant B. Higgs' crew. A tour was progressively increased to thirty then thirty-five combat missions. (via Bill Donald)*

1. 16 April 43 –
LORIENT, FRANCE.
Two vessels and a power plant. Milk run.

2. 17 April 43 –
BREMEN, GERMANY.
FW factory. Worst flak encountered so far. Windshield on pilot's side, cannon shell thru tail section, flak thru radio compartment. Pillow in windshield.

3. 1 May 43 –
ST. NAZAIRE, FRANCE.
Locks and sub pens. Plenty fighters and moderate flak. Poor bombing – clouds. 2 holes in lead edge of 1 & 2 cowling. Borrowed radio man shot stabilizer full of holes! Stirling's ship blew up and Walsh went down. Palmer's waist gunner shot dead thru heart with .30 caliber.

4. 4 May 43 –
ANTWERP, BELGIUM.
General Motors plant. Very good bombing. Spits and 47s with us – good cover. Flew #3. Calhoun and Clark Gable led mission. Real successful mission. Pentz ship shot up badly as it was approaching English coast. Co-pilot, Wallace, shot in calf with .30 cal. – tail gunner hit over, eye and in leg.

5. 13 May 43 –
MEAULTE, FRANCE.
Heinkle aircraft repair works. P-47s along – little fighter opposition. Excellent bombing pattern.

6. 14 May 43 –
KIEL, GERMANY.
Sub works, docks, harbor installations. Bombing excellent. Captain Bales/Dooley – Mathis – McColl went down about 50 miles from enemy coast. Not much chance of rescue. Few of crew baled out. Bales & McColl were our roommates. Plenty of fytrs & flak. B-24s along. We were high and got off easy. Good mission.

7. 19 May 43 –
KIEL, GERMANY.
Same target. Started out low-low in formation. Broke up half way over. Roller took lead element home, left Smitty, McClung and us alone in the hot spot. Plenty of fytrs & flak again. Worst running fight for us so far then. Holes in wing, cowling, nose and windshield. Quick got a Fw 190.

8. 21 May 43 –
WILHELMSHAVEN, GERMANY.
Sub pens and ships. Poor weather – poor formation. Heaviest fytr opposition yet. Hernan got 2 Fw 190s. Only one ship from 306th returned to base. Rest lost or crash-landed.

9. 13 June 43 –
BREMEN, GERMANY.
Target was dock installations and sub pens. Excellent smoke screen. No fytrs but plenty of flak over primary. Very poor bombing results. We bombed dummy airfield and missed it at that! Fytrs all went to Kiel and knocked hell out of that wing (26).

10. 22 June 43 –
HULS, GERMANY.
Big synthetic rubber plant. Bombing results excellent. Our group led wing. We flew #5. A B-40 flying #2 was shot down by flak over Target. Closest call for us yet. Most successful mission but very strong opposition. Flak closest yet – few hits on us (10 holes). Head-on attacks by fytrs. 3 of our bombs hung up due to violent evasive action. Nix flying behind us had an injured waist gunner when we pulled up to evade an incoming fytr. Have heard the kid might die.

11. 25 June 43 –
HAMBURG, GERMANY.
Flub-dub mission (Salvo). Lousy weather all the way, multi-layer clouds, etc. Very heavy and persistent contrails had us flying formation half on instruments half contact. Reached enemy coast with ships all mixed up in clouds & contrails. Kept our formation somehow and made it home OK after some fytr attacks amidst the clouds. Lost Palmer (Kieffer), Mack (Barrog, Cos, Smith, Stallings hit bad) they got back to England and baled out. Kelly got Silver Star.

12. 28 June 43 –
BEAUMONT, FRANCE.
FW field, good bombing, easy mission for a change. Hit Ammo Dump and really raised hell. Cemetery nearby. No fytrs – Spitfire escort.

13. 29 June 43 –
VILLACOUBLAY, FRANCE.
Flub-dub. 10-10s. Little fytr opposition. Flak hit us on way out at coast. No losses. Flew #13, low-low, ass-end. Beautiful sight on way home sun going down on overcast.

14. 4 July 43 –
LE MANS, FRANCE.
Airport & Pd repair depot. Fytrs very intense, hit us 15 minutes before Target. Ball Turret ran out of ammo before we reached Target. Shot up plenty of ammo myself. Bombing fair.

15. 10 July 43 –
ABBEYVILLE, FRANCE.
FW Airfield – missed Target completely. Flew with 379th – very poor formation and bombing. No fytrs or flak to speak of. 379th led show.

16. 14 July 43 –
VILLACOUBLAY, FRANCE.
FW sub depot (Bastille Day). We led 2nd flight of lead squadron, which led entire wing. Bombing pretty good. Fytrs weak, flak heavy as we came back at 16,000 feet for the Spit 5s (Wheww!) Swafford ditched. Small flak hole near tail.

(25 JULY 43 –
JOHN VAN WIE (WALSH, BLANK) SHOT DOWN OVER HAMBURG. #21 FOR MOST OF THEM. ANNIVERSARY OF HIS COMMISSION 1 YEAR AGO. RICE NOT WITH THEM.)

17. 26 July 43 –
HAMBURG, GERMANY.
Sub Works and ships. Bombing very good. Flak like a cloud!!! Fytrs didn't bother us very much. Flew #2 on Calhoun who led entire wing. No losses to our group. Lucky.

18A. 28 July 43 –
Scheduled to bomb Kassel. To be longest mission yet. Lost #1 just inside enemy coast so came home in cloud cover. No attacks. Later the whole wing aborted due to weather and aborts. NO CREDIT.

18B. 30 July 43 –
KASSEL, GERMANY.
FW factory near city. Bombing pretty good. Flak encountered at several points on way in, over Target, and on way out. Longest 8th AF trip yet. 4 hours on oxygen. Hit by most enemy fytrs yet. Came right thru formations. We led 2nd element of low sqdn. Hernan & Quick each got a Fw. Gas gone at English coast. #4 quit, started glide and found a field as #2 sputtered. Plenty of ditching, crash & emergency landings. One ship came in for emergency landing and one flat only came down – burned. Upper

Turret out of 02 over enemy territory – co-pilot had to feed him walk-arounds. Very rugged mission. Lieutenant Cogswell/Tippet ditched in channel – all OK.

19. 12 August 43 –
GELSENKIRCKEN, GERMANY.
Happy Valley! Synthetic Oil Plant. Results almost nil. Went in at 27,000 feet, leading 2nd element of low group, lead squadron. Flak was terrific & fytrs rough stuff!!! Lieutenant Pentz (Mulligan, Street, Philpot) shot down – afraid they burned on way down. Enlisted crew were roommates with our guys – swell bunch. Lost #2 supercharger just off enemy coast. #1 began throwing oil badly from oil cooler vent. #4 began to run rough. Feathered #1 on way home to save it. Lost Oxygen on right side. Several flak holes in bomb bay & #3 cylinder of #4 engine, wings, etc. Good smoke screen over target.

Above: *Exhausted 491st BG crewmembers at Metfield after returning from the group's first combat mission on 2 June 1944. (USAF)*

20. 17 August 43 –
SCHWEINFURT, GERMANY.
Ball Bearing plant, & Town & People. Bombing very good. Up at 0300 – Brief at 0400 – TO scheduled for 0700. Ground fog called it off until they finally called us in for eats and another briefing of Nav's. TO set for 1200 – Low group at 20,000'. Led 2nd element. 2 aborts from our squadron. Lot of flak over Antwerp on way in – couple of bold fytrs there, too. Little flak over Targ. – no fytrs. Plenty of ME-110s, Fws and ME-109s after Tgt. P-47s did a superb job! Saw incendiaries hitting in town. Coast really looked good. Lead Bomber hit in guts on bomb run. Longest, toughest and probably most important raid of war so far, by us. Hole in

left aileron and thru fuselage under Millers seat – piece hit pilot's hand. RAF failed to follow-up (went to Peenemunde). Other 4th Winger's hit Regensburg on shuttle to North Africa.

21. 6 Sept. 43 –
STUTTGART, GERMANY.
Flub-dub. Spark plugs & Magnetos. Longest so far in this theater by us. 10-10s over target. Stooged around dodging flak & waiting for clearing. Captain Barret of S-2 with us. General Travis led our group with Lyle. We led #2 element. Bombs from #3 ship were tossed out by evasive action – just missed us? Flak hole right in front of my face – small glass splinters in neck. Gas lites on with coast no where in sight. Plenty of ditching and bailing-out. We got all set for ditching but made it in to a field with no facilities along with 15 other ships. One cracked up when it was cut off on approach with 2 engines. What a mess, but no injuries! Life photographer was there. I took a couple of pics for him. Ninety degree cross wind on landing. Waited 7 hours for gas and took off at twilight. Just made it home as darkness really set in. Good job of navigation. Old Squaw ditched. C. R. Asher and probably Bugs Bunny went down.

22. 9 Sept. 43 –
ARRAS, FRANCE.
Fytr base. Bombing damn good. P-47s all the way. Milk run. Flak from Dunquerque on way out. 2 missions scheduled; #2 was scrubbed.

23. 16 Sept. 43 –
NANTES, FRANCE.
(MY 23RD BIRTHDAY) Supply ship in river port. Bombing very poor. Flak & fytrs terrific! Heard flak burst and then hit ship like hail. Lost #3 over target. Couldn't feather because we lost oil pressure. Pistons finally froze and prop broke off from crankshaft and kept windmilling. We were leading high squadron and had to fall back, but they stayed with us? Came back low, by sea. Jumped by 8 ME-110s. They got one which was flying alone on the deck. On the bomb run I held my bombs a good 25 seconds after the leaders left and theirs all hit way short.

24. 9 October 43 –
ANKLAM, GERMANY.
FW 190 factory making component parts. Bombing very good. NO FLAK!, plenty of fytrs. Deepest penetration and longest trip for me. Carried 3 x 1,000# plus 5 small incendiaries and one bomb bay tank. Crossed Denmark North of Kiel on way in and

out at 13,000'. Weather perfect. A beautiful, uneventful bomb run. Long running fight going home; little flak from Wannemunde. Saw men bailing out over No. Sea. Not a chance of 'em surviving. No escort. Lost around 30 ships that day. None from our group.

25. 14 October 43 –
SCHWEINFURT, GERMANY.
Ball bearing plant. Bombing excellent. Plenty of flak, most and boldest fytrs yet? Took off in 0–0 weather and rain on instruments. Climbed on runway heading to above overcast – 4,000' – did 180 and returned to field where we assembled 3,000' above overcast. First flak over Antwerp. Continuous fytr attacks from 45 minutes this side of target to one hour after target. Worst I've ever been through. Flak over Tgt. terrific and accurate. Right horizontal stabilizer hit by fytr right after target and we almost spin in. Pilot called up to stand by for bail out twice. Lost formation sometime in there and ended up with Grafton-Underwood – LOW!!! Pilot asked for course to Switzerland, but it was 200 miles, too far. Best and most violent evasive action ever by Manning saved us from the roughest running fight I've ever seen!! After fytrs left they didn't return. Escort never showed up. Nose guns worked off & on – tail guns out most of the way – 1 upper out most of way – Ball guns out most of way – waist guns OK. Over England, pilot gave us choice of landing with damaged stabilizer or bailing out. We all stayed and landed OK, at Halesworth. Last mission, Thank God. (Phelps and Rothman finished OK, too.)

Verbatim mission summary, Lieutenant William A. Boutelle, bombardier, Lieutenant Claude W. Campbell's crew, *The Old Squaw*, 359th BS, 303rd BG, 16 April 1943–14 October 1943

Lieutenant Jay R. Sterling's B-17 lost on 1 May cost six crew KIA, three POW and one evaded. Lieutenant Vincent X. Walsh's crew was shot down in *Joe Btfspik*. Seven men were KIA and three POW. 'Calhoun', first mentioned on the 4 May mission: Captain William Calhoun, 359th BS CO. Clark Gable, the famous Hollywood movie actor, was in England at this time, assigned to the 351st BG to make a motion picture of gunners in action. Co-pilot Wallace, on Pentz's ship, never flew again.

On the 14 May mission Captain Ross C. Bales (Lieutenant Campbell's roommate) and all ten crew were lost in *F.D.R.'s Potato Peeler Kids*. One of the crew was bombardier Mark Mathis, whose brother Jack had been killed over Vegesack, and was posthumously awarded the Medal of Honor. Quick, the gunner mentioned on 19 May getting a Fw 190, was one of the gunners on Lieutenant

Above: *B-17s en route to their target. (USAF)*

Claude Campbell's crew, as was top turret gunner, Howard E. Hernan, first mentioned on 21 May. On the 22 June mission the 'B-40' lost was a YB-40 Fortress gunship flying with the 92nd BG formation. Lieutenant James S. Nix got his B-17 back to Molesworth but was lost on 19 August flying *City of Albuquerque*. Four crew were killed and six made POW. On the 25 June mission Lieutenant Joseph F. Palmer and crew were lost in *The Avenger*. Seven men were KIA and four POW. Also on 25 June, Captain George V. Stallings and crew on *Qui-Nine The Bitter Dose*, FTR (failed to return) after ditching in the North Sea.

On 14 July the 'Swafford' ditching was actually Lieutenant Calvin A. Swaffer, whose crew of ten were picked up by ASR after they ditched in the North Sea in *Memphis Blues*. On 30 July Tippet/Cogswell ditched in the Channel. On 2 October Lieutenant Paul S. Tippet and crew of eleven were lost on *Yard Bird II*. On 12 August Lieutenant Arthur H. Pentz was lost flying *Old Ironsides*. One man was KIA and nine made POW.

On 6 September General Robert B. Travis, 1st Wing Commander, flew with Lieutenant Colonel Lewis E. Lyle, one of the 303rd BG's two acting COs – 1 September 1943–29 October 1944 (the other was Lieutenant Colonel Richard H. Cole). 'C. R. Asher' was Lieutenant Colman R. Asher of the 92nd BG who ditched with the loss of six crewmen. Two were taken POW and two evaded. *The Old Squaw*, a Fortress flown many times by Lieutenant Cameron's crew, was indeed ditched. All ten of Lieutenant Robert J. Hullar's crew were picked up and returned. On 9 October, Howard E. Hernan and two other members of Claude Campbell's crew flew their twenty-fifth and final mission of the war, when they flew in *The Eightball*, although Campbell's place was taken by Captain William Calhoun and General Travis took the co-pilot's seat. Campbell flew his twenty-fourth mission on 3 November and his twenty-fifth on 26 November.

Above: *B-24s of the 445th BG en route to their target at Glinde, Germany, on 6 October 1944. (USAF)*

… He read a name. The guy came forward and saluted. The major handed him his air medal and gave him a tight-lipped smile and a fast shake. They saluted each other as gallant gentlemen.

Next.

My turn pretty soon. I gave him my best salute … When I got back in line I opened up my box. It was a pretty medal. The metal part is better looking than the DFC, but the ribbon isn't. The box is blue with a thin yellow line for trim, and 'air medal' neatly lettered.

The citation was mimeographed, with my name typed in. The mimeograph was just about out of ink when it got to mine. The exceptional gallantry part was pretty thin.

Serenade To The Big Bird, 'Air Medal', Bert Stiles, 401st BS, 91st BG

After the first two weeks it seemed like I'd been here a hundred years, and all time before that was just a dream.

We were alerted eight days straight, and we flew six missions and were called back once, and had an abortion in that time. After that first trip to Eschwege we went on a short one to Calais, and clear down to Munich on our third one. We hit an airfield just outside of Metz and flew over the Zuider Zee (the Netherlands) again to Brunswick, and swung down through the wine country around Avord to hit another airfield on our sixth.

The raids went by so fast they got all mixed up, and I couldn't remember which one came first and what happened which day. If it had kept up much longer we'd have all been so flak happy we'd never have made it.

I was so tired of sitting in the co-pilot's seat I thought I was getting cancer of the left cheek. The cheek bone on that side was beginning to throb at high altitude, and when we got back from the ten-hour haul to Munich it was ringing like a gong, and I had to sit on half myself most of the way home.

… Air medals come in boxes. They are sent to each squadron by the medal department of the army which is a hard-working outfit. Whenever the boxes begin to clog up the works there is a presentation.

We got ours on a Sunday.

We never knew until the CQ opened the door and called 'Elliott' when the day would start. It could be anytime from midnight on, depending on the target and where we'd be in the bomber stream that day. Takeoff was as early as 0500 and as late as 1120. For a 0600 takeoff for a major target where we were #1 lead crew, pre-pre briefing came about 0100. This gave my bombardiers the first look at the target. Next came pre-briefing where all the day's lead crews saw the target – 0200. Breakfast would be at 0300 and all the crews would be up. We could never divulge the target, but we did occasionally suggest that maybe they ought to eat an extra good breakfast – or suggest that having fresh eggs that morning had a special meaning. Main briefing would be about 0500 with all of the crews in attendance. There was a guard on the door and you were checked off as you entered the briefing room. The officers sat together toward the front with the gunners in the rear. The map of Europe was covered by a curtain, and it was always a tense moment when it was opened and everyone could see the bomb route spelled out with a red ribbon. The briefing officer covered the details of the target and the route, the weather man gave us his guess for the day, and we got any special information available on expected flak and possible fighters, as well as what our own fighter cover would be. After the briefing we'd finish dressing and catch a truck out to the hardstand where our plane was parked. The Protestant chaplain was always around with a cheerful word or a prayer, if you so desired, and the Catholic chaplain would have communion for any Catholics who wished it …

Captain Ralph H. Elliott, pilot, 467th BG

Off we go into the wild blue yonder,
Climbing High, into the sun
Here they come, zooming to meet our thunder,
At 'em boys, give 'er the gun.
Down we dive, spouting flame from under,
Off with one hell of a roar.
We live in fame, or go down in flame,
For, nothing can stop the US Air Corps.

Here's a toast to the host of
Those who love the vastness of the sky
To a friend we send a message of his
brother men who fly.
We drink to those who gave their all of old
Then down we roar to score the rainbow's pot of gold

The US Air Corps song

'It was terribly cold in the air and just miserably cold on the ground. Two or three oxygen masks would freeze up on each flight. People would wear their flying gear on the ground to keep warm and it would absorb moisture, which would then freeze when they were airborne … adding to the frostbite problem, of course. It was just plain miserable.'

Colonel William Cameron, pilot, 44th BG

Combat is pretty good, if you make it back. Especially the money. But the raids are very tiresome as the oxygen and the cold temperature really wears you out. A lot of my good friends have gone down. At first it bothers you, but now I don't mind it so much. To think I used to be afraid of the dark and I wouldn't even ride the roller coaster. But I can say with truth that I'd rather face fighters than

Above: Short Snorter *of the 392nd BG at Wendling in 1944. (USAF)*

flak. At fighters you can shoot back; but flak you can't. You just have to ride through it and hope for the best. Another thing I sweat out is my heated suit. This damn war is getting tough. You have to beg to go on a mission; our pilot took another crew into Sweden. So we are just spares now. Hoping to stay together. The fellows are fighting over my cap as I leave it behind when I go on a raid. When you don't make it back they divide up anything they wouldn't send home to your next of kin. We receive a bar of candy and a package of gum. I am now in a different squadron, which gives you two Mars bars and a package of gum.

Staff Sergeant John W. Butler, gunner, 389th and 93rd BGs

They were over the Channel bound for Calais:
The crew knew for sure it was judgement day
No fighters, no flak, came up from the ground
But the brave crew's hearts began to pound.
Anonymous

COMBAT ORIENTATION

Combat time was at hand, so North Pickenham, the home of the 492nd Heavy Bombardment Group, was to be our home – our next assignment. We were welcomed with open arms and the usual 'You'll be sorry.'

Within a day, I noticed much tension and little talk from others. I thought it might be our newness or something personal. It wasn't. Their combat losses caused this behavior. This group with Colonel Snavely had been operational only six weeks, and during these missions, they had lost all but eleven of their original seventy-seven crews. The story was the same as it was for the Bloody Hundredth group ... The losses for the 492nd were so great that within a week after we arrived, it was disbanded. Drinking the bar dry is the last thing to do to close a base. This was my first bout with scotch whiskey as I remember it and can't remember it. Within a day or so, my crew was assigned to the 392nd Heavy Bombardment Group about ten miles distant and was to be our home for the next year.

Lieutenant Robert H. Tays, B-24 pilot

others of the crew didn't want. It all depended on how rough the mission was whether or not there was any whiskey left over. Since our last meal had been breakfast at about 0600, it also had a heady effect on most of us. We did carry a box of high-energy candy to suck on, but never any real food. Flight lunches weren't in the program for combat missions. Interrogation was to update flak and enemy fighter information, collect reports on aircraft shot down or that dropped out of formation, find out if anything unusual had happened, etc. It was always very thorough, especially with the lead crews who had bombing information to report. There was also an officer's critique session after supper in the mess hall ...

Captain Ralph H. Elliott, pilot, 467th BG

Below: *Cavalier of the 367th BS, 306th BG, which bellied in at Thurleigh on 15 November 1943. (Joseph Minton via Larry Goldstein)*

Most of the boys drank the whiskey at interrogation after a mission, but it was pretty strong stuff. The coffee and sandwiches tasted the best. Intelligence officers interrogated each of the crews after they landed from a mission, but there was always coffee and sandwiches to eat, served by the Red Cross girls. Each crewmember was also entitled to a shot of whiskey – which did cause somewhat of a problem if one of the fellows also drank the whiskey that

Beer, beer for old Pappy Wayne,
You bring the whisky, and I'll bring champagne
Send the 'N' crews out for gin,
Don't let a sober flyer in.
We never stagger, we never fall
We sober up on wood alcohol,
While our drunken 'S' crews are staggering,
Back to the bar for more.

Anonymous

MILK RUNS

'A "milk run!" The briefing officer described our mission and our route and it really sounded sweet. We would start our run over the water and only be over land a few minutes. "There are only about eight guns there that will be able to reach you," he said. Wow! This was really great! We wondered how the "Bloody Hundredth" happened to get such a soft mission.'

John A. Miller, gunner, 100th BG

'I'll see you at briefing,' I said.

'You'll love this. It will be a milk run.'

The next morning, sleep-stiff, I walked across the mud and found Bill McShane. It was Bill who had actually aroused me but I didn't remember getting up. I asked him where I could get some flying equipment. 'What for?' Bill asked.

'I'm going along with Mac.'

'You are not!' Bill said. 'Don't be a fool. Have you ever been on oxygen at 27,000 feet?'

'Well, no.'

'Alright. Wait until you've done a couple of test flights and try it out. You don't want to go up and pass out on these kids do you?'

'Well, no. I just thought. I've done a lot of flying, but not that altitude stuff I guess I'm a rhubarb merchant, eh?' I grinned.

'There's no rhubarb where these guys go. You stay home today.'

'So I didn't go with Mac. He was keenly disappointed. He even brought Staff Sergeant Gerald E. Murphy of South Bend, Indiana, over to try to kid me back on. Murphy was McCormick's gunner-radio man. When Mac wasn't looking, Murphy said *sotto voce*, 'Maybe you're getting out of something. I wish I could stay home today. I don't feel too good. I've got a cold.'

'Mac says it will be a milk run,' I suggested.

'Murphy adjusted his parachute straps and said: 'Maybe, but I don't think there's any such thing. There ain't any milk runs, any more.'

Arch Whitehouse, writing in *True Magazine* about

Above: Little Warrior of the 493rd BG shot down over Fallersleben, Germany, on 29 June 1944. This dramatic photo was taken by S/Sgt. Clifford Stocking Jr. of the 862nd BS, a waist gunner in The Green Hornet. (via Truett Woodall)

the last flight of *Vagabond King*, 389th BG, which was shot down by enemy fighters into the Skagerrak off southern Norway on 18 November 1943. One parachute was seen to leave the stricken B-24 but no survivors were picked up. Captain John B. McCormick and all eleven crew died in a watery grave.

From Bremen to Bordeaux
From Berlin to Oslo
Wherever those heavies go.
Anonymous

'After losing twelve hours yesterday on our longest raid thus far, and one which not only was long, but also pretty rough, we were all very tired and worn out at 0300 this morning when we were called for another mission. This last day of the week, which was to go down in history as the biggest week of aerial combat of the war, found us rather dulled at the prospects of another long mission. We had arrived at that mental state where one more extra long, extra tough raid, meant almost nothing to us. It was just another raid. As for myself, at least, I'd grown calloused. The tougher the raid now, the better I liked it.'

First Lieutenant Lowell H. Watts, pilot, *Blitzin Betsy*, 562nd BS, 388th BG, 'Big Week', February 1944. He was shot down on the mission to Berlin, 6 March 1944 when fighters shot part of the tail off. Watts and five of his crew were captured and made POW. Four gunners were killed.

Below: B-17 navigator's station. (MWB)

We went back to Berlin.

Coming along into the flak over the city, a Fort in a wing off to our left pitched over into a screaming dive into the flame below. The plane was on fire. All four props were turning smoothly. Maybe the pilot had a personal grudge to settle, and wanted to make sure his bombs went home ... or maybe the pilot was a bloody pulp in his seat, and the controls were shot away, and the co-pilot was a corpse, and the plane was afraid to stay up there any longer.

... The 109s knocked a whole squadron out behind us.

'They just went away,' Sharpe said later. 'This one just crashed head-on into the lead ship, and three others blew up, and the last two just disappeared.'

The sky was wide and blue and empty except for Forts. Some P-51s came over, heading for Berlin.

'Right on time,' Bird said. 'That guy had blue eyes.'

I could have counted the cylinders in his engines.

Now that they were gone we were all pretty shaky.

'They'll be back,' Sam said. ' Everybody get ready.' His voice was high and shrill the way it always was when he was excited.

But they never came back after that one pass.

Letting down in the Channel, Sharpe came up front. There was blood all over his shorts. He turned around and dropped them so we could see the wound.

'Mostly gore,' he laughed.

He had a gash on the left cheek.

'Plenty good enough for a Purple Heart,' Lewis said.

'For conspicuous gallantry and getting shot in the ass,' Sharpe said. 'No, thanks.'

A 20mm had exploded just in front of our wing and knocked out the feathering motor on number four.

Sharpe's kit was near the door, and all that was left was some powdered malted-milk tablets.

'That was what they call the Luftwaffe,' Crone said.

'I never even seen them till they were gone.'

***Serenade To The Big Bird*, 'The Big-B ...', Bert Stiles, 401st BS, 91st BG, 24 May 1944**

When a crew finished their combat tour they were rewarded with a trip back to the States. We were told about all the nice things that would happen to us when we reached the USA. Most of my crewmates left almost immediately, but I was chosen along with seven other men to train new crews that would be arriving in England. I was told that the assignment would be for three months, but I had a choice, accept a direct commission to Second Lieutenant and have to stay overseas for the duration of the war, or sweat out the three months. I chose the three months because I initially planned to ask Rose to marry me when I returned home. As things turned out, my decision was a wise one, as I remained just two months. When our students flew their first combat mission, I was released and left the base within hours of my notification. En route to my base to be shipped home I had to pass through London and who could miss a week of leisure in the international capital of the world. I was there for a few days when I met several US Army infantrymen. It was unusual to see anything but air force people in town, and when I inquired why they were there I heard something that immediately made me think that the invasion of Europe was about to occur. I decided to exit London before things changed and I was on the first train outbound to a small base near Liverpool. Most men in the 8th Air Force were certain that if they were still in England at that time, that their trip home would never come until the end of the war. We all believed that if the invasion happened, we would be forced to fly additional missions. This was definitely a good time to leave London and to proceed to the next base where I would be processed for the trip to the USA.

When I arrived, I was told that I would be there for about two weeks but after just a few days an announcement was made that Allied troops had landed on the beaches of Normandy, France. This was 6 June 1944 and within minutes a rumor began to spread throughout the camp that all airmen would be returned to fly more combat missions. There was a collective sigh of relief when we were notified before the day ended that we would all return to the States as scheduled. We were not

aware of the heavy losses that our fellow combat crews were undergoing. We were needed in the US as instructors for new crews in training. Finally, on 9 June I was on a large ship that left Liverpool, England for home. Not until the ship was two days out did I have the true feeling that I was really on the way home. It was a great day for me, I had finished my combat flying, and I was on the way home to be married.

Sailing into New York Harbor past the Statue of Liberty was a thrilling event to me. I had seen this scene many times before but on that day in June it was the most beautiful sight that one can imagine.

I was part of a group of GIs that were given the royal treatment. At this point in time, very few soldiers were returning from overseas, most were on their way over. We were treated as returning heroes, given steak, and fresh vegetables and fruit and extended all the help we needed including the promise of a long leave and the opportunity to bring a new wife to the next army facility, which in my case would be a stay in Atlantic City in

Above: *452nd BG Fortress over Berlin's Templehof airport on 29 April 1944. (USAF)*

midsummer. After we were fed and babied, we were granted twenty-one-day furloughs and told that we could bring our new wives with us for a honeymoon at Uncle Sam's expense.

I was ordered to Atlantic City for rest and recuperation, but first a stop in New York to talk about marriage, but when I returned to my home, my parents were away for the weekend so I had to wait several days to see them. Rose and I were young and in love and wanted to be married as soon as possible. I had to return to the army base for a few days to be processed as the army called it. Then

finally I was on my furlough and there was so much to do. For my first few days home I was welcomed and kissed by so many relatives that I was almost worn out. It was a terrific feeling to be with my family and Rose and right then everything seemed to be going well. I picked the most opportune moment to talk to my father about getting married.

Staff Sergeant Laurence S. 'Goldie' Goldstein, 388th BG

1. OSNABRUCK
2. COLOGNE
3. COLOGNE
4. MUNSTER
5. GELSENKIRCHEN
6. HANOVER
7. HANAU
8. KOBLENZ
16. HALLE
17. MESCHEDE
18. MAGDEBURG

The golden years seem to give one the ability to view one's youth with detachment ... even impersonally. God! if only I had known then what I know now! I literally wince when I think of some of the really dumb things I said and did in those days.

Most of us were cocky young extroverts. I'm sure I was ... and downright insufferable a good deal of the time as well. But this unshakable confidence was mother to a really professional attitude given time. Beginning with my days as an aviation cadet, I came to realize that personality had nothing to do with ability. The hard-nosed instructor was most often the best of the lot. Among the B-17 crews, the man who flew with a good buddy gunner who couldn't tell a ME 109 from a P-51 was trading amiability for security. The longer one was exposed to combat, the more one counted on expertise and less on good buddy relationships. I flew with some men who perhaps disliked me as much as I disliked them. Never bothered me one bit either way. If they were pros who knew how to keep their heads out of their asses, they were my kind of people; if not, I wouldn't give them the time of day. I had the same kind of attitude towards my superiors. Why should they care if I liked them or not? It didn't occur to me that I had to like them! Respect them yes, but who needs the other? Respect one earns in combat... the hard way ... Alas, there are always men and leaders who never mature to the stage where they have the sense to separate the sheep from the goats.

I have always felt that my long love affair with airplanes since I was eleven worked to my advantage, but today I'm not so sure. Flying was in my blood long before it became reality ... it was the great romance of my youth. I was sure it had a good deal to do with lightening the burden of combat on my young shoulders. There were times even in the middle of a combat mission when it was possible to enjoy the sheer beauty of flying ... the skies ... the panorama of the far-away earth for miles around ... viewed with indulgence like some demigod surveying his unlimited domain.

I was never really able to understand men who found flight a chore ... just another job. I had the tunnel vision of a true believer. I flew a few missions with a co-pilot who wore an expression of warmed-over death. I used to do a lot of looking around from the astrodome and remember one time when I grinned at him and gave him the thumbs-up salute. The poor bastard stared at me like I had lost my mind.

Men seem to either love or hate the machines they fly. My first co-pilot had been pulled out of B-25 phase training and transferred to B-17s. He never got over his love affair with the B-25 and accepted his lot with great bitterness. He was like a passionate young lover torn from the bosom of his true love and banished to exile among strangers by harsh and disapproving parents.

My affair with the B-17 was like an infatuation with a comely young wench. How was I to know that she would eventually lead me down the primrose path to perdition? She was lover, mother, comforter ... all that a young swain hopes for in his loved one. Then, alas, as in all earthly relationships, reality intruded and destroyed my dreams. I began to see her faults, her aberrations, and all the petty deceits that marred her beauty. I tried to come to terms but the advantages were all on her side

Above: *Mission over. (Richards Coll)*

Below: *A 367th BS, 306th BG lead crew preparing for the mission on D-Day, 6 June 1944. (Richards Coll)*

Above: *Abe Dolim (far left) and crew of Vie's Guys at Bury St Edmunds (Rougham). (Abe Dolim)*

Left: *Abe Dolim in the navigator's office of a B-17 in 1990. (MWB)*

Below: *Fuddy Duddy of the National Wartime Heritage, in flight over New York State in 1995. In WWII, Fuddy Duddy flew with the 708th BS, 447th BG out of Rattlesden and completed 96 missions before being lost in a collision with another B-17G over Mannheim the day before New Year's Eve 1944. (MWB)*

because of her great power over me...it was a true power of life and death ... and it became in time a love-killing death blow from which I never recovered. Love turned sour, I began to watch her every move. My nerves took a beating. She developed suicidal tendencies ... I had the feeling she wanted me to share in her death wish. I was terrified and fiercely resolved to escape her clutches the very instant she made any attempt to involve me in her wild schemes. The strain eventually got to me and I longed for an end to our deadly relationship. The last weeks and days were an agony. Finally it was all over, I was FREE, home safe, and I didn't give a damn if I ever laid eyes on the old whore again.

The very next day she destroyed herself, as I had feared. *Florencia* met an inglorious end in the middle of the English Channel. She had chosen to drown herself and her new crew but they cheated her and escaped in a life-giving vessel.

What had gone wrong? What happened to us? Why did she try to kill me? What changed this lovely young woman into a sullen bitch who wanted to destroy me in mind, body and soul? They say it takes two to tango ... perhaps I had grown too old too soon ... unequal to her fast, hard pace. Perhaps I never realized she too had problems. We shared all the trials and tribulations of the times ... but I had no appreciation for the fact that she was thrust into the hard cruel world, ill-prepared herself for the enemies we both faced in the innocence of our youth.

Maybe, just maybe, I wonder, weren't the lucky ones those who never cared for her type to begin with, who saw her as just another broad out to get her jollies out of some poor unsuspecting bastard ... gimlet-eyed men who took her and left her with no regrets? I resolved never to make that mistake again!

'Love Me, Love Me Not', First Lieutenant Abel L. Dolim, navigator, 332nd BS, 94th BG. A Hawaiian, Abe Dolim had stood and watched the Japanese bomb Pearl Harbor on the 'day of infamy', 7 December 1941. He was not to fight the despoilers of his island, but yet another enemy half way around the world. Abe flew his missions against Germany from Bury St Edmunds, Suffolk.

We were at 15,000 feet as no flak was expected. However, there was plenty of accurate flak at the target. I never thought I would be glad to see flak, but I was this day because it meant the fighters wouldn't 'come in'. We started out with ten ships in our squadron and on 'bombs away' there were six ships. We were glad to return from this one. There were so many holes in the nose that Wilk nearly froze sitting up there on the way home.

After this mission the mental and physical strain was so much that I was too tired to keep up the log of my missions. Missions were coming every day with no rest in between. I would return from a mission and the pilots' truck would be waiting to carry me to the mission critique. From there I would stagger over to the mess hall and gorge myself. After that I would waddle over to my barrack and fall in bed until the alert sergeant woke me the next morning for briefing. Following that schedule I didn't have much time to write notes on my missions. I planned to catch up on them in a couple of days while they were still fresh in my mind, but somehow I never got around to it.

Lieutenant Griswold Smith, pilot, 100th BG, mission to Hamburg, 7 April 1945

Above: *'When we returned, the left waist gunner, a bombardier from another crew on his last mission, hit the ground, kissing it.' Lloyd Murff, pilot, 491st BG (USAF)*

Right: *B-17 control column. (MWB)*

Above: *Boeing Maker's badge. (MWB)*

Right: *B-24 control column. (MWB)*

Above: *Clip of .5 ammunition in a B-17. (MWB)*

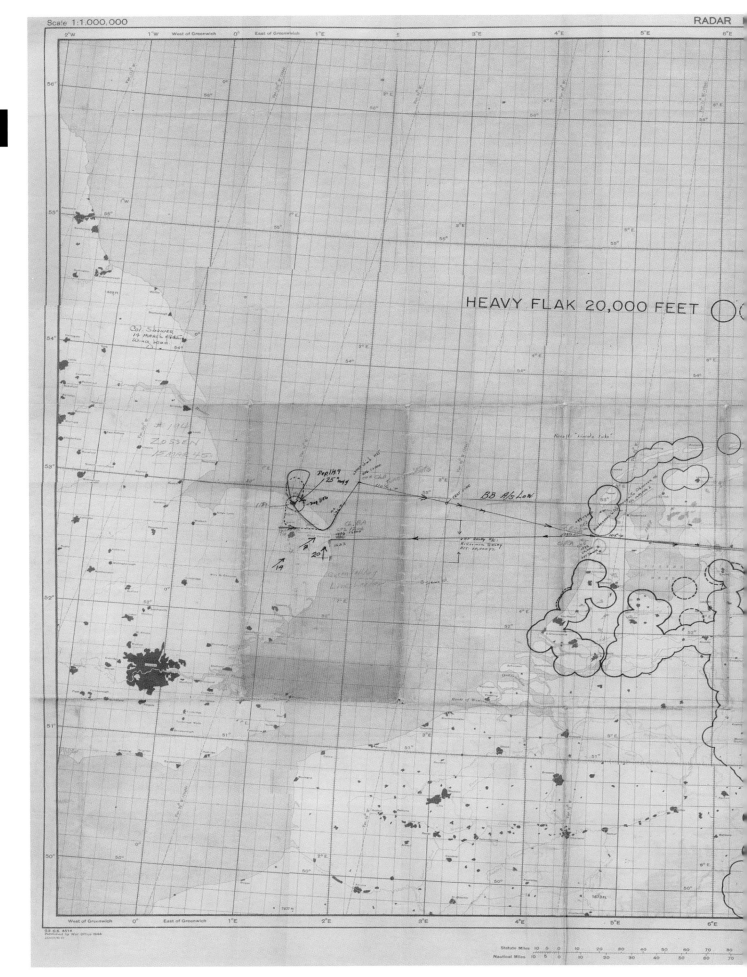

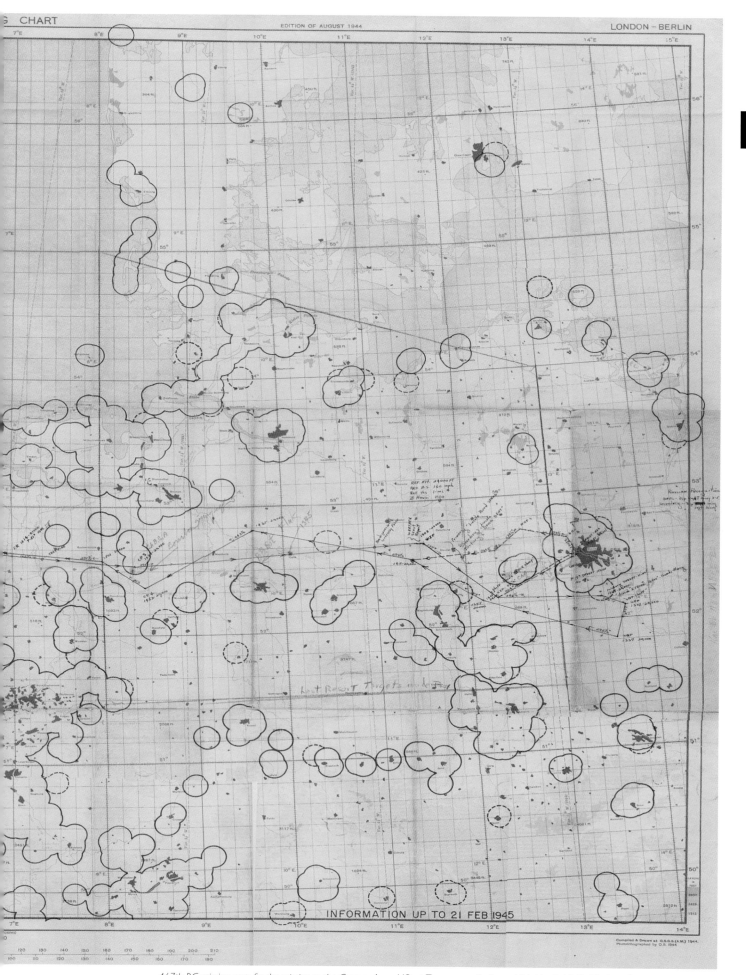

INFORMATION UP TO 21 FEB 1945

467th BG mission map for the mission to the German Army HQ at Zossen, near Berlin on 15th March 1945. (The late Colonel Albert J. Shower)

Right: *The crew of Windy City Challenger, 422nd BS, 305th BG, on their return from a mission to Caen on 10 July 1943. Kneeling, second from left, is the pilot, Lt. John H. Perkins Jr. one of seven killed on 14 July 1943. Four were taken prisoner. Perkins, who was from Chicago and whose father was English, was on his nineteenth mission. Originally, Perkins had been co-pilot on Chuck Wagon and his two best friends were the pilot and bombardier before they finished their tour and returned stateside. (USAF via Bill Donald)*

Right: *Staffelkapitän Georg-Peter Eder, 7./JG2, who on 14 July 1943 shot down Windy City Challenger south of Paris. (Steve Gotts)*

Failed to Return

'Way down in Ruhr Valley where black mushrooms grow
Way down in Flak Valley where B Two Fours go
You're briefed in the morning
No fighters, no flak
But the boys that go down there
Will never come back.'

Anonymous

One day at the GI club in Bedford, a young flyer due to fly a mission the next day, asked me for a loan of £5 so he could go out on the town with his buddies that evening. He was so persuasive and I had such a strange feeling about this boy that against my better judgement and firm principles, I finally agreed and handed him the money. He left a small, green marble with me as security on the loan explaining that he had nothing else of any value in his possession. The next day he went down in his B-17 and the little green marble was left at the back of my desk drawer for the next few months. It was only when I was clearing my desk, ready for the move to Cherbourg, that a friend told me that the 'marble' was actually a rare piece of jade and was quite valuable. So I had it made up into a ring and I have worn it ever since in memory of that young boy and the thousands like him who lived for the day, for there might well not be another one for them.

Anona Moeser, American Red Cross

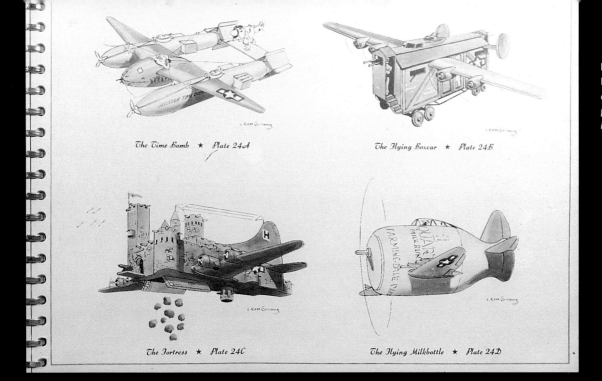

The Time Bomb ★ Plate 24A

The Flying Boxcar ★ Plate 24B

The Fortress ★ Plate 24C

The Flying Milkbottle ★ Plate 24D

Left: The Time Bomb, The Flying Boxcar, The Fortress, and The Flying Milkbottle, *painted by Col. Ross Greening in POW camp. (Ross Greening)*

'An old woman asked the soldier if I was an Englander. When he said I was American she exclaimed, 'American Devil!"

Staff Sergeant Lee C. 'Shorty' Gordon, ball turret gunner, First Lieutenant George E. Stallman's B-17, 365th BS, 305th BG, which was shot down on 26 February 1943 near Wilhelmshaven. Stallman and four crew were killed. At just 5ft 2in. Gordon was one of the few gunners who could occupy the ball turret and wear a parachute at the same time. In captvity Gordon repeatedly attempted escape and finally, on 1 June 1943, he succeeded. He escaped from a work detail and donning Lederhosen, dressed as a Tyrolean boy, he cycled to Switzerland. He became the first American airman to receive the Silver Star for escaping from captivity.

His crew was hit over France near Paris. They bailed out, hit the ground OK and were grabbed by the Free French. Instead of being hidden in a farmhouse, six of the crew were taken into Paris and hidden in a house of prostitution. This fellow said that when he was twenty years old he weighed 160 lbs. Several months later, when they were moved, he weighed 140 lbs. He said they could not be confined without sampling the merchandise.'

Staff Sergeant Laurence S. 'Goldie' Goldstein, B-17 radio operator, 388th BG

Below: *Lee C. 'Shorty' Gordon, 305th BG ball turret gunner, beside B-17G Sally B at Duxford in 1989. One of the few 8th AF gunners small enough to wear a chute in the turret, he parachuted out of the ball turret on 26 February 1943 when his B-17 was shot down near Wilhelmshaven. He later escaped from POW camp and was awarded the Silver Star. (MWB)*

We had four officer crews in one Nissen hut. The night before a mission I would go over to the barracks and write letters and get some early sleep because you never knew when you would be alerted to fly a mission the next day. One night one of the officer crews packed all their belongings. It made me wonder what insight they must have had when they knew they would not survive the next mission. Sure enough, the next day they went down.

We had another crew who went on a bombing mission with us to southern Germany. After bombing the target we turned around and came home, but this crew took off for Switzerland. When we got back I checked their clothes in the hut. Everything was there except for their Class A uniforms, which they had worn on the raid to prove their identity. They had just given up fighting.

Lieutenant Bill Rose, pilot, 92nd BG

The formations flew down across France, through the clean sky, and four miles below the world was soft and green in the sunshine.

The Alps poked up out of the haze in the south, white and jagged and endless. The Forts turned east paralleling the mountains, heading into Germany.

I checked the RPM periodically, and kept an eye on the manifold pressure and gave the cylinder head temperature a quick once-over now and then, and kept looking away into Switzerland.

Serenade To The Big Bird, 'Munich', Bert Stiles

We speak not in sorrow ...
that he died,
Though we miss him sorely. There are some who cried
Because they liked the man. They knew
His quirks, his laughter, and the way he flew.

His was not a gesture to vain strife.
He died pursuing that which filled his life
He loved to fly and to his flying gave
A mastery that made the sky his slave.

He knew the breathless beauty of the air,
Towering clouds the heavens fashion there.
He rolled and tossed o'er fleecy stratus fields
And drank the flaming glory flying yields.

His heritage was but a pilot's right
Outsoaring mighty eagles in their flight;
To zoom and play mid sunset's golden mirth,
High beneath the wispy roof of earth.

And though his taste for life was justly sweet,
He laid this precious gift at freedom's feet
And when he left, he went still in the fight
To keep intact all that he held as right.

(MWB)

The least we owe is faith, the best a smile
A faith at what he did was worth the while.
A smile we owe because he left us one,
A living tribute to the job he's done.

Untitled poem by Second Lieutenant John Edward Kerns, 22, of Kansas City, Mo., as a tribute to First Lieutenant Lynn W. Hair, 27, of Dallas, Tex, KIA 11 January 1944. Lieutenant Kerns, who joined the 370th after Hair had gone down, was assigned Hair's equipment locker. He said he was inspired by the 'sad beauty' of Hair's sacrifice and wrote the poem as a message to Mrs Hair and her two daughters. On 27 March 1944, over Chartres, France, Lieutenant Kerns was reported shot down in a dog-fight with Me 109s. He is listed as 'MIA' – presumed dead.

The first thing we heard when we got back from London and signed in at the orderly room: 'You know that ship you wanted?' one of the sergeants asked.

'Yeah.' Sam was ready to battle for it. They'd promised it to us.

'It went down.'

'Who?'

'Some guy named Mac something.'

It was Mac.

After a while I went to see some of the guys who went along on that trip. It was flak, right at the coast. He was the only one who went down that day in the whole 8th Air Force. One out of a thousand.

... The airplane Mac took down with him was officially ours. We flew it on three missions, and we named it the *Cool Papa*.

She was supposed to have her name painted on, while we were in London, with a picture of a dame with no clothes. A girl in the States drew up some sketches for us, and I gave them to the group artist down at the sub-depot.

'I'll draw her on there,' he said. 'I ain't got no time, but I'll do it.'

He was in demand.

The *Cool Papa* was Sam's name. When we were in school everyone called him cool papa, because he was such a major operator.

I wanted to name it the 'Witcherlybitcherly' or the 'Nancy Moonshine' and my mother wanted us to name it 'Colorado colleagues', because we went to Colorado College.

Most of the crew wanted to name it after Sam's sister-in-law, Mary Helen. She came down from Omaha one night when we were in Grand Island and she is about the best-looking dame in the world.

'We ought to name it for her,' Ross said.

'We ought to get a big picture of her and paste it on the side,' Crone said.

'You'd always be falling out the waist window,' Sharpe said.

'*Cool Papa*,' Ross said. 'What a hell of a name.

What's it mean?'

It didn't matter what it meant. The *Cool Papa* lived a short life.

Serenade To The Big Bird, 'Mac', Bert Stiles. *Cool Papa* and Lieutenant Albert F. McCardle's crew failed to return on 1 May 1944 when they were hit by flak at Troyes, France. Eight men were KIA and two taken prisoner.

What was it like? First of all, you probably married after your husband was already in the service, so you started out with an abnormal way of life. Private's – even sergeant's – salaries were next to nothing. Even that income was long coming sometimes when the guys were moved around and the payroll took time to catch up to them. You had to be frugal to make it to the next pay check. Later they got it set up so dependents' allotments came via the mail.

You still paid for your own doctor and hospital when you had a baby. This usually followed pretty regularly after a furlough. Chances were that the husband/father was elsewhere at the time of birth and may not have seen the baby for five or six months.

Then, of course, most everything was rationed – gas, shoes, coffee, sugar, canned goods, etc. If you could find them, new sofas and chairs were hard as bricks because they had no springs. You listened to the war news on the radio each morning. The first reporter to give the news made it sound very bad, and you started your day feeling pretty down. Later in the day another reporter gave the same news almost word for word, but his tone of voice or something made it not sound so bad after all. This was all we had to go on as to what was happening – along with the newspaper. One thing for sure, coming out of high school into this type of situation sure made you grow up fast.

'A GI Wife During WWII', Virginia Bergman

'A life sentence.'

Major Ronald V. Kramer, 713th BS, 448th BG pilot, on arrival on 29 May 1944 at Stalag Luft III. On 9 May Kramer had been flying in the co-pilot's seat with Captain Richard T. Lambertson, whose B-24 was hit by flak and burst into flames just as they released their bombs on the marshalling yards at Liege, Belgium. Nine men were made POW; the right waist gunner was KIA.

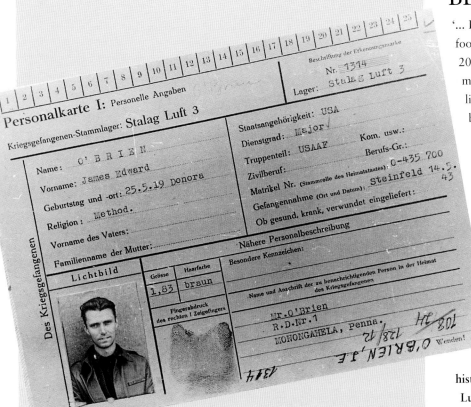

'I turned around and saw a German soldier on one knee with his rifle pointed at me. I threw up my hands. He came toward me, still holding his rifle on me and said the words I dreaded to hear.

"For you the war is over."'

Lieutenant Loren F. Jackson, pilot, *Crash Wagon III*, 551st BS, 385th BG, shot down on his tenth mission on 12 June 1944 while bombing lines of communications in Normandy. He became a prisoner in Stalag Luft III until the end of January 1945. Fred Martini, his assistant flight engineer/gunner evaded and masqueraded as a Catholic priest in France. He was finally betrayed and sent to Buchenwald concentration camp before being sent to POW camp. Sam Pennell, one of the waist gunners, also spent some time in Buchenwald after evading with Martini. The Germans captured the rest of the crew.

BLOODY KASSEL

'... During that time I got soaked from head to foot with gas. Before I could move, one or more 20mm shells went off under my feet, wounding me in the right foot and both legs. The blow lifted me up and hurt my back and I fell on my back on the catwalk. Then I saw a blinding flash and I was on fire from head to foot. I felt my face burning and that was all I remembered as I thought I was dying.'

Technical Sergeant Theodore J. Myers, top turret gunner, *Hot Rock*, piloted by Lieutenant William J. Mowat, 445th BG, 27 September 1944. Some 315 Liberators of the 2nd BD flew to the Henschel engine and vehicle assembly plants at Kassel in central Germany. It was a mission which would live forever as one of the most tragic and was probably the most disastrous raid for a single group in the history of American air warfare. In six minutes the Luftwaffe shot down twenty-five of the 445th BG Liberators. Five more crashed in France and England. Only five made it back to Tibenham. (Myers regained consciousness to find himself hanging in his parachute. He and Frank T. Plesa, tail gunner, who was also badly wounded and burned and blown out of the B-24, were reunited in a German hospital.)

I was helpless as the Fw 190 streaked past. He couldn't have cleared us by more than six feet. We were in the high right squadron and I could see the fighters attacking the lead squadron like a swarm of bees ... At this time I heard the bail-out bell ringing, so I got out of the turret and found the navigator putting on his chute. The whole nose compartment looked like a sieve. Those exploding 20mms had blown up right between us but neither of us was hit. By this time we were nosing down and the whole left wing was on fire. We opened the nosewheel door and bailed out. I hadn't really looked at the ground until I saw our ship crash. I then realized that the ground was coming up rapidly. We had been trained to hit going forward and roll up in a ball. However, I was unable to reverse my direction and hit going backwards. My feet and fanny hit just about like a machine gun. Had I landed as I had been trained, I'm sure I would have had three tongues in my shoes because I hit so fast and so hard.

Second Lieutenant George M. Collar, bombardier, 702nd BS, 445th BG, Kassel, 27 September 1944, describing the sad demise of Lieutenant James W. Schaen's ship, which went down 800 metres south of Forstgut Berlitzgrube. Collar was among five of the crew captured. There were 236 empty seats in the mess halls at Tibenham that evening. Altogether, the 445th lost 117 men killed. At least nine airmen who landed in or near the village of Nentershausen were murdered or executed by German civilians, and in one case, by a German soldier home on leave. Forty-five officers and thirty-six enlisted men were made POW. Some, like Collar, were ordered by the Germans to collect the burnt and charred remains of their colleagues from the crashed aircraft ....
'In an orchard, there, lying on the ground, was the body of one of our flyers ... The victim had obviously been blown out of the plane as he landed without a chute. Every bone in his body was broken ... We traveled up and down the hills and forests all day, picking up approximately a dozen bodies, some of them horribly mangled. In the middle of an open field we came across a radioman. He had a bad leg wound but came down in his chute. He was lying in a pool of blood and was dead.'

I noticed an unusual red glow in the sky around us. As I turned my head to the right, through my co-pilot's window I saw a parachute floating down. Then the plane in front of us burst into flames. Other parachutes appeared on all sides. Suddenly, a Fw 190 swooped in front of us from underneath and behind. At the same time my co-pilot, Newell Brainard, was pounding my arm. One engine was on fire and other German fighters came into view. All around us was on fire ... black smoke ... planes going down ... more parachutes ... machine guns firing ... the shudder of 20mm shells hitting ...

another engine gone ... intercom out ... plane out of control ... a gripping fear – near panic ... then, fire!'

First Lieutenant Raphael F. Carrow, pilot, *Patches*, 700th BS, 445th BG, 27 September 1944. Carrow bailed out and landed in a field near a group of buildings surrounded by a high fence. A German soldier who approached him, pointed a rifle at the American and asked, '*Jude?*'. Carrow had landed near a slave labour camp!

'I asked my co-pilot to unbuckle my seat belts before he bailed out. Just as he stood up to do so a 20mm cannon shell cut him in half.'

Second Lieutenant William Bruce, pilot, *Bonnie Vee*, 445th BG, Kassel, 27 September 1944. Only one other member of his crew survived. Bruce broke his neck and his right pelvis and badly damaged his right shoulder. After capture German officers fractured his jaw with a pistol butt. Almost totally paralized and black-and-blue all over, Bruce spent three days on a train which took captured airmen to a Frankfurt interrogation centre and then another week on a train before his severe injuries were at last treated by a German doctor. Bruce was finally sent to Stalag Luft I.

When you've feathered your third prop
and there are Focke-Wulfs up top
Then it's time for you to stop
Because friend — you've had it

If you land in sight of Dover
and some Nordic type sea rover
Says 'For you the War is Over'
Then friend — you've had it
Anonymous

'Twas May the ninth that I did spring
From a B-24 with a burning wing
Into the cold I leapt, nine thirty exact
Midst a silence interrupted only by flak

Belgium lay 20,000 feet below
Dimly visible in the sun's early glow
Jerry was thick there as everyone knew
But nothing to worry about – so said S-2

The farmlands near Liege awaited my descent
I steered the chute as down I went
A quick reconnoitre on reaching the ground
Did not disclose the enemy around.
Anonymous

MISBURG

'I told myself that I had better pull the ripcord. When my chute opened I looked for other parachutes and they were all tiny specks above me. One of the 109s flew past me at about 50 yards distant. The pilot took a good look at me and flew on.'

Staff Sergeant Carl W. Groshell, tail gunner, 854th BS, 491st BG, First Lieutenant John S. Warczak's crew, Misburg, 26 November 1944. Warczak was thrown clear. In all, the 491st BG lost sixteen Liberators in rapid succession to enemy fighter attacks.

'Three of our men were killed in the plane and six more were killed by German civilians when they touched down. I was almost killed by a farmer but a Frenchman talked him out of it.'

Staff Sergeant Kenneth M. Pieffer, tail gunner, and only survivor from Lieutenant James A. Wynn's crew of *Scarface* in the 854th BS, 491st BG, Misburg, 26 November 1944. The 854th BS lost seven of the sixteen 491st BG B-24s lost on the disastrous raid.

Below: Airman's silk escape-map of France, printed on both sides. (via Truett Woodall)

'The ship was on fire. The pilot gave the order to abandon. Since I already had my chest pack on I probably was the first to get out. I kicked out the escape hatch and was gone. Four others managed to get out before the plane disintegrated.'

Staff Sergeant Jasper C. 'Clyde' Crowley, bombardier, Second Lieutenant Charles H. O'Reilly's crew, 95th BG, shot down on his thirty-third combat mission, to Hamburg, 31 December 1944. Four men were KIA, five were taken prisoner.

'At Frankfurt (Oberusel) we were put in solitary confinement, interrogated and accused of being spies unless we gave the information our interrogators needed. I said my dog tags were proof enough and refused to answer any questions. Finally, I was handed a piece of paper with answers to most of the questions and told to sign it. I refused and was taken back to my 8-foot by 13-foot cell. The truth was they knew more about what was going on than I did.'

Second Lieutenant William B. Sterrett, navigator, Lieutenant Billy C. Blackman's crew, 418th BS, 100th BG, who were shot down on their thirteenth mission, to Hamburg, on New Year's Eve, 1944. Four crew were killed. Sterrett, and four others, including Blackman, who was blown out of the nose of the B-17 when it exploded, survived and all became prisoners of war.

'Write a big letter
Send it to me
Send it in care of
Stalag Luft III.'

Second verse of
'Down In Ruhr Valley'

What was life like as a 'Kriegie' (POW)? A typical day would have us getting up shortly after dawn, jumping down from our high sacks and falling out for appell (the count) taken twice a day. We usually had all our clothes on in winter because the rooms were freezing. We stood at attention in a large field at one end of the compound in set formations from all the individual blocks, about 150 men in each. The 'goons' would then carefully count the entire compound (over 2500 men) one block at a time and record the tally. God help us if there was even one missing Kriegie in the count. The guards would then proceed to count again and again until the problem was resolved. Any escape would trigger turmoil. The entire camp could be standing for hours, in snow and rain. After appell we were free to do as we pleased. Most went back to their rooms or would walk the perimeter. We organized touch football games; if we had the energy.

The washroom facilities were very skimpy to say the least. We did have a Saturday inspection by our own senior officers to maintain a minimum of morale and check for a clean shave and decent hair length. Truthfully I can't remember where we got our safety razors or scissors, because the Germans would not allow any cutting instruments.

The blocks were divided into rooms big enough for four men, into which were crowded fifteen or more, sleeping on five triple-decker bunks. Each room prepared its own food from the monotonous Red Cross parcels that were rationed to each man. One man was elected cook and usually he prepared some very tasty dishes by mixing the ingredients of the parcels with other perishables that the Germans allowed us. But we never had enough to eat, while at the same time our captors continuously cut our supplies of food. Needless to say, the cook was always the best fed in the room.

We always kept the tin cans from the parcels. The 'craftsmen' in the room made our pots and pans and dishes from the sides. It was unbelievable what they could do with such little to work with. Each room had a small iron stove and we cooked on it. We were given just enough fuel to barely warm the food – none to keep the room warm.

A Kriegie's life, especially in the last few months

Left: *Roland L. Douglass' escape photo. Douglass, a ball turret gunner in the 351st BS, 100th BG, went down while flying as tail gunner in Lt. Clifton Williams' B-17 on 31 December 1944. Their Fortress was struck by Fools Rush In which nosed down after it had been hit by flak on the bomb run over Hamburg. Williams and five others were killed. Douglass never got to use his photo. He and two others were captured and made POW. (Douglass)*

of the European war, was miserable at best. As the vice closed on the Third Reich, our captors, already hungry and war-weary, were much less willing to abide by the Geneva Convention that stated enemy POWs were to be treated as well as their own soldiers. The Germans had little regard for us who had sacked their homeland. They had a serious food shortage themselves. In addition they had much difficulty getting any American Red Cross parcels to the POW camps because of the bombings and strafings. As a result we suffered much hunger.

American Kriegies never had the slightest doubt about eventual victory. However, we all expected it sooner than it happened. I remember a fear I had while behind barbed wire in the west camp of Stalag Luft III. I worried that when the end came the enraged, brainwashed Nazi mobs from the cities would attack and kill us all before we were freed. This secret fear I kept to myself, but it was real.

In the coldest winter on record, the Russians advanced towards our camp. To avoid falling into Soviet hands, we evacuated the Stalag and started our death march across Germany. It was then that I found out that people in the nearby cities and towns were petrified that the POWs would ravage them when we were released. Neither happened, and I'm sure they had a lot more to fear from the Russians.

Mike O'Shea

'A crowd was there when he stopped his crate.
"Where am I?" he asked, "It sure looks great."
"Why where," they asked, "were you heading for?
This my boy is Stalag Luft IV."'
Willie Green's Flying Machine
Anonymous

Left: *This remarkable colour photo of George Michie was taken almost immediately after landing by parachute in the village of Diefflen, 2 kilometres east of Dillingen on 11 May 1944. Oberleutnant Herbert Kunz, a bomber pilot and Knights Cross holder, who was home on leave, had watched the scenario unfold after Lt. Marion W. Holbrook's B-17 in the 366th BS, 305th BG was shot down returning from a raid on Saarbrücken. Kunz ran home to get his camera and ID card and returned to find a crowd gathered around an airman (Michie, the crew's engineer) whom two Reicharbeitdeinst, (Labour police) had taken prisoner. Waving his ID card, and introducing himself as an officer of the Luftwaffe, Kuntz took charge of the situation. Michie, who was terrified, started to calm down and asked for a cigarette, which a bystander gave him. The group then made their way over a small bridge where Kunz took this photo. (Bill Donald via Stefan Reuter)*

We received a little horsemeat once in a while, a few potatoes, rutabagas, salt, German brown bread, ersatz coffee, some sugar and ground barley. The bread was extremely heavy even after the sawdust and wood slivers were brushed and picked off. It could be sliced less than a quarter of an inch thick. The ground barley was always a treat. We boiled it in a bucket all day so it would swell up to many times its original volume.

We were so hungry that we could not keep our minds off food and recipes. We all became expert cooks in our minds and our conversations often centred on food. Everyone got out their little blue Red Cross books and wrote down marvellous menus. Our diet consisted of four thin slices of very black bread, only about an eighth of an inch thick, and a bowl of soup a day. As a consequence, I lost about 45 lbs in weight.

There was a period of six weeks to two months when Red Cross parcels were not delivered and things got pretty bleak. There was a cat that used to wander around the compound. It disappeared during this time. I was told it tasted like rabbit.

We were allowed to write very few letters and postcards per month. I received a few letters from my mother and aunt but none from my wife. Up to a year after I was released from captivity her letters were returning to us. It appeared that most of them had not left the US. I had received one book parcel

My crew and I were shot down in July 1944. Going up to Luft IV, they put us in boxcars. One night we stopped on the outskirts of Berlin and they left us locked up in the marshalling yards. The RAF hit us that night and boy that was something else! We were jammed up so you couldn't stand or sit. I made up my mind that night, if it was meant for me to die, I had to be out in the open. I would never get locked up that way again! As long as I could walk, I would stay out on the road. And that's just what happened to us, during the winter of 1945.

Sergeant Carmelo Frontino, 351st BG, in Stalag Luft IV. (Not unusual considering nearly everybody from the ETO who got shot down, wound up there; 9,200 sergeants!)

'The quarters in the South Compound at Luft III were terrible. Two hundred men were living in barracks containing sixteen rooms with one night latrine each. The rooms were dim, smoky and poorly ventilated. Several of the men went crazy from the confinement; others developed complexes.'
Lieutenant Karl W. Wendel, POW, Stalag Luft III, 1944–45. Wendel, a twenty-year-old navigator in the 711th BS, 447th BG, was shot down on only his second mission, to Merseburg, on 7 October 1944, when his B-17, *T.N.T. Kate*, was shot down by flak. Two of Lieutenant Robert I. Harwood's crew were killed by German civilians and seven were made POW. Wendel, who struck the roof of a house on landing and bounced off into a back yard, could speak German and it was this that probably saved him from the same fate as the two others in the crew.

from my wife with two books censored out.

First Lieutenant Dean H. Sanner, de Havilland Mosquito pilot, 25th BG whose aircraft was brought down in the explosion of a 2,600 lb GB-4 Batty glide-bomb dropped by a B-17 he and cameraman Staff Sergeant Augie Kurjack were filming on 13 August 1944. Kurjack was killed. The blast threw Sanner out of the aircraft and he was captured and sent to Stalag Luft I.

I was given a bowl and spoon and cooked my meals in the washroom near my bunk. With others cooking, the room became quite smoky. We had no cooking stove at this time. We got hot water from the camp kitchen and the Germans gave us boiled potatoes or boiled rutabagas for our noon and evening meals. Sometimes we would get spinach or pea soup. The pea soup had bugs in it and we threw most of it out or gave it to the Russian POWs. They were so hungry they ate it eagerly. Every day we got

a ration of dark bread from the Germans. I would try a piece and put a slice of cheese and fried Spam on it. It was good. Sometimes we got blood sausage but I did not eat much of it. A few mornings we got barley for breakfast.

Our barley ration to the kitchen has been cut twenty-eight per cent and 'spuds' fifteen per cent. There are enough Red Cross parcels for a couple more issues and they are being given out one for two men per week. Most of the time we get spuds once a day. The other two meals we get hot water. Living conditions are poor. There is good news from the fighting fronts. Maybe we won't be here much longer.

Corporal John L. Hurd, diary entry, Stalag 17B Krems, 9 March 1945. Hurd, ball turret gunner in *Battlin' Betty*, flown by Second Lieutenant Francis L. Shaw in the 614th BS, 401st BG, was shot down on his eleventh mission, to Politz, on 1 April 1944. All ten men in Shaw's crew survived to be taken prisoners of war.

Above: B-17G 42-97991
joined the 305th BG on 9
August 1944. On 24 August
Lt. Roland B. Heusser and crew
failed to return from the
mission to Merseburg. Beverly
A. Hayes, the radio operator,
and Maurice F. Thomas, the
operator, were killed, and the
rest were made POW.
(Lockheed)

When half parcels are the thing
And there will be no mail till spring
If it's verboten not to sing
My sympathy — you've had it

When the bells ring out the cheer
If the boat just left the pier
And you're still looking for a souvenir
Then chum — you've really had it.
Anonymous

'The march was a nightmare. Our German guards were as miserable as we were and many wanted to escape with POWs, but we had orders to remain together as a group. When roll call was taken at Stalag Luft VILA, Moosburg, thirty-one South Compound men were missing, having escaped using 'X' committee maps, compasses and equipment distributed before the march began.'

Colonel (later General) Delmar T. Spivey, who was in Training Command and had been flying on 12 August 1943 as an observer on B-17F *USS Aliquippa* of the 407th BS, 92nd BG, flown by Lieutenant Gene Wiley, when it was shot down by Unteroffizier Hein Heuser of 2./JG26 east of Arnhem. Spivey was on only the first of his five scheduled missions as part of an inspection tour. Spivey's first – and last – of his planned five mission tour, a 'milk run' over the Ruhr,

'When we stopped for our five- to ten-minute rest each hour, many of the inexperienced POWs would kneel in the centre of the road and start rocking back and forth on their hands and knees, not knowing that they were freezing to death. Some others and I did everything we could to get them back on their feet. We dragged them, kicked them in the "fanny", swore at them – anything that would cause a spark to get them moving.'

Second Lieutenant Franklin F. Cotner, 784th BS, 466th BG POW on the 'death march' from Stalag Luft III, winter 1945. Cotner, pilot of B-24 Liberator *Play Boy*, had been shot down on his eleventh mission, to Berlin, on 29 April 1944. Two of his crew evaded, one was KIA, and seven were captured and taken prisoner.

'A most wonderful day: the 609th day of imprisonment. The war was still going on but for us, as the German lady wistfully said on the day I was captured, "For you der war is over."'

Robert 'Bob' O'Hearn, 96th BG, POW, day of liberation, April 1945

ended with his capture. All the crew survived and they too were taken prisoner.

'The Germans said they would shoot stragglers. Very tired, I kept numbly plodding like the others, concentrating on each step.'

Robert 'Bob' O'Hearn, POW on the 'death march' from Stalag Luft III, winter 1945. O'Hearn had been flying as navigator on Lieutenant Silas S. Nettles' 96th BG crew when they were shot down on the 14 October 1943 mission to Schweinfurt. All ten crew were captured and made POW. O'Hearn endured life behind the wire until 28 Febraury 1945 when the POWs at Stalag Luft III were moved westwards by the Germans to prevent them being overrun by the Russian advance.

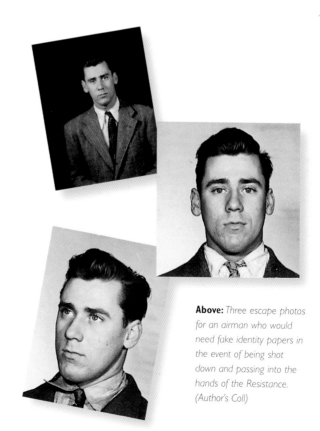

Above: *Three escape photos for an airman who would need fake identity papers in the event of being shot down and passing into the hands of the Resistance. (Author's Coll)*

Left: Blue Streak *of the 834th BS, 486th BG, hit over the oil plant at Merseberg on 2 November 1944. All the crew perished. (USAF)*

Death

'Your Son, my Lord, has paid a soldier's debt; He only lived but till he was a man;
The which no sooner had his prowess confirm'd
In the unshrinking station where he fought,
But like a man he died.'

Macbeth, William Shakespeare

Early in the mornings we would hear the drone of the planes overhead as they assembled, layer upon layer, ready for their attack on the enemy. When they returned, often shot to pieces and limping home with sometimes only one engine left functioning, our thoughts would be of those men. One particularly tragic occurrence was when a Liberator crashed in Sheringham woods after it had been on a raid to Kiel Canal, and was hit by flak. It circled over Upper Sheringham, finally crashing into a corner of a field at the 'Butts Lane' near Pretty Corner. My father, Henry William 'Joyful' West (the legendary lifeboatman) was in the area that cold winter afternoon. It was icy cold and snow was

'Neville Shute, in his fine portrait of wartime England in pastoral, drew on the contrast between peaceful countryside and death in the skies.'
Technical Sergeant Forrest S. Clark, 67th BS, 44th BG

falling. He realized the plane was crashing and went into the woods, thinking it might explode. He then went back to the Liberator and was able to get the men out, on to a nearby bank, where he gave them a cigarette each. He told us it was a terrible sight to see bodies of other men in the crippled aircraft. The US ambulances arrived and my father held the arms of the men while they received injections. When my mother and I got to the field, we saw debris scattered all over the place. A terrible sight. Actually we never knew if the five or six men recovered, but my father thought that four were dead. For many years on the anniversary of the crash, a wreath was put at that spot. Over the years

I have often wondered, did any of the survivors ever return to Sheringham?

May Ayers, recalling the crash of *Alfred*, a 392nd BG Liberator at Sheringham on 4 January 1944. Four crewmen were killed in the crash and another died four days later at Cromer hospital.

'I saw many men who absolutely refused to fly another mission after seeing their buddies killed on a raid or be victims of mid-air collisions.'
Staff Sergeant Laurence S. 'Goldie' Goldstein, radio operator, 388th BG

'I can still remember a mid-air collision in dense fog. It happened in front of us and the resultant explosion burned a clear hole in the fog that must have been at least a quarter of a mile in diameter.'
Lieutenant Colonel Tom S. Belovich, 446th BG

The clouds had continued their build-up and as we climbed on course, we suddenly found ourselves surrounded by fog so thick that we could barely see our own wing tips. Everyone was really scared, but all the pilots could do was maintain a set rate of climb at a set airspeed, with absolutely no deviation in course. We finally pulled up through the tops of the clouds at about 25,000-foot altitude. Luckily, our group came out in perfect formation, but the group ahead was not so lucky. We were eyewitnesses as two of them came together just as they emerged. There was an explosion and both ships disappeared back into the clouds.

Second Lieutenant George M. Collar, bombardier, 702nd BS, 445th BG

I forget which day it was.

I was there when the ship came in.

One flak shell had burst just outside the waist window. The waist gunner wore a flak-suit and a flak-helmet, but that didn't help much. One chunk hit low on his forehead and clipped the top of his head off. Part of his brains sprayed as far forward as the door into the radio room. The rest of them spilled out when the body crumpled up, quite dead. The flak-suit protected his heart and lungs all right, but both legs were blown off, and hung with the body, because the flying-suit was tucked into electric shoes.

Nobody else on the plane was hurt. The waist looked like a jagged screen. The Fort got home okay.

Above: *On 30 November 1944 returning from a raid on Lutzkendorf, during landing peel-off at Rougham in rapidly deteriorating weather, two 94th BG Fortresses were on short final, one directly above the other and converging when the tower advised the aircraft on final to go around. 42-97985, the lower aircraft, piloted by Lt. Owen W. Winter, 331st BS, responded immediately and pulled up into the aircraft above. It crashed and burned in a nearby field and all except the tail gunner, who was critically injured, perished. The other aircraft crash-landed in a field without injury to the crew. (Abe Dolim)*

I climbed in with the medico, and, getting through the door I put my hand in a gob of blood and brains that had splattered back that way. I took one look at the body and climbed out again, careful this time where I put my hands.

I felt no nausea, just a sense of shock, just a certain deadness inside.

Serenade To The Big Bird,
'Blood on my Hands', Bert Stiles

Gasper Cangemi, a ten-year-old boy in South Ozone Park, Queens, New York, was shooting marbles with his friends when a Western Union delivery man arrived in front of his home at 109-48 133rd Street. It was September 1944, and a flag trimmed in blue hung in their window, indicating the family had a son serving overseas during World War II. Gasper noticed the deliveryman's little bow tie, and he figured it had to be bad news. His parents accepted the telegram and then, 'there was a lot of screaming.' Gasper's twenty-year-old brother, John, had been shot down while on a bombing raid over Germany and was missing in action. For a while the family pinned its hopes on the word 'missing.' But the weeks turned into months and the family started to accept the fact that their oldest child was not coming home. After two years, John Cangemi was legally presumed to be dead, but the family was frustrated because it was never able to learn anything about the circumstances of his death or where he was buried.

On 8 September 1944 Sergeant John Cangemi was one of the crew of B-17 (43-38348) *Roxy's Special* flown by Lieutenant David McCarty Jr., in the 332nd BS, 91st BG. Cangemi was one of seven men killed when the B-17 was hit by flak over Ludwigshafen, after which it exploded and broke in half while still in the air. One of the crew, believed to have been John Cangemi, parachuted out and lived for several weeks after the crash. Two other crewmen, including Don Brazones, parachuted to safety and were made POWs. Don Brazones landed in the Rhine. As he was swimming to shore, he recalled, he saw a man waving to him. This man turned out to be a slave labourer, probably Polish, and he directed him to a

bomb shelter and gave him food and started explaining how he would help him travel by night to make contact with advance units of Allied forces. An SS trooper who pointed a luger at his head and informed him that he was a prisoner interrupted the conversation. Initially, John Cangemi was buried in Germany but then was moved to St Avon Cemetery in Metz, an American military cemetery in France. His body was taken to Fort Snelling Cemetery in Minneapolis in 1950. His tombstone lists the date of death as 6 October 1944, some four weeks after *Roxy's Special* was blasted out of the sky. He may have lived for four weeks after the crash.

If I didn't listen to the engine roar it was quiet up there. The sky was a soft sterile blue. Somehow we didn't belong there.

There was death all over that sky, the quiet threat of death, the anesthesia of cold sunlight filled the cockpit.

The lady named death is a whore …

Luck is a lady … and so is death … I don't know why.

And there's no telling who they'll go for. Sometimes it's a quiet, gentle, intelligent guy. The lady of the luck strings along with him for a while, and then she hands him over to the lady named death.

Serenade To The Big Bird, 'Leipzig', Bert Stiles

NOSE TORN OFF BY FLAK, BUT B-17 RETURNS FROM RAID
A direct flak hit over Cologne, Germany, instantly killed a member of the crew and literally tore off the nose of the Fortress he was in.

'Just after we dropped our bombs and started to turn away from the target,' First Lieutenant Lawrence M. deLancey, pilot from Corvallis, Ore., related, 'a flak burst hit squarely in the nose and blew practically the entire nose section to threads, obstructing my vision and that of my co-pilot (First Lieutenant Phillip H. Stahlman, of Shippenville, Pa.). What little there was left in front of me looked like a scrap heap.'

The altimeter and magnetic compass were about the only instruments still functioning. The oxygen system was knocked out and there was no hydraulic pressure left in the brakes. Without instruments and maps, Second Lieutenant Raymond J. LeDoux, navigator from Mt Angel, Ore., managed to navigate the bomber back home, where the pilot set the Fort down without further mishap.

Stars and Stripes, 1 November 1944

Above: *1/Lt. deLancey brought his crippled 398th BG Fortress back to Nuthampstead on 15 October 1944 after losing the nose and his togglier, Sgt. George Abbott, to a direct flak hit over Cologne. DeLancey recalled: 'We were flying through heavy flak. I felt the plane begin to lift as the bombs were released, then all of a sudden we were rocked by a tremendous explosion.' Co-pilot Phil Stahlman added: 'The instrument panel all but disintegrated and layers of quilted padding burst into a million pieces.' DeLancey received the Silver Star for a 'miraculous feat of flying skill and ability'. (USAF)*

We were over the target in Hanover and had just dropped out all of our bombs on the target, which was a gun factory. As we made our right turn to come home to England all four engines stopped running. We thought the Germans had some new weapon, but we fell several thousand feet and they all four started up again. They checked over the ship when we got home many, many times, and tested the bomber out many times. Another crew took the bomber the next day, and over Berlin all four engines stopped. Crews saw them plunge to their deaths just out of Berlin with all four engines out.

Staff Sergeant Richmond Henre ('Dick') Dugger, B-24 Liberator top turret gunner, 712th BS, 448th BG, Hanover, January 1945

Just as I stepped out of my barracks building, I saw smoke rising beyond the perimeter of our field. I realized it could be nothing but one of our planes that had crashed (I found out later the pilot had committed the ultimate sin in a four-motor bomber, he had banked into a dead engine, could not recover, rolled the plane onto its back whereupon it fell straight down. On board was a full load of gas and bombs as well as nine other men). Later that afternoon, I decided to cycle to the site of the crash, which I found easily by following the back roads leading to the still smoking ruins.

When I came upon the scene, the utter destruction of a once-proud bomber was difficult to comprehend; wreckage was scattered over a large area. I was the only person there except for the

Above: *When I came upon the scene, the utter destruction of a once-proud bomber was difficult to comprehend; wreckage was scattered over a large area ... I proceeded to within a few feet of one of the craters caused by an exploding bomb. Not all the bombs went off as I saw several scattered about, still unexploded. The bottom cone of the hole was filled with aluminium that had melted from the intense heat of the burning wreckage.'* Lieutenant John W. McClane (USAF)

British Bomb Disposal Crew. The area was roped off, which I ignored. I proceeded to within a few feet of one of the craters caused by an exploding bomb. Not all the bombs went off as I saw several scattered about, still unexploded. The bottom cone of the hole was filled with aluminium that had melted from the intense heat of the burning wreckage. Not too far away was a crew of three men, they had placed a rope around the trunk of the body of one of the pilots. Both of the unfortunate pilots were still sitting in their heavy metal bucket seats, their arms had been burned to stumps as were their legs. Their entire bodies, including their heads, were burned charcoal black. The clean-up crew gave a tug on the rope, expecting to extract the body but instead, the torso simply pulled apart like an overdone roast. I saw no other bodies, but on the way to my observation point, I saw an unburned electric flying glove. We always needed an extra glove so I was not above usurping this one for my emergency bag. When I picked it up, it took me no time to let it go again, as I noticed it still had a hand in it.

One of the men pointed to my feet and said, 'Look what you are standing on, Governor.'

I looked down; my left foot was on top of a man's skull, cut off at the hairline. Another man

said I should move further away as they were going to defuse some bombs. By this time, I had seen more than I had bargained for, so I cycled back to the 68th Squadron area. Even though I find words inadequate to describe the sights I saw that day, I'll never forget them.

Lieutenant John W. McClane, navigator, 44th BG

> 'Death and courage and devotion to duty were a part of our history.'
> **Allan Healy**

One grey morning in the early winter of 1944, a Liberator fell out of the skies. One of a squadron cruising in the northern skies from east to west, it turned slowly out of its place. 'Hullo', we thought, 'something wrong; that plane's turning back.' But it was not turning back, being instead, obviously out of control. Now below the level of its fellows, it reeled slowly this way and that, and then slowly – so slowly it looked like a slow-motion film – it began to fall. Gradually the nose dropped, and then, with ever-increasing speed, it plunged earthwards in a vertical dive. For a few surprised seconds there was no sound – the earth might have opened and swallowed it up. Then the air was rent by an ear-splitting report as the bombs went up. The squadron had turned south, and now streamed overhead, with a deafening roar of engines. Whatever the feelings of pilots and crews might have been as they saw their comrades crash to death – they were hidden within the shells of those insensible machines. Smaller and smaller into the hazy skies – the voice of engines now a diminishing murmur; they went to accomplish their mission. A mile or two away, bits of a Liberator lay scattered over a wide area, and nearby a farmhouse stood roofless to the skies. Somewhere, were the crew who had accompanied the bomber in its dive to death. It was a fraction of what America has paid in the flower of her youth for liberty.

**Local newspaper column by R.D. Clover,
15 August 1945**

Our group started with nineteen planes, but was down to fifteen before we even got into enemy territory. As we approached the IP, the message for visual bombing was received, and we started taking interval for group bombing. It was about this time that a direct burst of flak tore Lieutenant Roy's *My Yorkshire Dream* in half at the waist. We saw no parachutes, but found out later that the ball turret gunner, Sergeant L. K. Black, had managed to get out of his turret and snap on his chute while the plane was in its death dive. He later said that the bombardier managed to get out also, but his chute didn't open properly. Sergeant Black said that First Lieutenant L. E. Weiss went past him with a 'streamer' and was never able to open the chute properly. Sergeant Black was the only survivor of this ill-fated B-17.

Lieutenant Roy's co-pilot, R.E. Quint, had told me that he was going to be a father in just a few months. This baby girl was born on 4 January 1945 and was named Tawny.

The crew of Lieutenant Roy were on about their sixth mission.

In two days, there were eight empty bunks in our barracks. This is what really brings it home to you. In the combat area when a plane went down, my reaction was, 'Thank God I wasn't over there.' It was later that it hit you that they were truly gone.

Lieutenant Richard 'Dick' Johnson,
co-pilot, 303rd BG

Below: *Madingley Cemetery, Cambridge, 1944. (via Pat Everson)*

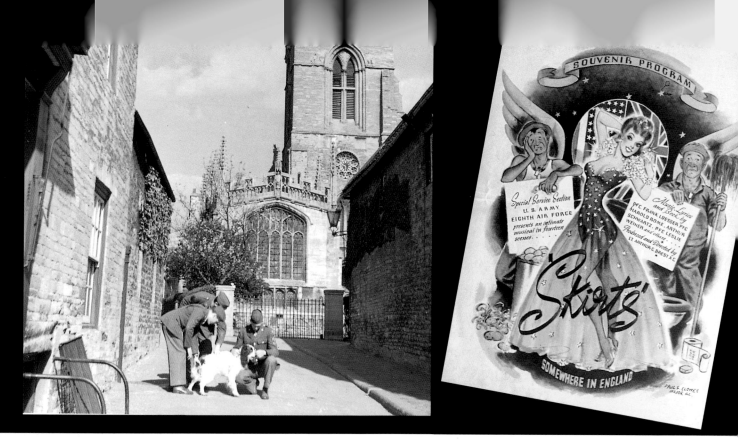

R & R

'Every man has his own story to tell of life in England, his friends there, and where he went and what he did … England gave compensation for the life of combat and work. We lived in the cold of its winter. The peace and beauty of its spring and summer were salted with the bitterness of war. Its people were our friends, though to some they were too like us to be considered foreign and their tolerance of bad plumbing, cold, and what we thought was a lack of progress did not too much endear them to us.'

The 467th Bombardment Group, **Allan Healy**

During the late afternoon of 25 November 1942, an orderly room clerk came through the barracks looking for persons from Boston, Massachusetts. He instructed us to get dressed in our Class A uniform and get on the truck in front of the orderly room pronto. We were to take a 'special excursion' to Boston, England. Thomas 'Joe' Kasberovich and myself from our barracks got in the back of a 6 x 4 GI truck with several other GIs and off we went to Boston, a town located in Lincolnshire, near The Wash. When we arrived we found a few other trucks from a couple of other airfields also there.

Above left: *Three GIs stop to pat a dog in front of St Mary's Church, Higham Ferrers. (H. E. Bates)*

Above right: *'Skirts' played all over England for 8th Air Force bases and English theatres on 4 July 1944.*

I remember the following day's events because of a special 'programme' given to us as we attended a reception given by the Mayor, George H. Bird, at the council chambers. As we waited in the assembly room for the entrance of the mayor, I was impressed with the 'pomp' of the master of ceremonies as he announced, 'His Worship, the Mayor.' In came a short middle-aged man bedecked with gold chains and medals around his neck. I couldn't help but think how ludicrous this must have seemed to most of the American GIs attending.

After a short ceremony, we were led on a tour of

the guildhall and cells. This was where Nottingham puritans, who sailed to Boston, Mass. (via Holland) in search of religious freedom, were caught before embarking and tried in the guildhall courtroom. Some were placed in the adjoining cells. Following the short tour we assembled at the South Square from where we paraded to the parish church, called the 'Boston Stump.' As our group of Americans, consisting of about 35 to 40 men, marched down the street to the church, people were standing along the route cheering and waving American flags and giving the 'V for Victory' sign as we passed by. Our appearance was not very military. I doubt whether any two wore exactly the same uniform. Some wore Class A with variations, some wore field jackets or raincoats, and a few wore non-regulation scarves – even some with flying boots. A real motley crew if there ever was one. However it did not dampen the spirits of the British civilians lining the route. This was November 1942 and few people in Lincolnshire had yet seen American personnel.

We reached the church and watched as Lieutenant Colonel A. L. Streeter (US Army Medical Corps) laid a wreath at the monument for the five men associated with Boston, England who later became governors of Massachusetts. Then we attended a special Thanksgiving Day service conducted by Canon A. M. Cook. The bible lesson was read by Captain James Lawrence, USAAF, and a short address was delivered by Chaplain Herbert Hamburger, USAAF. Following the playing of the anthems of both countries and a blessing by the Archdeacon of Lincoln, we proceeded in the mayor's procession to the assembly hall for the Thanksgiving luncheon. Food in England in 1942 was not sumptuous by any means, but they did their best with clear noodle soup, cold ham and beef, roast potatoes, vegetable salad, stewed apricots, and cheese biscuits. Personally my memory of the meal is blurred and my recollection is primarily of the toasts to His Majesty the King and to the President of the United States. Water was used for the toasts, of course.

Following lunch, we had a conducted tour of St Botolph's, the parish church. St Botolph's is on the site of a seventh century monastery, founded by St Botolph, a pious Benedictine monk for whom the town was named. The name Botolph evolved into Boston. The church's 290-foot tower was called the Stump because it did not come to a point like most of the churches of the time. In 1620, the first journey of the Pilgrim Fathers to America was the

Above: *One of the most famous entertainers to visit England in wartime was undoubtedly Bob Hope, here with singer Frances Langford and Tony Romano with Lt. Ellsworth F. Kenyon's crew in the 364th BS, 305th BG and Lallah VIII at Chelveston on 5 July 1943. Kenyon and his crew were shot down on the mission to Schweinfurt, 14 October 1943. Radio operator Russell J. Algren was KIA. Kenyon and eight others were made POW. (USAF via Bill Donald)*

vanguard of a great tide of migration in which the town of Boston was closely involved. A second and greater puritan exodus began in 1628. In 1633, the Puritans under John Cotton sailed from Boston to the Massachusetts Bay capital, renamed Boston. These events tied the two Bostons historically and was the reason we Bostonian GIs were invited to celebrate our first Thanksgiving in Boston, England. These historical ties resulted in a gift (in 1931) of £11,000 to help in the restoration of the church. The money was used to 'restore the tower, which now stands firm and secure in all its loveliness.' The preceding quote is from the book, *Boston – Botolph's Town*, which was given to each of the Americans in remembrance of the day's events.

After the tour of the church, we went to the Scala Theatre for a variety show especially dedicated to American personnel. The acts included singers, dancers, musicians and comedians. Unfortunately, we hadn't been in England long enough to understand the British accent or their humor. By this time, Joe and I had had enough of all the formalities, so we decided to rent a room at the Peacock and Royal Hotel. We had dinner at the hotel's Silver Grill. Can't remember what we ate, but it was an improvement over lunch and cost all of ten shillings.

The next morning, we took a train to Bedford and back to the base at Thurleigh. Luckily, no combat missions were scheduled during our absence. It was a memorable visit to an extremely historical and interesting place, one of many to be enjoyed during my three-year stay in England.

Paul G. Tardiff, 306th BG

Below: GI cartoon at Mendlesham in 1973. (Chris Gotts)

'They moan about our lukewarm beer
Think beer's like water over here
But after drinking one or more
You'll find them on the floor'
'The GIs' by a WAAF at Shipdham

I always carried a money belt but by the time we finished leave, the money was gone and all we had was the return train ticket back to London. We did every pub in Brighton, a resort town noted for its pubs. There was something like a frontline mentality about this seacoast city because it was only about 40 to 50 miles across the Channel to Nazi-occupied France. During this time Brighton was the target of several hit-and-run type German bombing raids. But we thought there were more girls in Brighton.

It was Tom Kinder, from Boontown, New Jersey, who got us lodgings in a small rooming house on Marine Parade, overlooking the sea. All the old Georgian style sea front hotels were filled with servicemen and women mostly on some kind of leave. The landlady was a Mrs Sutherland. She was very English and I had trouble understanding her. She referred to her establishment as a 'billet'. Even in the darkest days of winter she had flowers in the living room. She put us Yanks up for a couple of nights, but I am sure she wondered what we did all day. The beach was off limits and was filled with barbed wire barricades. I saw the Royal Pavilion and that was quite a spectacular sight for Americans.

When the damp mists rolled in from the sea our wool uniforms became musty, and I can still recall the smell of that musty wool and the way it scratched your neck. We had to wear the winter uniforms by order. We tried to look jaunty but it was difficult with those bulky uniforms and the wet climate of southern England. After a few days of pubbing we presented a raunchy looking group and must have scared off many girls. Dave Edmonds, our bombardier, was a favourite drinking companion of the pub-jockeys I went on leave with. Dave was a handsome, tall fellow, the biggest man in our small group. He died tragically, as so many did in the air combat of World War II. I liked him because he reminded me of a loner, a lost sheep and yet in his loneliness he managed to summon enough courage to fly combat missions, and that is the way he died. Perhaps in many respects he had more to overcome than we did. He would go through several transformations during the drinking hours. During one of these transformations, his eyes, which were dark, would turn the colour of mince in a pie. Therefore, we called him, simply, 'Mince'. We would all take turns looking intently at his eyes to see when they would turn this mince colour; a sort of mushy yellow-brown hue. It was at this precise time we knew he was getting drunk and so were we.

Kinder, 'Mince' and I, along with the Aussies, tangled with many Limey soldiers, but it was the Royal Marines who did us in. This was before D-Day and the Marines didn't think much of the so-called flyboys of the American air forces. We challenged them to all kinds of contests but it was chug-a-lugging that was the real test. Kinder would line up ten beer mugs and start chug-a-lugging them. He got to five and collapsed. Then I would take over, followed by 'Mince', until all ten would be consumed. Not to be outdone, the Marines would line up fifteen mugs and chug-a-lug them down, next twenty, and so forth. Now, I knew our limit was about fifteen mugs of beer. Kinder downed seven mugs; I did about five and 'Mince' the last three mugs. The Marines, however, beat us by downing twenty mugs. We were flat out after about three such contests but the Marines were still going upright. The Aussies came to our rescue and downed the required twenty. We couldn't take too much of the warm English brew and preferred Scotch. It was the Aussies who were the greatest beer drinkers.

Our favorite pub was one owned by the British boxing champion of the time, Tommy Farr, a big bulk of a man who often tended bar. He liked Americans, having fought some bouts in the States. We would arrive a few minutes before the pubs would open, stake out our favorite pub for that day, and be there when the doors opened. We would start drinking Scotch or English liquor with mild and bitters for chasers. We started out from the first pub, making the rounds up every little alleyway and street and returning to the first shortly before closing time. The next day we would repeat the routine.

These pub forays into drunkenness and oblivion were to obscure the grim realities. Many of those young gladiators-of-the-air didn't make it through the war; the Royal Marines, who hit the Normandy beaches, were among them. Nothing can detract from their heroism in the face of impending combat. Even their drinking had a noble quality to it, like youthful gods who died young, sampling the divine nectar, living and loving deeply and above all, loving each other.

We had done much drinking from pub to pub and late that day we found ourselves in a roller skating rink, each of us with an English girl we had met somewhere along the way. We were just intoxicated enough to whirl our girlfriends around that rink at breakneck speed, clearing the floor of all others. We were having a great high time sending the girls flying in all directions, when suddenly, the air raid siren sounded. Immediately, the place was cleared; the girls and the English disappeared, leaving only us Yanks and a few Aussies still skating around and around. An air raid warden came in and shouted, 'Come on Yanks, you've got to get to the shelter. Make it quick!'

We paid no attention and continued to skate, led now by the Aussies singing 'Waltzing Matilda', directly down the street and toward the seafront! Now and then we could see the glow of bomb bursts but we never did go to the shelter. We must have skated into a plush beachfront hotel in the early morning hours. I awoke between satin-like sheets in the bridal suite. I don't know how I got there but I suspect it was the stalwart Aussies. The girls had difficulty explaining what they were doing in our hotel. One of them got our GI shoes, which we had left at the skating rink. She was told, 'Don't bring those crazy Yanks back here again.'

I felt very ashamed as I gathered my clothes together, dressed hastily and crept downstairs through the large ornate lobby and past the gaze of dozens of officer types. I thought it was a dream because the hotel was full of majors, colonels and high-ranking RAF officers. I may have saluted a few very weakly as I made my sheepish exit. As I stepped out on the broad avenue that was Marine Parade on a bright sunny morning, a squadron of RAF fighters went over the beach and headed out toward France. I wished them luck.

Technical Sergeant Forrest S. Clark,
air gunner, 67th BS, 44th BG

BICYCLE TRIPS TO THE PUB

I remember the Yanks coming to Shipdham airfield, and how they roamed the local villages, looking for the rural pubs, which they very much enjoyed. They bought anything that looked like a bicycle and learnt to ride. I remember them coming from the pub riding single file, wobbling all over the road, and shouting at each other, so it was quite easy to know they were coming. We were organizing 'saving week' for the benefit of the war. My wife was secretary. We invited local folk to give all kinds of articles, which I would auction in the village hall. On one occasion I auctioned a duck, and twice a little boy bought it but his father wouldn't let him have it. So I put it up again and a Yank bought it and he said, 'If the little boy wants it, he shall have it.'

J. Gogle

... I saw a stone cottage with a thatched roof against a background of green and red and yellow hills, framed in a sky full of all different colored clouds, the light varying the shades of the clouds and of the picture. I've been surprised to find so many thatched roofs instead of red tile, but they are by no means crude affairs. Some of the thatching must be over a hundred years old, and to do the work is an art. The roofs seem to be almost a foot thick and are very solid looking. It does look queer to see grass growing out of the roof ...

Captain Ralph H. Elliott, pilot, 467th BG

(Bill Cameron)

... Most of the bikes were Raleigh and another make, but there were a few Royal Enfield models. The Royal Enfields were far superior in quality to the others, and it was a status symbol to 'drive' a Royal Enfield. Since I was ranking NCO in Base Ordnance, naturally I had the best Enfield on the base! There became such a problem with bikes being lost, stolen or left at pubs in town; and with the identification of each one's bicycle, that we had to actually issue license tags. Never will forget mine – No. 2121! The first three 3SAD SD men lost were killed while riding bicycles. One crashed head-on into a GI truck; one lost control of a bike and was killed when his head struck the concrete runny. A truck hit the third at night by Griston church. And for every death, there were 5000 injuries! What few bicycles left in serviceable condition when we left Griston were loaded up and given to an orphanage in Norwich, maybe some to Ipswich.

Technical Sergeant Wiley S. Noble, 31st HQ & HQ Sqn, Base Ordnance at Watton-Griston

Herman B. Shrew was an American airman. He was a ball turret gunner on a B-17 bomber. We met Herman and his crew on our way to a very popular wartime pub in town. 'Hi there!' he greeted us. 'Ma name is Herman B. Shrew, and these guys here are ma buddies. Now ... y'all have drink with us ... y'hear?'

'Sure!' said his buddies. 'Have a beer with us, you guys!'

It was all so instantly friendly, with much backslapping as we crowded into the bar. Our newfound friends insisted on paying for all the drinks all the time, in spite of offers from us to help with rounds of beer, gin and cider.

We also found ourselves smoking huge cigars, handed round by a giant American sergeant. 'Okay? Call me Joe, you guys!' he grinned, puffing furiously at his own cigar, as we drank our pints and forgot the war for the time being ... Everyone was having a good time, including the army girls

grim Victorian buildings which we would soon be vacating, the dreary banshee of the siren warned once more of enemy planes sneaking in.

George Greengrass. In 1943 George was a soldier at Gibraltar barracks in Bury St Edmunds. It was late summer and he and his comrades would soon embark for service as infantry replacements to the 8th Army in the fourth year of the war.

On our days off from duty we would often stroll in the abbey gardens. It was so quiet and peaceful there that it was almost impossible to realize that not far away a great war was being fought. I remember a canteen for women in the armed forces. It was run by a lovely lady who, with a helper, served tea or coffee and the best powdered-egg sandwiches in town. Along with the food and drink, she dispensed solace and advice to us girls, alone and far from home. I also remember never being in the least afraid when leaving the canteen at night and having to walk through the churchyard alone in the dark.

'Memories of Bury St Edmunds,' Frances Nunnally

sitting at tables, who had plenty of admirers from the US of A.

'Have you been with your crew long?' I asked Herman. He nodded. 'Oh, sure,' he said. 'Together … on a lotta raids, lotsa missions. We gotta great ship,' nodding again, 'great guys … all great guys, yeah, they sure are …'.

I looked around, and I thought everyone there was having a happy time, especially the ones in uniform, so young and eager and vulnerable. Then someone sat at the old piano and began to play and sing. We all joined in: Yanks and Tommies and girls together, trying to remember the words of the songs through all that smoke and beer. We sang 'Break the news to mother, please tell her that I love her' and all the ladies sitting on chairs by the wall, clutching glasses of stout or gin, had tears in their eyes. But they laughed at 'Bring me back a banana, sailor boy!'.

Then … a special song, for all the bomber crews, for the RAF, and Herman and his buddies and all who flew in freedom's cause. As the landlord vainly called 'time', we sang louder than ever so they could hear it all over Bury, 'Comin' in on a wing and a prayer'.

As we made our unsteady way back to those

Above: *Regulars and American friends gather at The Fortress pub on the site of the HQ of a USAAF ground unit on the WWII airfield at Bury St Edmunds (Rougham). Note the* Twelve O'Clock High *Toby jug (see p. 216). (MWB)*

Right: *The Memorial Rose Garden in the grounds of the Abbey commemorates the Americans stationed in the area in WWII. A marble column with a bronze plaque is in memory of the 94th BG stationed at Rougham nearby, 1943–45. The garden has a seat presented to the city by the USAF and is made out of a wing of a B-17 Flying Fortress. Royalties from the book,* A Suffolk Summer, *by J.T. Appleby go towards the upkeep of the garden. (MWB)*

Above: *American sightseeing tour by the Women's Volunteer Service (WVS) at John Bunyan's statue in Bedford on 24 April 1944. (Beds & Luton Archives)*

My twenty-fourth mission was my last as co-pilot, and it was a bad one. Now I would take two-and-a-half weeks off from combat. During my first twenty-four missions, I had been to London twice for overnight passes, but I preferred going to Bedford, where I had met an English family named Lowe. I don't know the first names of the adults, but their two daughters were named Beryl and Marjorie. Beryl was in the Royal Air Force as a WAAF, while Marjorie was still in high school. Beryl had a steady boy friend while Marjorie was pretty protected. A good thing, since she was a very pretty girl. I was attracted to her, but didn't have a chance to get to know her very well.

Mr Lowe sometimes took me fishing on the River Ouse. I caught a 3-inch fish one day and was about to throw it back when Mr Lowe reminded me that they never threw back a fish that size. I found it difficult to imagine the rationing and hardships that the British had to endure for so many years. We had rationing in the United States at that time, but nothing approaching what the British had.

Mr Lowe was the plant superintendent at a local Spitfire assembly plant, and one Sunday he said that he had to go to the plant and I could ride along. Since Marjorie wasn't home that day, I said that, sure, I would ride along. The assembly plant was in a converted auto garage. It was a very large building, and inside were about ten Spitfires in various stages of assembly. There were only three or four people in the entire building, and I asked Mr Lowe where all the workers were. He said, 'Oh, we don't work on Sundays. They will all be here tomorrow.'

I was dumbfounded, since I knew that in the United States, defense plants were working twenty-one shifts a week, every week. I didn't comment about this, since they had been through so much. Besides, I reasoned that they may have been short on parts, and so decided to take Sundays off.

In my high school at McLeansboro, Illinois, the book *Pilgrim's Progress* was required reading. It was here in Bedford, England, that the author, John Bunyan wrote this Christian anthology while he was in prison. I was impressed by this fact and was dismayed in 1992 to find that the prison had been torn down. John Bunyan was the rector of a large church in Bedford.

While visiting the Lowe family in Bedford, I stayed overnight in the Red Cross billet there. One night as I was getting ready to go to bed, Glenn Miller and David Niven walked in to spend the night also. They both spoke to me briefly, and Glenn Miller asked me if I had caught their show. I told them that I didn't know about it. He said that they had just completed his first band concert in England. And I missed it.

The Red Cross billet was in a large auditorium that had been partitioned off with 8-foot high walls to form two-man cubicles with an open top. I stayed in one cubicle by myself, and they shared the one next to me. They stayed awake for an hour or so telling each other the latest off-color jokes. Many I hadn't heard. The next morning I got up early, since I seemed to be used to it. I was having breakfast when they walked in and they asked me what was good. I told them what I was having, but didn't follow up on the conversation. My shyness kept me from even asking either of them for an autograph, because I didn't want to seem pushy. I never saw either of them again, since Glenn Miller was later killed in a lost UC-64 Norseman that disappeared on a flight on 15 December 1944.

Lieutenant Richard 'Dick' Johnson, 303rd BG

A SOJOURNER IN HUNTINGDONSHIRE

While I was recuperating I visited a lot in nearby towns and villages. Kimbolton was nearby and Thrapston, too. These picturesque villages with thatch-roofed cottages were a delight to me. I was fond of the dignified, sturdy villagers, who were friendly and hospitable once I learned a few 'ice breakers'.

Our base was in a lovely section of England on the perimeter of what is usually referred to as the Midlands. The countryside was unbelievably green and rolling. Many stately groves of trees ringed the base, and I was fond of taking long walks and bicycle rides in the countryside. I loved this verdant country. Somehow, I had the feeling that I had been here in another life. I knew that my roots were here – that my people had all come from England in earlier times. Anyone with a passion for literature could not help being in love with this lovely pastoral land. Beginning with Mother Goose, this land had shaped my life from childhood on. I knew it intimately from my books. So I bicycled constantly over hill and down dale, rejoicing in the lush greenery of Huntingdonshire. The war seemed far away.

The English had been cultivating the same farms for thousands of years, but they were still fertile and productive. These people had a deep reverence for the land; they did not exploit it. The farmhouses were quaint and attractive with flowerbeds and rose gardens in profusion. One never saw a bad piece of landscaping. It had been going on for centuries, just

getting better and better. A cottage would be set down in the perfect place, every tree and every shrub in proper place and scale. Yet it was not a studied effect at all but completely artless and charming.

I could almost believe someone was arranging these things for my personal delight. Bicycling around a bend, I would see a chuckling brook spanned by an arched stone bridge, then a hedgerow with a stile over it, then a little farther an antique haywain parked in an orchard. Every foot of this land was steeped in history. Near our base there was an old Saxon church, St Swithin's. It was a thousand years old and still being used for worship. There were many such churches scattered throughout this part of England. The parish church in Kimbolton was registered in the Domesday Book; the census ordered by William the Conqueror in 1085. Catherine of Aragon spent the final years of her exile in nearby Kimbolton Castle. This was the country of John Bunyan, the great Puritan preacher. He had preached in all of the glades and hamlets hereabouts and had written his great allegory, *Pilgrim's Progress*, in Bedford Gaol only a few miles away.

At that time I had a passion for the English landscape painter, John Constable. Constable has been able to capture the beauty of the English landscape as no other artist has. His paintings do not exaggerate. There are still many areas in England where these lush landscapes may be seen. Curiously enough, I never felt depression here. As

Above: *High Street and Vicarage Lane, Podington – little changed over the centuries. (Mike Fuenfer)*

soon as I was away from the base and out in the countryside, I was transported to another realm.

I was quite taken with the country inns and pubs and never intentionally passed one by. These were venerable institutions, nothing like saloons. They were homey places, family-oriented. Misbehavior was not tolerated in them. I eventually learned to appreciate the English ale and beer, served unchilled, and came to prefer them to the American, probably because they were much more potent. Their lager was phenomenally good. All of it had much more of a malt taste than our own.

There was always a plink-plank piano and the Limeys and Yanks liked to gather around it and sing the old World War I songs: 'Long, Long Trail', 'Tipperary', and 'Pack Up Your Troubles.' 'Roll Out the Barrel' was a standard, but the most popular of all was 'Roll Me Over in the Clover.' At least three or four times an evening there would be bawdy renditions of it. The Yanks were as fond of it as the British. There were at least a hundred verses, each describing more graphically a new violation of the unfortunate lassie, the heroine of the song.

These were the best times of all to me. I loved to sing, and I loved to drink. I remember the blazing logs and the hearty camaraderie of these places. It was not difficult to believe that I was set down in the time of Dickens, for these places had in no way changed from those times. Many of them were hundreds of years old.

Many of my friends felt that the English were a backward people, slow to accept changes and new ideas. This was precisely what I liked about them. I was a traditionalist; so were they. They held on tenaciously to their enduring monuments. The British had a sense of history and were fully aware of the greatness of their past. They did not demolish old churches and other historic landmarks to make way for junk food places, gas stations, and other forms of visual pollution. This was all to the good as far as I was concerned. They did not compromise with the quality of life in this respect and I hoped they never would.

Some of our people were quite vocal in their criticism of English institutions, and I, for one, was greatly embarrassed when it occurred in my presence. I was quick to apologize for the rudeness of my countrymen. The English merely ignored these few loudmouths. They never attempted to defend their customs and way of life; indeed, they had no need to as far as I was concerned. I think it is significant that in our own country when we want to give something a touch of class, we give it an English name.

Chick's Crew, Ben C. Smith, radio operator, 303rd BG, Molesworth

---

Whenever we were in London or on leave anywhere and some member of the crew had a date, before he took off to meet his date we would join in singing to him, 'Roll me over, lay me down and do it again'. On a few instances I recall some crowd in a pub singing and the girls joining in the verses. Being Americans and in uniform, we could not go far without being stopped by girls. One night a Norwich girl stopped a group of us, placed herself in front of us, and she started, 'Roll me over.' We were quite stunned by this until we realized that none of us had time to comply with her wishes. We merely brushed past her on our way to the train and London. One of my friends said, 'You know, I always regret that we never picked that girl up in Norwich.' To which another replied, 'Would it have been worth missing the train?' To which another said, 'She would probably want to marry you after one date. Who wants a wife to sing, Roll me Over?'

Technical Sergeant Forrest S. Clark, air gunner, 67th BS, 44th BG

ROLL ME OVER IN THE CLOVER

*Now this is number one
and the fun has just begun
Roll me over, lay me down
and do it again.
Roll me over, in the clover
Roll me over, lay me down
and do it again.
Now this is number two
whatever shall I do?*

'The public house tradition is outstanding. First throw out all your old concepts of American bars and start over. Begin with a neighborhood house that opens its doors to all strangers. It welcomes those who desire a pint or two of ale, invites them to a game of darts, hopes they will join in with others in group-singing regardless of quality of voice. Friendly conversation and discussions abound. Even though I cared little for the warm ale or scarce Scotch whiskey, I fell in love with the pub tradition, where I met many friends, Polish allies speaking little English, English soldiers, etc.'

Will Lundy, 44th BG

It was at Coventry, that I saw the most impressive bomb ruins of my life. I recall walking along a sloping street up to the cathedral or what was left of Coventry Cathedral. I can still see the jagged spire and rubble, the place where the altar was and, strangely enough, I see flowers growing in the crevices of the ruined stones. It was a beautiful early spring day in 1944 and in each of the little houses along the street leading to the cathedral ruins, flower pots and gardens were a fantasy of color, as only English gardens can be. I walked slowly because some children were on the streets, which was strange for that time because many of the children had been evacuated to avoid the bombings. I shall never forget those bomb ruins not only because of the contrast of flowering gardens but also because amid the devastation there were children playing and their cries echoed among the rubble. I think it was the first time in my life when the fullest impact of war hit me. I can only compare it to the sights and sounds of war and years later seeing the flower children of the 1960s presenting flowers to the soldiers. It was that kind of a vibrant, poignant mixture of darkness and light, colour and drabness, order and chaos. Coventry sent me on my way back to my airbase with the smarting realization that war can visit anywhere and even houses of worship are not immune from its ferocity. It was that rather small, bright and seemingly unruffled town with its ruined cathedral that

Above left: *Sgt. Kenneth J. Smits (right) and the landlord of the Bedingfield Arms (wearing a trilby) watch T/Sgt. Emory A. White perform some magic. (Don & Peggy Garnham)*

Above right: *'Down at the local' – The pub is the Bedingfield Arms at Eye, Suffolk. (Don & Peggy Garnham)*

Right: *'It was at Coventry, that I saw the most impressive bomb ruins of my life. I recall walking along a sloping street up to the cathedral or what was left of Coventry Cathedral. I can still see the jagged spire and rubble, the place where the altar was and, strangely enough, I see flowers growing in the crevices of the ruined stones.' Technical Sergeant Forrest S. Clark (British Official)*

FOR U.S. ARMED FORCES IN U.K.

Coventry

" For many years the City of Coventry has occupied a position well-nigh unique among the centres of Britain.

" It is at once a very old and a very modern city, one that occupied a place of importance in civic and industrial life a thousand years ago, and it continues, despite the attentions of the enemy, to occupy a place of even greater importance in civic and industrial life to-day."

Emily Smith

MAYOR

presented the most powerful sermon against war and man's war against man and God. I could only get some sense of the horror of it all when I saw the later pictures of magnificent Cologne Cathedral standing stark, brave and daring amid the ruins of that great German city devastated by our air forces and our bombs. Then I think of Dresden, Hamburg, Berlin and scores of other cities.

Four hundred German bombers droned over Coventry in November 1940, and they were responsible for the Coventry to be seen today. They left a city of smoking and ruined buildings in their passing. They left more. They left a new verb – to coventrate – to express the Nazi idea of war. They left a heroism that enabled yet another English city to defeat hate. They left a courage that enabled its citizens to carry on.

America was the first of the nations to express its horror at the German method of war, and many US newspaper correspondents told the people of the United States of Coventry's ordeal and Coventry's courage ... Today, in streets with many gaps, in a city centre full of ruins, and a cathedral that is a shell, Coventry industry continues to forge the weapons which are helping to bring victory.

'Coventry', for US Armed Forces in UK

Coming out to Oxford on the train from London I recall how quiet and reticent the English passengers in the same compartment were. I remarked that the countryside looked beautiful and complimented the gardeners. One woman passenger turned and said, 'That's one thing the Germans can't take, the gardens.' It made me think of the flowers in the ruins. We passed through Reading and I thought of Oscar Wilde and Reading Gaol. As we neared Oxford I could see the spires of the colleges and the ornate facades of the town buildings and green squares. I had visited Cambridge and Oxford but they were relatively untouched by war in the physical sense. They were touched in another way as many of the students were in the Allied forces or the Commonwealth forces. When we got off the train at Oxford, a group of English girls came running over seeing our American uniforms. They asked if we wanted to go to a dance that night. Sergeant Abe Sofferman said he didn't want to go because he was in Oxford to learn something about history. Sofferman was a bookish fellow in that way. We ended the day by visiting all the college buildings open to the public and then went to a pub near the station. We dwelled for a day or two amid the Gothic splendors of Oxford, visiting the rooms and dorms, the pubs and the river bank. For a brief period we were in that citadel of learning away from the dreariness and danger of our bases.

Sofferman was to die on the missions in an enemy land and all of us were to suffer fear and anguish, but on that day at that time, we were as immortal as the flowers among the ruins. I was to take Sofferman's place on the crew after his death but our friendship was deep and enduring while he lived.

I remember the damp days when stopping at a railway station, the first thing one would see were the flower boxes on the station building; roses blooming amid the damp fog and penetrating mists of England at some remote railway stop. Nearby, huddled over a fire would be a British woman or girl dressed in the home services uniform handing out huge heavy mugs of hot tea and soft, sticky buns. You would have to juggle your gas mask and kit to grab the steaming mugs and pour down the warm tea.

In London it was said a very special rose or flower bloomed amid the wreckage of bombed-out buildings. This tiny red flower became the symbol of the will of the people, the spark for survival and hopes. Perhaps it was growing at Coventry. I am sure other flowers, perhaps of different species, blossomed in the bombed-out cities of Europe. It was indeed strange yet redeeming what one could find among the ruins.

The rest is lost in memory somewhere ... memory eradicates time. It is a victory over that most dread enemy of mortals. It is the only way ordinary men and women can defeat this arch enemy and it is sought by all of us as our weapon. Time will win in the end but memory mocks its victory by the bright sunshine we recall of summer days, the joyous moments of life, the romances, the tragedies, the good and bad and the beautiful that endures in memory. Thus Coventry, Oxford, London and the scenery of wartime England remain my weapons against time.

Among the Ruins, Technical Sergeant
Forrest S. Clark

A fair imitation of a movie theater was maintained on the base and we saw many old pictures and some new ones. Monthly dances were held, where our own orchestra, the 'Airliners' played and the base trucks brought the girls from Norwich and took them home – most of them. USO shows came occasionally, weekly 'situation' talks were given, beer nights were held in the clubs, and Special Services and the Red Cross kept us sane. There were frequent dances in the Rackheath village hall on the edge of the field and other dances close about.

... We began to explore our corner of England. Many had bicycles, those fine, low-geared, light English bikes whose handlebar brakes caused many a spill, arse over teakettle. On them we went pubbing in the long, light, spring ... we rode the old lanes to Coltishall, Wroxham, or Horning Ferry, through that beautiful village – Woodbastwick, or to Brundall, or Acle, or Norwich. We saw new birds: the sweet singing blackbirds, wood pigeons, the English robins, small and cocky. The chaffinches flashed their white wing bars everywhere, mistle thrushes searched the grass, kestrels passed overhead. Everywhere, too, there seemed to be noisy flocks of rooks and crows. We smelled the perfume of English hedgerows and saw woods blanketed in bluebells. Poppies grew in profusion on the sides of the air raid shelters and along the roadways. The massed bloom of many-colored rhododendron was magnificent along one complete driveway into the field. There were many places we went to. We saw the cathedrals, Ely, Peterborough, even York or Durham. The ruined abbey at Walsingham was not far off. Some few got to Devon and Cornwall, some to Liverpool, or the Lake District. Best of all,

Above: *American Red Cross minstrels show at Seething. (Newton L. McLaughlin)*

perhaps, was Scotland. The girls seemed prettier there, the people less reserved, life a bit more like that in America and yet more foreign too. Maybe you could catch a ride on a plane running a check and get set down somewhere near Edinburgh. Maybe you sat up all night in an English train compartment. A few days for Princes Street and the castle, some time in the Highlands, Luss and Loch Lomond, Glasgow, Aberdeen, and you had had a fine time, found hospitable people who seemed to like you, and had gotten a long way from the war and the life of the base.

Allan Healy

Since nothing was doing yesterday afternoon, Archie, Nat and I decided to go take a look around Great Yarmouth. We took a noon train and came back about 8.55 p.m. last night. We had quite a good time. First thing we did was walk along the waterfront. The beaches are all closed off now with barbed wire and pillboxes, and, since the beaches are mined, it's a poor place to go anyway. From Brittania Pier we walked south on the big, wide walk for several blocks. It was quite a resort area in peacetime as the postcards show. There were two enormous dance pavilions, one all glass, and several amusement places including a big roller coaster.

Then we went to see a show before supper. It was called *Rose Marie*, with Jeanette McDonald and Nelson Eddy. I enjoyed the singing as much as I did the first time I think. Then we had a real good supper, chicken and ice cream in fact, in a restaurant there. By then it was time to catch our train back. It got kinda rainy then, but I didn't mind – although it was too late to write by the time we got home at 11.30 p.m.. That seems to cover the day, Vonny. We want to go to Cromer if it warms up and lay out in the sun on the beach since they've been cleared now of wire and mines. Might even go swimming ... R.
Captain Ralph H. Elliott, pilot, 467th BG

THE BROADS

'I remember the flak house on the broads. I went there for a rest and went pubbing by boat and learned to play hearts with shillings.'

Mary Carroll Leeds, American Red Cross girl, Attlebridge June 1944–May 1945

That summer many of us rented boats on Wroxham Broad and sailed dinghies on that pocket-handkerchief of a lake, or had parties aboard with the girls we had met ... The Broads were a lifesaver to some. There we rented cruisers or sailboats that had been brought up for protection from the seaports, boats that had comfortable bunks and galleys. You had a sailing dinghy to go out to them and could sail on the small lakes and through the narrow channels. It was a pleasure to be able to sleep away from the base in the summer nights, to have the calm of being on the water. Swans flew in marvelous flight, ducks were about and the war could almost be forgotten until a buzzing Liberator or Mosquito came past at mast height.

Allan Healy

Right: *'That summer many of us rented boats on Wroxham Broad and sailed dinghies on that pocket-handkerchief of a lake, or had parties aboard with the girls we had met ... The Broads were a lifesaver to some.' Allan Healy (MWB)*

Today has been beautiful out, Vonny, just like summer almost ... We've been figuring on whether or not to get a yacht for the summer, and this afternoon, Nat and Frank went down to the Broads to see about a boat. There's about 200 miles of river around here to sail on, and it's not far from here so that most any evening we could go up by bike. On a two-day pass we figure we could have a swell time with a 16 or 20-foot sailboat. After talking it over, the five of us have about decided to invest in a three-bed, 24-foot yacht. It's going to cost us each about two pounds a week, but we figure it will be worth it just for the fun and relaxation.

Captain Ralph H. Elliott, pilot, 467th BG, in a letter home to his wife Vonny.
(Elliott added, 'Actually it was a houseboat that we poled down the waterway and managed to anchor out in the Broads for the summer And I had to carefully explain what we meant by the 'Norfolk Broads' to stay out of trouble at home. Yvonne and I went back there in 1982; the same boat was still anchored out in the Broads in exactly the same place as we left it in 1945.')

A popular British pastime in Norfolk, where we were stationed, was to go sailing in small sailboats along the canals and small streams. This pastime prompted us to develop another sport of trying to blow over or capsize these boats while on training flights. On one occasion (George must have been at the controls), we made a couple of passes but couldn't capsize one, so we made another pass very low and directly at it. This must have been too much for the sailors because they dove in the water as we pulled up to go over the top of the mast.

Lieutenant Alvin Skaggs, pilot, 448th BG, Seething

'BRANDON, LAKENHEATH, SHIPPEA HILL, ELY, CAMBRIDGE, AUDLEY END, BISHOP'S STORTFORD, LONDON'

There was the time you stood from Thetford all the way to London, your feet numb in the draughty corridor, the windows steamed so that even the bleak Suffolk landscape was hidden in the November curtain of cold. There was the jerking, stopping, backing, starting, and there was the inevitable twenty-minute stop at Ely. You cursed the heat-lever over the seat; it never worked. But then it was April, a half year later. You left your overcoat behind in the belly-tank crate that served as a wall-locker, stuffed some shaving articles in your musette bag and hopped the 5.50 or the 9 or the 11 p.m. bus from the MP gate. You were taking off on a '48 to London.' It was spring and you felt eager.

No tickets now at fourteen-bob a round trip. In April 1945 you began getting reverse lend-lease in travel warrants to any point in the UK. You waited on the platform for the train to pull in from Norwich, buying a *Daily Express*, *Sketch*, *Mail*, *Post* or *Illustrated*. Then you read the signs, 'There'll Always Be Mazawattee Tea' and watched a Thetford farmer herd two goats off the Bury train through the passengers. And you looked over the local civilians, the British officers, and the scores of American airmen, a few of them with all their gear starting the trip back to the States.

Local trains from Swaffham and Watton arrived with schoolkids in shorts and high wool stockings, clutching their books like the schoolkids in all countries. The British Indian soldiers looked up from the freight cars they were unloading and silently watched the trains. Thetford is a small town, but its station carried life in and out by day and night: Girls from Knettishall; Scotch [sic] officers in kilts; GIs starting on pass clean-shaven, and returning un-pressed, unshaven and unwell; goats, dogs, bicycles, and boxes of aromatic fish.

And there was the morning a few months after D-Day when your train was an hour late and then you saw why: a hospital train steamed in to pick up a score of US wounded, casualties headed for the States. There was no ceremony, no coffee and doughnuts or brave smiles. The wounded stared back at those who stared at them, their eyes dull and tired …

You sat in the compartment and slept most of the way. That is you sat when there was a seat, one of the eight that could be crowded into each compartment. Opposite you was a minister who smiled in a kindly, professional way; three gunners from the B-17 field near Bury, invariably sleeping; two civilian women next to you reading a cheap-covered book and holding boxes and babies; a civilian smoking steadily, his pipe acrid and penetrating, tobacco shreds sprinkled unnoticed on his well-worn overcoat.

Again you read the signs in the train … 'If danger seems imminent, lie on the floor,' advised the poster next to the watercolor of the cathedral. 'It is dangerous for passengers to put their heads out of carriage windows,' warned the message over the door with the window you opened by working the heavy leather strap.

'48 To London', 359th FG

History

Left: *'There was the time you stood from Thetford all the way to London, your feet numb in the draughty corridor, the windows steamed so that even the bleak Suffolk landscape was hidden in the November curtain of cold. There was the jerking, stopping, backing, starting, and there was the inevitable twenty-minute stop at Ely.' '48 to London' (359th FG History)*

Below: *'You waited on the platform for the train to pull in from Norwich, buying a Daily Express, Sketch, Mail, Post or Illustrated.' '48 to London' (MWB)*

My stay in Lavenham during the war was a rewarding, heartwarming and memorable experience, because the locals were so kind, considerate and friendly. At that time I was a first lieutenant and worked in Operations or 'Flying Control' as the RAF called it. During my time off I usually went to the Swan Hotel for a pint or two and a chat with the regulars. On one occasion I was invited to attempt to meet the requirements of the 'boot record' – to consume a large volume of ale from the glass boot without stopping. I did manage, with some distress, to accomplish the task and I was asked to sign my name on the wall of the Swan. Those wonderful people in Lavenham who befriended a young American during WWII were so kind and considerate. They served so well on the 'Home Front' as civil defence members, air raid wardens, aircraft spotters, firefighters; and those who worked side by side with the Womens' Land Army recruits in the fields, or those folks who worked in the Red Cross clubs.

Bob Clements

Below:
Clyde Colvin at Carleton Rode windmill near Hethel.
(via Pat Ramm)

AN AMERICAN'S IMPRESSION OF BRITAIN

I may be leaving England, perhaps never to return. Before I go I want to tell some of the things I shall never forget – the scenes and episodes that have impressed me during my two years as an American soldier in Britain.

I remember that first night in England, standing in a wheat field in East Anglia and watching cascades of green incendiaries drifting down. 'This is it,' we told ourselves. 'We are in it at last.'

But it was hard to convince ourselves, for here were these crazy English standing in their gardens watching the bombing raid as if it were a Fourth of July spectacle. It was hard to boast about our own experiences when all around us were five-year-olds who had lived through more than we have ever known.

The blackout was so black. It gave us the feeling that the houses behind the staring windows were abandoned.

The atmosphere of rural Suffolk, the workers in the fields, the stillness, the emptiness of the roads, the quiet of the village streets – these made us feel we had come to a country where all but a remnant of the population have moved away.

Memorable days ... Watching our first cricket match on the fields of St. Albans, in Hertfordshire, within sight of the Roman ruins and later having a beer with Eric, the Warwickshire soldier.

Boxford in Essex where two girls waited at their window every morning for eight months to wave as we drove past. We never once spoke to them, but we were friends.

I shall remember a Sunday in June, punting on the river at Cambridge, and talking to the don who badly needed a shave, a haircut and a press, but who had (we later learned) just been knighted.

Biking to Lavenham, Suffolk, with Vivian for a look at that perfect Tudor village and a drink at 'The Swan' ... Walking across the meadows with Joan to listen to the skylarks, those most irresponsible of sun-struck birds.

I shall not forget the friendly evenings at 'The Unicorn' where we would buy each other rounds of ale and argue about the blue haze and settle all the problems that baffled the world.

Derby Day at Newmarket, Suffolk, where 9,000 came to see a race that was run behind a hill, and the same 9,000 tried to get back to London on one train.

There were churches … the don who spent hours showing us Durham Cathedral and the woman verger in Canterbury Cathedral … Lincoln Cathedral, Peterborough Cathedral, Ely Cathedral, and the beautiful smaller churches … Above all, Boston Stump, lit up like the last rays of the setting sun, shining across the fens like a white sward.

We shall remember Piccadilly Circus after dark. The girl who sang operatic arias on the Bakerloo platform, as everyone cheered … the sailor who played his violin and danced in the modern train when everyone joined in 'Dear Liverpool'. This was England with it's hair down.

But we shall remember, too, our Christmas parties for the orphans and evacuee children. No one could ever forget those parties, with the kids yelling and gobbling ice cream, sitting on our shoulders and singing for us … going home along the lane clutching armfuls of toys and candy, chewing gum and biscuits. Fifteen hundred we had at one party.

It was not all fun. There was the mud in the airfield building, the tents that leaked, the north wind that blew.

There were trains that did not arrive on time, and the telegrams that did not arrive at all … We got stranded in the overcrowded towns. One night it was in Hull, Yorkshire, and another night it was Chesterfield (the police helped us here) and again in Grantham, Lincolnshire. But we always seemed to find a bed somewhere, a friendly welcome, and the month's egg ration on our breakfast plate, now matter how loudly we protested.

There were haunting scenes, the mist hanging over the silent mountains round Loch Lomond, that day when everything dripped, and the solitude of

Right and Below:
USO and Stars & Stripes War Correspondent uniform flashes and badges.

the place heightened by the wail of the bagpipes far up in the hills.

The steady drone of the bombers going out over the coast at night, a prayer on our lips for each.

Sombre pictures too. The shelters each night in the London underground; the faces of the children sleeping on the floors under the feet of passers-by, in draughts of dusty air. There it is, or a small part of it anyway. There you have the face of Britain as we have seen it, these two years.

We thank you for your hospitality, for opening your homes to us, for smiling at us and dancing with us, for marrying some of us, for being patient with our faults, for listening to our talk with tolerance, for struggling with our quaint tongue and then adopting it.

For playing host to this vast army of foreigners without letting it get you down. For showing us quiet courage and stamina and patience that is your greatest virtue and worst handicap. We will remember England.

Daily Express, Robert Arbib, January 1945

Left: *A GI poses by an MG in front of the American Red Cross club (Bull Hotel) in Trumpington Street, Cambridge. The city boasted six clubs, five for enlisted men and one for officers. G. M. Trevelyan 'one of the great historians of England', was available to meet GIs at the Bull Hotel every Saturday at 4 o'clock. (via Steve Gotts)*

Right: *Punts on the Cam. (MWB)*

A Comfortable Blend of War and Peace

'Our entire squadron was given a 24-hour pass today. Our crew and Granahan's took the train over to Cambridge – about an hour's ride. One of the nicest towns I've seen in England. The Cambridge University and several other colleges are located there. It's a typical college town. The streets are crowded with students (most of them on bicycles) each with a book or two under his arm and a bright scarf around his neck. These scarves represent their individual schools and have the school colours. The graduating class also wears a black cloak. Saw a show and visited a few of the pubs. Didn't have time to visit Cambridge University. Hope to get back there soon.'

Diary entry, Andy J. Coroles, bombardier, 331st BS, 94th BG, Bury St Edmunds

The town of Cambridge is as comfortable a blend of war and peace as you could find anywhere in the United Kingdom, and all the side effects and currents of a world conflict can be seen and heard right from the time of arrival at the railway station. In one corner, a large group of Italian prisoners in their maroon wool uniforms, squat on their barracks bags and leather suitcases and smoke, whistle, or doze in the autumn sunlight. They are a cheerful, sunburnt, bored, well-fed bunch, probably on their way to work on the farms of Norfolk. In the station restaurant American soldiers surround

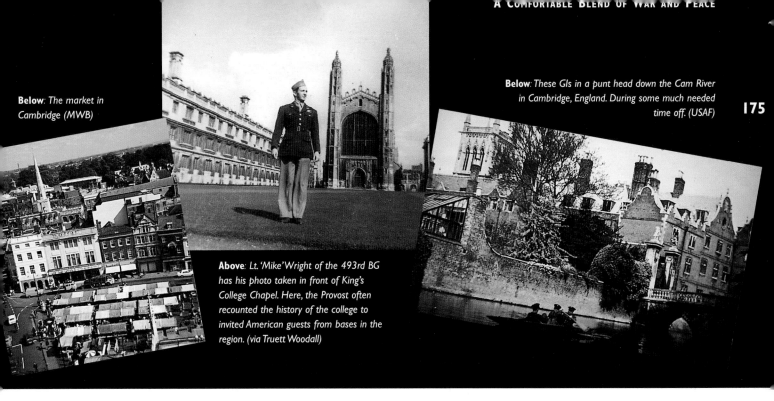

Below: The market in Cambridge (MWB)

Above: Lt. 'Mike' Wright of the 493rd BG has his photo taken in front of King's College Chapel. Here, the Provost often recounted the history of the college to invited American guests from bases in the region. (via Truett Woodall)

Below: These GIs in a punt head down the Cam River in Cambridge, England. During some much needed time off. (USAF)

the counter eating meat pies and discussing the excellence of the coffee. The English are now turning out good coffee and this comes as one of the climaxes of the war as far as we are concerned.

Walking through the town you are made aware of the fact that this is a great center of university life until you reach the Red Cross club on Trumpington Street. This is an ex-hotel right next to the smoke-gray battlements of King's College. The soldiers lounging in the doorway of the Red Cross, wondering what their next move is going to be, can look straight across at King's College Chapel and the clouds of pigeons wheeling outside the boarded-up stained glass windows.

Along the streets the excellent book stores, and print and liquor shops are filled with customers. Students flow and sweep along on either foot or bicycle in their blue and black gowns and long, trailing college scarves worn over turtle necked sweaters and tweed suits.

Down on the river bank, the Cam, choked with leaves, winds slowly along, encircles some of the colleges like a moat, and finally wanders off towards Grantchester under a bridge. Here there is a small, mild waterfall whose noise is sometimes lost in the sudden roar of a Marauder flying low and fast over the tree tops.

The surface of the river is strewn with GIs in punts and canoes, and the man who rents out the boats is pleased by the sight. For him the American Army has been an unqualified godsend in providing tourist trade that he never expected to see again after 1939.

'We really enjoy seeing you Yanks here now. Of course, some of you get drunk and lie around the marketplace all night, but that's all right. It makes it seem like the old days again.'

The rest of the people in Cambridge feel as he does and the only complaint that the college authorities have to make is that the average US Army visitor does not show the proper amount of curiosity about the place and does not make use of the free lectures and other sightseeing privileges.

This lack of curiosity might account for the fact there were so few GIs at the town meeting held in Cambridge on the night of 8 October. When the meeting broke up, a number of the audience went over to the Eagle Hotel across the street from the Exchange. Here, Ethel, the well-set brunette barmaid, was setting them up right and left across the counter. She is one of the livelier institutions of Cambridge, and her large public among the 8th Air Force all swear by her. Even on flying pay, aerial gunners and the like have a habit of going into a

Above: The Eagle in Benet Street, Cambridge. (MWB)

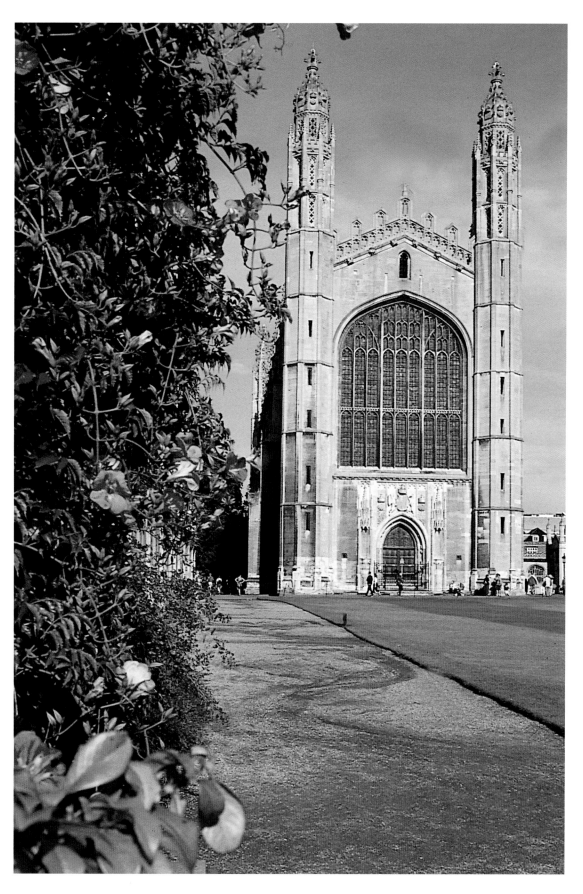

Left: *King's College. (MWB)*

Right: *The Airman's bar in The Eagle. The Gls took readily to the wartime pastime of autographing walls and ceilings of local pubs. Most of this graffiti was removed in post-war years, however, in a few places it has been preserved, notably in the Eagle public house with its Aviation Bar and wartime memorabilia. (MWB)*

Above: *Part of the ceiling from the Airman's bar in The Eagle. (MWB)*

fiscal collapse when they least expect one, but Ethel has always tided her friends through such dark periods in their lives. What is more significant, she is always paid back.

On the wall of the Eagle Hotel's washroom among the usual frescoes and epigrams is pencilled this inscription: 'Never before in history have so many known so little about so much. Signed Benito Mussolini, Guard House, Italy.' This does not seem a bad motto either for an army educational program of a university town during wartime.

Yank magazine, 'A Day at Cambridge', **John D. Preston**

Near the end of my tour of operations I obtained a three-day pass and visited Cambridge, the lovely old university town. It was only about twenty miles from our station.

I fell in love with the place. Its fine old Gothic buildings, many of them dating from the thirteenth and fourteenth centuries, were deeply satisfying to me. I could not get enough of roaming its medieval streets. Everyone walked or rode bicycles; the streets were almost too winding and narrow for automobiles. Here the timbered veneers of Tudor England were very much in evidence. Some of the houses and inns were many centuries old. The university owned all the land thereabouts, and they did not countenance any of the tomfoolery called progress. They wanted Cambridge left just as it was, a decision I would have to applaud wholeheartedly.

The university was made up of a number of colleges, thirty-five to be exact; each having its own identity, such as Queen's College, Trinity College, St. John's College, and the like.

I learned that in ancient times Cambridge had been a monastic establishment built in the fens of East Anglia. Eventually it began to be a center of learning. It was already a great university when it was visited by Erasmus, the foremost prophet of the Reformation. He came to Cambridge in 1500 and remained there at Queen's College for three years.

The finest of the medieval edifices was King's College Chapel begun in 1446. With its inspired fan vaulting, it was the supreme example of the perpendicular Gothic. I had only a rather general understanding of the decorative vocabulary in those days, but there were many knowledgeable people about who were glad to explain these things to me.

The loveliest area of all was that part of the university called The Backs, where the tree-shaded lawns and gardens ran from the backs of the colleges down to the picturesque River Cam, from which the town derived its name. I strolled along the grassy banks of the green river with its weeping willows and ancient stone bridges and thought to myself, 'This is the loveliest spot in the world.'

I happened upon a cricket match and was fascinated. The players were immaculate; it seemed a very antiseptic sport to me, but as I watched I could see that a lot of coordination and agility were being displayed. I never did fathom what was going on despite a friendly bystander's attempts to tell me.

The Backs had once been marshes but in the seventeenth century had been filled in by one of the distinguished alumni, Oliver Cromwell, the Great Protector, to become the beautiful garden spot that one now sees.

I was told that a great summer fair had been held annually on the Commons in olden times. The Commons was a great grassy expanse near the river. Here the stout English yeomen had come from every part of the Midlands and East Anglia to socialize, carouse, shoot their longbows in competition and vie with each other in feats of strength. Farmers, merchants, and artisans hawked their wares on all sides, drinking and wenching betimes. It was said that the fair was the model for Vanity Fair in Bunyan's *Pilgrim's Progress*. It was a lusty, brawling time. Now a hearty new breed had invaded the Commons. The Yanks were to be seen everywhere, intruding with a jarring note upon the timeless, pastoral scene.

I wandered again along the banks of the Cam

and saw an apple-cheeked underclassman poling a punt down the meandering stream. His passenger, an upperclassman, was eating an apple and reading a book. Being an American, I did not understand why the boatman was not rebelling at the supine role he was forced to play. This custom, which to me seemed an anachronism, had wide acceptance, going unchallenged by the underclassmen. But who knows what noble concepts had germinated in these verdant surroundings. Here the young Tennyson might have dreamed dreams, which became *The*

Above: *Gonville and Caius College with Trinity College behind. GIs were invited to discuss subjects of 'common interest' with Cambridge University undergraduates. (MWB)*

Left: *At Cambridge many Yanks got their feet wet on idyllic punts on the River Cam. (via Paul Wilson)*

Above: *Corporal Harold M. Middlemass, 361st FG at Bottisham, punting on the River Cam in 1944. (via Steve Gotts)*

A lively place, it held great fascination for me, as I had never seen an open-air market before.

What a delight to rest in an ancient inn drinking the excellent light brown ale! While chatting convivially with the other customers, I exulted in a milieu of Jacobean tables and chairs, mullioned windows, exposed ceiling beams, rich dark oak wainscoting, an open-hearth stone fireplace, and finally church warden pipes on the wall, not added as a decorator's touch but centuries old and once used by the patrons of the inn. A jewel of a setting for one who needed no such encouragement to drink. Had this genteel place once been the favorite haunt of Edmund Spenser or John Milton? Had the youthful Wordsworth and his friend Coleridge sat in these very chairs quenching their thirsts from the lovely old pewter tankards? I did not know, but I did not doubt it, for this was a place of poets.

The next morning I resumed my exploration of the old medieval town. In the narrow streets I saw the handsomest shops I had ever seen. I had a thing about bookstores and here was the oldest one in England, Bowes and Bowes, founded in 1581. Bookbinding had been a major craft in Cambridge for centuries, and the shop was a treasure-trove of

Idylls of the King, or the youthful Charles Darwin might have explored broad vistas of the intellect, which eventuated in the *Origin of Species.*

Since the Middle Ages, Cambridge had been a market town. Farmers from the surrounding country brought their vegetables and produce to the great open marketplace behind St. Mary's Church.

Right: *Gls strolling along King's Parade, Cambridge. (via Steve Gotts)*

handsome and rare volumes. Moving along, I was delighted to find a shop that had an amazing collection of jazz records. The proprietor told me that the college students and many of the professors not only loved jazz, but there were many connoisseurs of the idiom at the university. These were collector's items, some of which could not be found at home. I bought an album of a recording session by Louis Armstrong and Earl 'Father' Hines, featuring the venerable 'West End Blues' and 'Tight Like That.' This was really vintage jazz, and I was amazed to find it in this place. It only increased my esteem for the kind of people to be found hereabouts.

I had seen the genius of Sir Christopher Wren at St. Paul's and St. Mary-le-Bow's in London. I hadn't realized he was here also. The outstanding examples of his art in Cambridge were the magnificent Wren Library at Trinity College and the Emmanuel College Chapel. There were many quaint churches in the city. I was fond of poking and prowling about the graveyards. I was no necrophile, but the epitaphs on the tombstones were an unending source of delight to me. I sought out these places. They did not depress me. On the contrary, I rather fancied the idea of resting in one of these lovely old churchyards one day, for they did not seem like places of death to me but rather fitting ambiances for departed spirits.

And now I began to understand why Cambridge held such fascination for me. I had been looking for a place like this all my life. I felt that I was part and parcel of this greatest outcropping of the human spirit. In those days I only dimly understood the great thirst of the spirit that was growing in me, but I sensed that somehow in this place was the repository of every value that I held near and dear. My very soul sped across the centuries to unite with the antique refrain of the old medieval town.

In desperation I began to think of ways that I could manage to stay here. It seemed logical that every human being should be in a place where he was contented and happy and safe. I was in such a place. Here in this green Eden was peace and sanctuary. Twenty miles away the apparatus of death and terror was in ceaseless operation, but

now it seemed to have nothing to do with me. I did not want to be wasted just as I had begun to catch a vision. I knew that I belonged here. The other Americans did not care about this place, but I did. So my mind raced – was there a way? In the end I knew it was no good – I had to go back to Molesworth and finish the other business, one way or the other. It would have been better had I never come to Cambridge. Sadly I turned my back on the place and boarded the bus.

Chick's Crew, Ben C. Smith

Cambridge was not too far away and for some there was great attraction in its university atmosphere: the Cam, and the 'Backs'; King's College Chapel; the Bull Hotel taken over for GIs; bookstores and antique shops. The 467th, like other American organizations, brought back their share of souvenirs from England: old silver, coins, china, books. Oxford was farther away but it, too, was visited. A few even took the special week's course there that gave some insight into English history and places, took them to Stratford and gave them teas with interesting English people.

Allan Healy

At the Red Cross in Cambridge, I got the name of an English family that entertained American flyers on weekends. Their name was Newman; and they lived in Royston, a town nearby. I was to spend many happy hours with them. Their home was a fine old Georgian mansion with lawn tennis courts, orchards, formal gardens, and beautiful groves of trees. These people were very kind to me. Each night my bed would be turned down. A glass of milk and a bowl of fruit were on the nightstand by my bed. Sometimes there would be a book of poetry or a magazine, too. They treated me like a son, and I shall never forget them.

Chick's Crew, 'The Ties That Bind', Ben C. Smith

Above: *'Along the streets the excellent book stores, and print and liquor shops are filled with customers. Students flow and sweep along on either foot or bicycle ...' Yank magazine, 'A Day at Cambridge', John D. Preston (MWB)*

Flak happy isn't the word for it

'Down in Ruhr Valley
Flying so low
Some chairborne bahstaad
Said I must go
Flak loves big bombers
Fighters do too!
P-51 Boys how I love you'

Anonymous

I was well established in the sack when a bunch of guys came in the room and turned the lights on. A bombardier and a navigator were putting their co-pilot to bed, but he'd broken away into my room.

He was pretty drunk, and he really had the bright stare of death in his eyes.

'So you made the team?' this co-pilot said.

Above: *B-17s of the 851st BS, 490th BG flying through flak-filled skies. (USAF)*

I said, 'I guess so.' I was about half asleep.

All he did was laugh, just stand there and laugh, until the whole room was full of it, and shaking from it.

The bombardier and navigator got him under control then and took him away to bed. The bombardier came back after they put him away.

Above: *S/Sgt. Bruce P. Prosser, gunner, 1/Lt. James S. Munsey, pilot and S/Sgt. Walter J. Thomas, waist gunner, 453rd BG, inspect the damage to Queenie at Old Buckenham on 20 April 1944. A flak hit on the rear of the aircraft decapitated the tail gunner on the mission to Wizernes in the Pas de Calais. Munsey, who was flying with the new crew on their first combat mission, and four of his crew, were killed two days later, when Cee Gee II, named after his daughter Carol Geane, was shot down by Leutnant Nommining of 2./KG51 in an Me 410 15 miles off the east coast returning from Hamm, Germany. Munsey was posthumously awarded the DSC, which was later presented to his 2-year-old daughter. (USAF)*

Above: *Captain Cunningham and crew of the 365th BS, 305th BG with a teddy bear wearing the air medal at Chelveston beside B-17 Patches on 7 June 1943. Below the name are repairs to two flak holes. Patches and 2/Lt. Douglas L. Mutschler's crew failed to return on 17 August 1943 when fighters shot the Fortress down over Belgium. Three men were KIA and seven were made POW. (USAF via Bill Donald)*

little chunks of bones and meat, blown all over the sky. Or he was cooked; burned into nothing.

Serenade To The Big Bird, 'First Mission', Bert Stiles, 401st BS, 91st BG, 19 April 1944. 'La French' is First Lieutenant John E. LaFontin, pilot of one of three B-17s in the 91st BG lost flying as part of the high squadron in the 381st BG's 'B' Group on the mission to Eschwege. Stiles called him 'La French' because he 'could never remember the last part.'

'That baby's got it bad,' he said. 'He won't last much longer. He's seen too many guys go down.'

When the lights were out again I lay there for a while, not ready to go to sleep.

… Nobody saw the fighters. They came out of the sun, and they only made one pass. One Fort blew up and one went down burning. La French was in one of them and the drunk co-pilot that woke me up the night before was in the other.

'That poor bastard could see it coming,' somebody said.

'He knew it was his turn.'

They were talking about that co-pilot.

But La French wasn't like that. He was all alive the last time I saw him. He rode that bike of his like it was Seabiscuit. And now he was just blood and

The excitement of my first mission over enemy territory crowded out almost all thoughts except an expectation of seeing fiery Messerschmitt fighters flashing past with cannons blazing. But all my expectations were in vain. Nothing exciting happened. No fiery fighters, no flashing cannon, no exploding anti-aircraft shells nearby. Frankly, I was disappointed. At approximately 1500 I was swinging my B-17 about the circular concrete hardstand and the big ship halted in its sharp arc. As the engines were being cut, I could already see the crew chief, Sergeant Jim Haley, racing down the taxi strip in a jeep, heading towards our Fort. I believe he got his jeep training at Le Mans! The jeep

184

Above: *A Liberator receives a direct hit in the starboard wing and goes down in smoke and flame. (USAF)*

straight down and started for the ground by the shortest road. It must have dived five thousand feet, and then by some miracle it pulled out, level and into a straight-up climb. It stalled out somewhere below us, and fell off on the right wing and spun in.

'Two chutes,' Sharpe called up. 'There's another.'

You don't remember much when the missions come fast.

Serenade to the Big Bird, 'Kiel', Bert Stiles,
[22 May 1944]

The Germans threw a box formation of ten fighters high and ten wide. We were flying in the diamond slot in the high element of the 452nd. Our P-51 escorts, which were above us (we were flying at 38,000 feet), on sighting the German fighters jettisoned their belly gas tanks; one of which went and put a hole four feet in diameter through our left aileron. There was flak and Lutz, the ball turret gunner, who could not wear his heavy B4 sheepskin jacket in the turret because of the cramped conditions, would leave his outer uniform thrown inside the plane.

This crazy sergeant was tracking a German fighter and he put about one hundred and seventy-five .50 calibre shells through our tail assembly. A good many shells shredded Lutz's flying jacket. We also sustained two 20mm cannon holes in the waist area. On the return to Deopham, Lutz was amazed to see his B4 jacket in shreds. He saved it and only wore it on rare occasions, I assume to impress the girls. He was later issued a replacement. We lost quite heavily on that mission.

John A. Holden, navigator, 452nd BG

stopped just short of the No.1 engine propeller arc, just as the props were coming to rest and Jim was coming to meet me as I swung down through the bomber's forward escape door, 7 feet to the concrete below.

'Boy,' I yelled at him, 'if all my missions are like this milk run, I've got it made.'

Jim was a veteran. He had already wet-nursed six Fortress crews, efficiently keeping their ships running smoother than any in the group. I detected a rather incredulous look on Jim's face. He said, 'Lieutenant, let me show you something.' Then he methodically guided me on a tour around the Fort. Before we were finished, he had shown me no less than twenty-seven jagged shrapnel holes in my ship, all from enemy anti-aircraft fire!

Jim added, 'It's the ones you don't see that get you.'

Lieutenant Bob Browne, pilot, 487th BG

On the Kiel job I got my first close-up of a Fort blowing up. The flak tightened up on the group just ahead of ours, and right out at ten o'clock, not very far away, a great red wound opened up, and then the drifting pieces, and ten men and a couple of hundred thousand dollars' worth of airplane, powdered in a hundredth of a second.

And while we were watching the streamers of flame from that one, another Fort nosed over

The flak is real when it clanks on the wings, and knocks out your number one oil-cooler. The rest of the time it is only a nightmare of soft black puffs and yellow flashes outside the window.

The 190s are real enough when they swing in

from one o'clock high and start blinking their landing-lights. They're plenty real when the top turret opens up, and the nose-guns start shooting, and the 20mms blow away half the tail-end of the ship.

I'd seen Sharpe in bloody shorts, wrenching his neck to see the wound on his left cheek. I'd seen what a knee looked like with the kneecap clipped away, and a waist gunner with his brains all over the Alclad, and his legs shot off just below his flak-suit …

But most of the time you don't live with death in a Fort the way they must in a ditch. The smells don't get to you, and neither do the sounds, and every night as long as the luck holds out, your sack is in the same place, ready and waiting, soft and dry.

Serenade To The Big Bird, 'D-Day …', Bert Stiles

On 11 July 1944 we flew to Munich. We were supposed to bomb a jet plane assembly plant at Riem airfield, if visual, and if not, to bomb the centre of Munich. It was undercast, so we did not bomb the airfield. The flak was very intense. Since we were not successful, we went again to the same target on 12 July 1944, with exactly the same results. These were maximum efforts (1500 bombers and 750 fighters) and were long gruelling flights approximating nine hours. We saw quite a few bombers that were hit by flak, and saw several of the damaged planes peeling off for Switzerland, which lay on our left as we returned. We had a breathtaking view of the Alps projecting up through the clouds.

Second Lieutenant George M. Collar, 702nd BS, 445th BG

'Somebody's hurt,' Sam said. 'They shot a red flare at the approach.'

We heard about it later.

A shell came up through the squadron navigator's table, through his map, past his nose, out the top, and burst about ten feet above the ship. A big chunk came ripping back through and

Above: *'We had a breathtaking view of the Alps projecting up through the clouds.' Second Lieutenant George M. Collar (MWB)*

smashed the pilot's knee, just clipped off the whole kneecap.

The bombardier told us, 'We just went up and put a tourniquet on his leg. He didn't yell much. The co-pilot flew home okay.'

One ship took three bursts almost inside the bomb bays. There were at least 250 holes in the waist and radio room when the pilot crash-landed at a RAF base. One of the waist-gunners had a stitching of wounds just above his flak-suit across his throat. When they lifted him out they could see his lungs.

'He was so slippery with blood, they dropped him once,' one guy told us.

He died in the night.

The radio-man got a chunk in his left eye that tore away most of the eyeball. The other waist-gunner lost his hand later. It was shredded.

'He just kept staring at it,' this guy told us. 'He'd try to shake it, and he couldn't feel anything, and he didn't seem to believe it was really his hand when he looked at it. All chewed to hell.'

Serenade To The Big Bird, 'Metz', Bert Stiles

The day was as bright and crisp as I have ever seen; more like a Technicolor movie than real life. There were a few small wisps of white cotton clouds interspersed through the picture but mostly it was clear. The sun glittered back from reflections of the

Above: *Flak 'thick enough to walk on'. (USAF)*

shiny aluminum skin of the other ships in the formation. Before we reached the IP, I could see the stretch of this great city. The streets were like a chequerboard beneath us and once in a while, an ant-like motor vehicle appeared on the streets. The movement of the scene below was unbearably slow and we seemed as though we were motionless. The black bursts of flak were also hanging ahead and right; at our altitude the sky was completely peppered with the stuff. As I looked ahead I said to myself, 'and we're going to have to fly through that?'

I turned the ball turret to the right, at about three o'clock position, and I could see the lumbering hulk of a Fortress, which was probably from another squadron, about 4,000 feet below us going in the opposite direction. Its nose was pointed downward with its right wing toward my left. Its right outboard engine was engulfed in red-orange flames streaking back about ten feet. There was no

doubt that the plane was going down.

I watched the scene transfixed and uttered silently to the crew of the plane, although really to myself, 'Get out, Get out!' As I watched, one, two, three and then four small white blossoms appeared behind the craft. Some had made it out. I changed my gaze to one of the small white parachutes in the air with something hanging below; an airman, another American. As I watched, small black puffs appeared around him as he slowly floated downward. The Germans were shooting at him with anti-aircraft fire. They could have used the 88mm ammunition better by going after the rest of us still flying.

As we proceeded over Berlin, the ship lurched and twisted from impacts, but we kept going and finally unloaded our bombs onto a railroad station in the heart of the city. Once away from the city, the flight back was uneventful. When I turned my turret to about two o'clock, I could see strips of aluminum skin peeled back from the right wing.

When we landed we found we had taken what must have been a 105mm anti-aircraft shell through the wing. It left a hole that a man could put his head through near the inboard end of the Tokyo gas tank. There were hundreds of smaller holes throughout the main body, wings and tail sections but no one was hit. I had learned what accurate and intense flak was.

William C. Stewart, ball turret gunner, 92nd BG

'Bill Kuban, who was on our crew, had a habit of knocking his head against a post in the barracks the night before missions. He claimed it cleared his head and relieved the tension. He was wounded on the Oslo mission. The last time I saw him he was stretched out bleeding by the ball turret and I thought, here was a goner.'

Technical Sergeant Forrest S. Clark, air gunner, 67th BS, 44th BG

'The squadron flight surgeon drank with us and palled around with us but kept a very watchful eye on us. He knew what shape we were in, how many combat missions we had flown and what the crew situation was. He was the one who dispensed the pills. In February–March 1944, I was on pills to put me to sleep and on the morning of a mission I was on pills to wake me up and get me going. Sleeping at night became so bad that we started taking pills from our escape kits.'

Bill Rose, pilot, 92nd BG

One of the boys from the Bronx came back and caused quite a disturbance. He got drunk every chance he could. He knew he would get killed the next time out but this particular night he did not come straight in. He went out to the ship in a stolen jeep, rounded up the Very pistols, burned up several wheatfields during his riot and finally ended up in our barracks. He opened one door and started firing Very pistol shots into the barracks, setting fire

to clothing and bedding. The door on the other end of the barracks had a traffic jam. Because of the firing, they got down on their hands and knees and crawled into the ice and snow. I went next door and called the MP. He was interested in the information but said there was no way he could make his appearance until things quieted down. They still did not send the boy home. They just confined him to barracks and counseling.

Emmett D. Seale, 446th BG

'The crew that we resided with were on their twenty-eighth or twenty-ninth mission and they were all crazy. One in particular would wake up in the middle of the night and shoot his .45 off at mice. A .45 reverberates and makes quite a bit of noise and disturbs your sleep!'

John A. Holden, navigator, 731st BS, 452nd BG

'In the 410th, we had this crazy radio operator. Who wasn't crazy, especially radio operators and navigators? His name was Miller, on Shead's crew, as I recall. Between missions, Miller urinated in condoms, tied the tops neatly and securely, and stored the condoms on a shelf above his bed for future use. The future use was to take them along to Hamburg or wherever, freeze them, and toss them out here and there, shouting, "Piss on you Bastards!"'

Bill Mulroney, 94th BG

'Some of the boys were developing the equivalent of 'shell shock', in spite of all our doctor's efforts. The nervous strain of continuous raids had been more than some of them could take. It raised the very rough command problem as to how long these lads would be fit to fly a combat mission, especially the pilots, whose nine-man crews were trusting him with their lives. I finally had to go to Colonel Castle about one pilot who was rapidly coming 'unstuck' as the British say, and they sent him to the 'rest home' in southern England. He didn't like it and I felt real sorry for him, but Colonel Castle agreed that it was no longer safe to send him on combat raids.'

Captain Franklin 'Pappy' Colby, CO, 410th BS, 94th BG

I got out my typewriter and started a letter to my folks.

And then it came in again ... all those guys ... all those good guys ... shot to hell ... or captured ... or hiding there waiting for it.

... waiting for it.

Then I came all apart, and cried like a little kid ... I could watch myself, and hear myself, and I couldn't do a goddamn thing.

... just pieces of a guy ... pieces of bertstiles all over the room ... maybe some of the pieces were still over there.

And then it was all right. I went in and washed my face. Green was calling up about trains, standing there in his shorts.

'I think the boys need a rest,' he said, 'You going in?'

'I'll meet you in London at high noon,' I said. 'Lobby of the Regent Palace.'

'Okay,' he said. 'Get a good night's sleep.'

'Meet you there,' I said.

But I didn't.

They sent me to the flak-house. There was an opening, and the squadron sent me.

Serenade To The Big Bird, 'Leipzig', Bert Stiles, co-pilot, Green's crew, 91st BG, 20 July 1944. Stiles had completed his bomber tour but instead of returning to America on leave now due to him, he asked to be transferred to fighters, and he moved to the 339th FG and to P-51s. At age twenty-three, he was shot down and killed on 26 November 1944 while escorting bombers to Hanover.

I was sent for a 'flak furlough' at Coombe House shortly after the Brunswick mission of 11 January 1944, when we lost eight B-17s. We were in such bad shape our flight surgeon, 'Doc' Miller, went along with us! He too was getting 'flak happy' riding along with his boys.

Cliff Hatcher, pilot, 94th BG

Below: *Walhampton House at Lymington, Hants, which opened as a rest home on 17 February 1944 to accommodate fifty enlisted men. (via Truett Woodall)*

THE FLAK SHACK – COOMBE HOUSE

Left London (Waterloo Station) the morning of 13 February for Lemley. A station wagon picked us up there and drove us out to Coombe House (an AAF rest home for combat crews). Coombe House was a lot nicer than I had anticipated, operated by Red Cross women and army personnel, all under Captain McCarthy. The house itself was built in the 1800s – a large English mansion belonging to a very rich wine merchant. It was later converted into a hotel, then purchased by the USAAF to be used as a rest home. Situated on one of the few hills in England, the grounds include many acres of trees and grass. Spent a good deal of time shooting skeet, playing snooker, and pitching horseshoes.

The food there was delicious and I developed an enormous appetite. Mike, a civilian working there, woke us each morning at 0830 and served us each a glass of orange juice in bed. What a life! They furnished us with civilian clothes to lounge around in. First time I've had on 'civvies' since I entered the cadets. Met Captain Mahurin while I was there. He's one of the leading fighter pilots in the ETO. Has sixteen Jerries to his credit. A regular fellow and not a bit conceited although he wears the DFC, Silver Star, and DSC.

Andy J. Coroles, bombardier, crew 19, 331st BS, 94th BG

21 February–1 March 1945 – Spent seven days at the flak shack at Shaftesbury, Dorsetshire, in southern England at an old English mansion and had a swell time. Horseback riding, archery, golf, skeet shooting, badminton, sightseeing and sleep and good food. After being alerted for about ten days in a row, we were all worn out and ready for a rest. The butler came in about 0830 each morning with a glass of orange juice and a call for breakfast. The mansion had ninety-six rooms and was really a beautiful place. Had a good rest.

Captain Ralph H. Elliott, pilot, 467th BG

Above: *Frederick G. Keiferndorf (left) a bombardier in the 493rd BG, with a Red Cross girl and a fellow flyer, in the grounds of Eynsham Hall, Witney, Oxon, which opened as an 8th Air Force 'flak shack' on 22 July 1944 to accommodate sixty-five officers. (via Truett Woodall)*

Right: *Captain Ralph H. Elliott, (centre, standing) 791st BS, 467th BG, and his crew on 26 October 1944. (via David Kibble-White)*

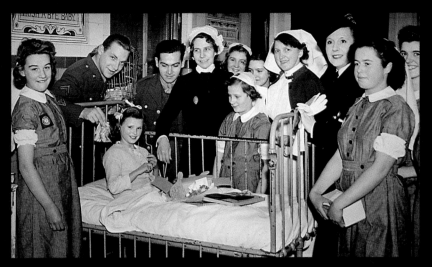

Above: *306th BG personnel deliver presents to children at the Bedford County Hospital, Christmas 1942. Third from right is English novelist Barbara Cartland, a volunteer worker. (via Richards)*

Right: *A young English girl at a Christmas party at Chelveston on Christmas Day 1943. (via Bill Donald)*

Yuletide

'On Christmas Day our base served dinner to the London children billeted in our neighborhood and many of our men were guests in English homes.'

Major Newton L. Mclaughlin, Special Services Officer, 448th BG

THE NIGHT BEFORE CHRISTMAS

'Twas the night before Christmas and all through the group
The 'big wheels' and 'wigs' were grinding out 'poop'
The bombers were parked on their hardstands with care
Waiting for ammunition soon to be there
The flyers were nestled all snug in their beds
While visions of 'milk runs' danced in their heads
When out of the darkness there came quite a knock
We cursed the OD and looked at the clock
Briefing will be in two hours he said
And if you're late you'll wish you were dead
Time marches on and the minutes fly by
So it's out of our beds get ready to fly
We rushed to the mess hall quick as a flash
And ate cold powdered eggs with hideous hash
Then a long bumpy ride to the group briefing room
Where the 'big wigs' preside and dish out our doom
The target is told and the first six rows faint
For lo and behold Berlin – it ain't.
The 'brains' had slipped up – oh my poor aching back
We're bombing a place that throws up no flak
So it's back in the truck and off to the line
The road is now smooth and the weather is fine.
The crew is at stations – the checklist is run
The engines run smooth as we give 'em the gun
Then suddenly the pilot wails in despair
'Look at the tower they just shot a flare'
We dash to the window with a heart full of dread
The pilot was right – and the darn thing is RED
So its back to the sack and we sweat out our fate
For there's a practice formation at a quarter past eight.

Anonymous

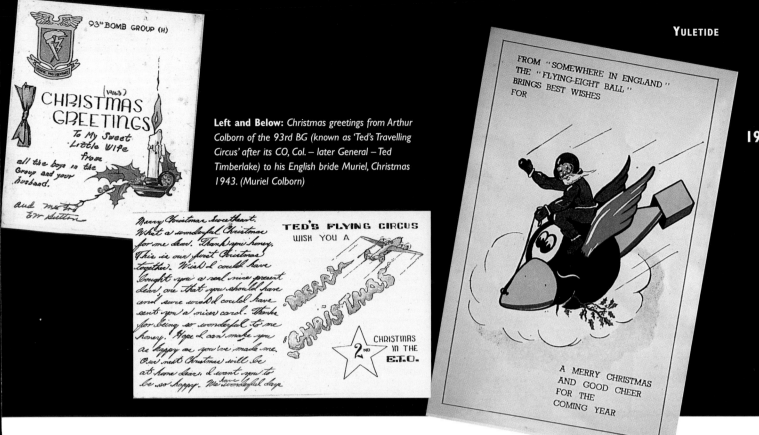

Left and Below: *Christmas greetings from Arthur Colborn of the 93rd BG (known as 'Ted's Travelling Circus' after its CO, Col. – later General – Ted Timberlake) to his English bride Muriel, Christmas 1943. (Muriel Colborn)*

I was in a base hospital for Christmas 1943. I had narrowly escaped with my life in a crash of a B-24 a few days before and had an injured back and legs. The crash left me in a blur but I recall Christmas because of two or three odd things that happened. There was a makeshift Christmas tree in the hospital and I could see it from my bed. Also, we had male nurses or hospital aides and I do not recall seeing or hearing any women nurses in the hospital. One of the odd things that happened had to do with a so-called secret cache of alcohol in one of the hospital cabinets. We were all supposed to be injured combat crew men but somebody, I think one of the male nurse aides, got the idea to open that cabinet and pass around some unadulterated alcohol for a little Christmas holiday cheer. The stuff was so potent that after a snifter or two all the patients and the hospital aides were getting high on it. It was decided that this was the best way to celebrate and combined with the contents of some Christmas gift packages of goodies we were having a high old time. We were all in this elevated state when one of the officers from the wing decided to make a little holiday visit. We could hardly restrain our glee as the officer and aides passed around the row of beds wishing each of us a happy holiday. We had a happy holiday all right but it wasn't because of the official visitors. The Christmas card that year on the base was a picture of a Flying Eight Ball and wishes for a Victorious New Year with the Morse code signal of the victory sign on it.

> **Technical Sergeant Forrest S. Clark,**
> **air gunner, 67th BS, 44th BG**

They came and collected us from our homes in ambulances and took us back to the hospital where we had a great time. We saw a film show and were given toys and sweets galore. (In Morley as elsewhere we were only allowed two ounces a week, we were rationed. But not here!) There was candy as the Yanks called it and gum by the yard. The toys were fun – some having been made by the wounded men, while they were convalescing. Then we had an enormous feed to end the party. We had fish, chips, meat, pickles, mince pies, Christmas pudding, crackers, and for drink it was either Coca-Cola (American only in those days) or cocoa. We were on rations at home. We thought we were in Canaan as it were, for it was certainly a place which flowed with milk and honey.

> **Derek Daniels, one of the local children who were**
> **entertained at a Christmas party in the Red Cross**
> **clubhouse at the 231st base hospital, Morley, near**
> **Wymondham, Norfolk, on 23 December 1944.**

Above: *'The Christmas card that year on the base was a picture of a Flying Eight Ball and wishes for a Victorious New Year with the Morse code signal of the victory sign on it.' Technical Sergeant Forrest S. Clark (MWB)*

Above: *Ghosts of Christmas past. (MWB)*

Below: *Childrens' Christmas party at Seething. (via Pat Everson)*

Christmas 1944 at Station 145, Rackheath, was the one I will never forget. It was a mixture of happy times for some, excitement for others and a very sad time for many. This was the best Christmas for the schoolchildren from Rackheath since the war started. In the morning they were thrilled to bits when they were all shown over the B-24 *Slick Chick*. This was followed by a tea party in the mess hall, with Spam and dried eggs, ice cream, candy bars, oranges, and chewing gum. What made it so special was the fact that it was the first oranges and ice

cream most of the children had ever seen, as the war had been on for almost five years. What made the ice cream so special was the fact that it had been taken up to 25,000 feet in the bomb bay of the B-24 *Wabbit* to keep it frozen until it was needed.

I felt rather envious at the time, missing out and having to go to work. The next day, 24 December, I was working at the timber yard next to Wroxham railway station with four more men, stacking and checking timber for the government stock used to build landing craft and RAF rescue launches which saved hundreds of RAF and USAAF aircrews who had ditched in the North Sea.

Long before I set off on my bike that morning, the noise of the B-24 ground crews pre-flighting and warming up engines had gone on much longer than normal. Arthur Harris had told the people that he would give Hitler and followers a good Christmas present. People were beginning to feel that the war was being won. Berlin had been bombed by 700 Halifax and Lancaster bombers the previous night, and the fires could be seen over one hundred miles away.

We had just started work when the 467th aircraft started their take-offs, using the main runway heading north, towards Cromer. First to appear was *Pete the POM*, followed by planes from Q2, 4Z, then from 6A and X7 squadrons. The planes came almost over the top of us and I would count them off in little blocks of five, like I had to count the timber.

This day I counted fifteen from each squadron, a total of sixty plus *Big Pete*. What a Christmas present for the Krauts, and icing on the cake for the 467th when they all returned safely to Rackheath. We finished work early that afternoon to start the Christmas holidays. As I cycled from Wroxham everything was still, apart from the hum of the pumps on the gas tankers and the strong smell of 100 octane petrol as they refuelled some of the B-24s ready for Christmas Day's mission.

I passed the Green Man pub and was almost home to my gran's when I heard the ping and clink of the tannoy system being turned on, then a voice wishing everybody a Merry Christmas, followed by Bing Crosby singing 'Silent Night'. As it echoed

around the hardstands and all the mess halls, living quarters, headquarters, Ops block, and hospital site a few seconds behind each other, it was the loveliest sound I have ever heard!

That Christmas lunchtime at Rackheath was very sad for my family; just Gran, Granddad, my uncle and myself. Dad was one of 600 who lost their lives when a U-boat sank their troop ship in April 1943. Mum was cook in a canteen at an aircraft factory at Coventry, and was killed when it was bombed as they were all at lunch on 12 April 1942, and my brother was prisoner in a Japanese camp when he was only eighteen years old. When the Australians were getting near the camp and the Japs knew they were losing the war, they smashed all the prisoners' kneecaps before they withdrew from the camp. He was in hospital in Hong Kong for three years, but sadly never made it home again. When he was found at the end of the war he only weighed 72 pounds.

Christmas Day was also a sad one for the 467th and by mid-afternoon the local people had noticed that three of the planes were missing from their hardstands. One of these was *Bold Venture III* that stood nearest Wroxham Road. Later it was known to have crashed on the Hereford and Wales border but no crewmembers were found. Much later some

of the crew got back to Rackheath after bailing out over France. After the pilots, engineer and radio operator had already left the plane over enemy territory, the Liberator was flown back to France on autopilot by the navigator and bombardier and then flew on to Wales where it crashed.

My gran did the laundry for two sergeant gunners from one of the other B-24s lost on Christmas Day. Gran had a little cry when the duty officer and an MP called to collect the laundry on 27 December.

Then came the 467th's saddest day of all. This was the morning of 29 December 1944. This was when four of the planes out of twelve were lost trying to take off in thick, freezing fog. We were unloading timber from the rail trucks at Wroxham station yard and everything was so still and covered with white, raw frost that sound carried that morning. We heard the first B-24 start its take-off and the noise of the engines got louder than normal and in the end they were whining and seemed to be pushed far beyond their safety limits. As it passed over us it was much lower than normal take-offs with white and purple flashes coming from the exhausts. We could barely see the numbers on the nose, as it seemed to part of the swirling fog. It was 161 Squadron code 6A. It had only just made it and

Above: *American personnel enjoying Christmas dinner. (via Pat Everson)*

old bike. He loved Coltishall down by the river, the Old Horstead water mill, and Woodbastwick with its little and very old thatched cottages. He said he would have liked to take one back to the States if he could have done so.

Fifteen-year-old Tommy Dungar

'One of my most poignant memories is of Christmas Eve 1944. The Germans permitted us to be out until 9 p.m. that night (normally we were locked up in our blocks at 6 p.m.). We were visiting back and forth, greeting our friends and wishing each other a Merry Christmas. We expressed our strong conviction (and ardent hope) that the Germans just could not hold out much longer. One memory in camp during the Yuletide season is the Kriegie parody on the song "I'll Be Home For Christmas".'

POW

'We won't be home for Christmas,
Don't depend on us.
We'll have snow
But no mistletoe
Or presents on the tree.
Christmas Eve will find us
Standing at appell,
We won't be home for Christmas,
We know that very well.'

must have been very low indeed as it passed over the first houses in Wroxham.

As the next B-24's engines got louder, there was a sharp crack like large branches of a tree breaking off, followed by a loud bump. This was followed by sets of small explosions as flares and ammo went of. We could hear the engines of another B-24 starting its take-off and at the same time there were about six to eight loud explosions all in a matter of seconds; one single and deafening explosion that seemed to be in the air; and at almost the same time, a lot of thuds and crunching sounds. The second B-24, *Topper II*, exploded in the air as it passed over the first crashed B-24 whose bombs exploded. It was blown to pieces in the air and the wreckage fell almost on top of the first crashed B-24. The tail section and part of the waist area of the first B-24 broke off as the plane hit the trees. A gunner survived and staggered along the rail line and back to the base.

My gran had done the laundry for one gunner killed at Wroxham that fateful morning. He would have been twenty-two the next day and his wife was expecting their second child any day. I remember he had shown Gran photos of her and their little girl. I think he came from Arkansas. He was a man who loved the countryside and he often borrowed my

It seemed that the war might be over by Christmas. Then came a shock. On 16 December 1944 German panzer divisions punched a hole in the American lines in the Ardennes. In East Anglia, the bombers, grounded by fog, were unable to intervene fully. Finally, on Christmas Eve 1944, a record 2,034 bombers and 500 RAF and 9th AF bombers, took part in the largest single strike flown by the Allied Air Forces of the war, against German airfields and lines of communication leading to the 'Bulge'.

12/31/44 ... New Year's Eve and still in England, Honey. I had hoped by now to be nearly through and on the way home to you, but it looks like luck's against it. It's hard to realize that 1945 is nearly

This panel:
Christmas cards for the servicemen. (via Truett Woodall)

here and that time has passed so rapidly – and yet so slowly. Looking back, a lot has happened, hasn't it? Just a year ago tonight we went to a show after getting out of a very crowded officer's club, and at midnight I kissed my wife and we wished each other the best. I'd give everything to be able to do that again this evening, but I'll do the next best thing and say, Happy New Year, Sweetheart. If only you could enjoy London with me ... not much fun alone.

Captain Ralph H. Elliott, pilot, 467th BG

Below: *93rd BG B-24 Liberators on a mission on Christmas Eve 1944. (USAF)*

Left: *S/Sgt. Maynard 'Snuffy' Smith MoH and his English bride, Mary Rayner, emerge from the Harpur Street Register Office in Bedford. (via Richards)*

Romantic Interludes

'Her mother never told her
The things a young girl should know.
About the ways of air force men.
And how they come and go.
Now age has taken her beauty.
And sin has left it's sad scar,
So remember your mothers and sisters,
Boys
And let her sleep under the bar.

You are their love, their life, their all,
And for your mother they would fall.
They'll love you dearly, 'till death do part,
If you leave them, you'll break their heart.
And they leave you broken hearted,
The camp has moved, your love departed,
You wait for mail that doesn't come,
Then you realize you're awfully dumb

In a different town, in a different place,
To a different girl, with a different face,
'I love you darling, please be mine'
It's the same old Yank with the same old line.'

'The GIs', by a WAAF at Shipdham

Left: *Silk handkerchiefs embroidered with the AAF badge. (via Richards)*

WITH THE REAR OF THE FORTRESS AN INFERNO, MEN BEGAN BAILING OUT.

AFTER GIVING MORPHIA TO THE BADLY-WOUNDED TAIL GUNNER..

SOMEONE'S GOT TO KEEP THESE GUNS SHOOTING!

UNAWARE OF THE DRAMA IN THE REAR OF THE PLANE, PILOT LIEUTENANT JOHNSON BROUGHT THE CRIPPLED SHIP DOWN.

CHIEFLY RESPONSIBLE FOR SAVING THE PLANE AND THE LIVES OF EVERYONE ABOARD, SERGEANT SMITH HAS BEEN RECOMMENDED FOR THE CONGRESSIONAL MEDAL OF HONOR.

Left: *Comic strip in the Sunday 25 July 1943 edition of the Washington Sunday Star showing 'Snuffy' Smith's heroism in the air on 1 May 1944 during the mission to St. Nazaire. Lt. Lewis P. Johnson Jr.'s aircraft was hit several times, and it caught fire in the radio compartment and in the tail area. Smith, the ball turret gunner, who was on his first mission, hand-cranked his turret to get it back into the aircraft. He climbed out and discovered that the waist gunners and the radio operator had baled out. Smith remained in the aircraft and fought the fire with a hand extinguisher. The Fortress did not show any signs of leaving formation, so Smith assumed the pilots were still on board and went to treat the badly wounded tail gunner. Then he jettisoned the oxygen bottles and ammunition in the radio compartment, manned the waist guns during an attack by enemy fighters, stopping to dampen down the fires and treat the tail gunner. Johnson put the B-17 down at Predannack, near Land's End, after Smith had thrown out all expendable equipment. He was the first Enlisted man to receive the Medal of Honor. (Anona Moeser via Richards)*

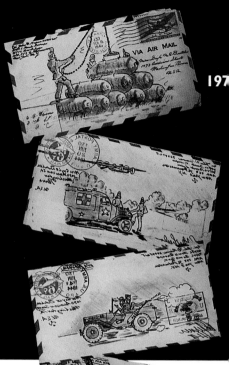

While I was waiting for the time for my first mission as pilot in command I had additional duties as mail censor. The enlisted men had their mail censored by officers, who looked for information that the enemy might use in case the letters were intercepted, or went to a talkative friend or relative in the States. The letters had to be written on one side of the paper so that offending words or confidential matters discussed in the letter might be cut out. There were a few high spots in this duty, as some of the letters were very entertaining. The best one was from a Lothario who wrote a very passionate love letter to a girl in the States. I had nothing to censor, so I picked up his next letter, which was almost identical to the first, but addressed, to another girl. And then a third, which was identical to the other two, but addressed to a third girl.

An evil thought passed through my mind. 'Suppose I accidentally put the letters in the wrong envelopes, and sent them on to the States? Nah.'

Second Lieutenant Richard 'Dick' Johnson, pilot, 303rd BG, Molesworth

V-MAIL (V STANDS FOR VICTORY)

Mail was very important to the morale of the soldiers at the front and the people at home. While people used their own envelopes and writing paper, many also used V-Mail. This was a way the Post Office cut down the weight and number of mailbags. Here's how it worked: a V-Mail blank was obtained at any post office. The blank was a piece of paper measuring 9.5 x 11 inches. After writing a letter on this, it could then be mailed free to a serviceman.

This letter had to pass through the military censors, who read it and blacked out any parts that they felt should be kept secret. After they had finished, the letter would be stamped and sent to be photocopied onto tiny film. This film was then sent overseas. The original letter would later be destroyed. When this film containing letters arrived near its destination, it was enlarged back to full size by special machines. Now it could be delivered. Mail coming into and going out of the country was censored. Servicemen and women also used V-Mail when writing from overseas.

Above: *Letters home from Jack Krause, a ground crewman in the 458th BG, to his fiancée, Gail, with cartoons on the envelopes drawn by a base artist. (Jack Krause)*

Below: *Joe Micksch (392nd BG, Wendling) and Elia May on their wedding day in Cleveland, Ohio, 20 August 1942.*

Life was good for a while, but then the 'Dear John' letters started arriving, from wives who had got tired of waiting. Of thirty-six men in my barracks, fourteen received 'Dear Johns.' I was lucky in a way. I had no children but the older men had the pictures of their children by their bunks, and they lived for daily mail-call. We all survived by helping each other (there were some that didn't survive, they were not in our barracks). Mostly we got each of the fellows to go to London or Norwich. After meeting some of the English people it helped change their feelings.

Right: *'Every day they seemed prettier and there weren't only a few that one might marry – and did.' Allan Healy, 467th BG (MWB)*

Mel Bourne, a 'ground-pounder' at Old Buckenham, December 1943 – June 1945, got his 'Dear John' letter on Thanksgiving Day 1944. He and his best friend, Bill Schlacher, cheered themselves up by going absent without leave on their days off to visit a couple they knew in Luton, scrounging food from the mess hall to supplement their host's meagre wartime rations. The couple called their first child Ian Melvin, after him.

Below: *Cartoon on a wall, now demolished, at Mendlesham, in 1972. (MWB)*

'It did not take long to meet girls. You met them at the Cottage, a pub, or the Samson and Hercules called the 'Muscle Palace'. They were brought in truckloads to our monthly dances. They gave us a royal welcome. We learned not to judge them by their clothes, for these were shabby to us, nor by beauty – drugstore or otherwise. Every day they seemed prettier and there weren't only a few that one might marry – and did.'

The 467th Bombardment Group, **Allan Healy**

The English look like they hadn't had any new clothes for years. For the most part their features [English girls] are coarse and they know little about using cosmetics. I've yet to see a really neat hair-do. Most of them have ruddy or reddish complexions and there are few neatly dressed women. Their legs (no stockings, but cotton) are usually dirty and very muscular, from so much walking I suppose, but a shapely leg is uncommon. Their shoes are usually low heeled but not well kept. So you see quite a poor description of English women and the boys agree. The war has been partly responsible but not entirely by all means ... R.

Captain Ralph H. Elliott, pilot, 467th BG, Rackheath, in a letter home to his wife Vonny

DELECTABLE DORIS

We passed through the park at Norwich – the one with the balloon barrage anchored in it. Standing under the balloon, I asked Doris, 'What would you say if I asked you to marry me?' I found out later this was not the first time she had heard this line. She had the answer ready,

'I hadn't given it any thought. I don't know.'

I persisted. 'Well, you'd better think of an answer, I just asked you.' She took it as a joke. After all, we Yanks had our reputation, and we had only just met! As soon as I could arrange a head cold, I got grounded and another three-day pass. Off to London. To Eltham Well Hall and a meeting with her parents. They invited me to stay with them, and I gladly accepted. I had brought some rations from the base, and they were most welcome – as was I.

Next morning I dragged Doris, and her companion, Pamela (I really think she was a pre-arranged chaperon) to London: to Goldsmiths and Silversmiths, Regent Street, by appointment to the Queen. Doris almost broke off the engagement before it began. She finally was persuaded to accept my ring. Really, the one she chose was more like a friendship ring than an engagement ring. Pam confided, 'Birdie (her nickname) will never marry you. Don't let it break your heart.'

I hung tough. When we got back, I told her parents that I needed letters from them and Doris, in accordance with army rules and regulations, stating that she was free and unencumbered, and willing to marry me, and that neither she nor they expected any privileges resulting from such a union. That she would not obtain US citizenship by virtue of it, nor any of the expenses of transport to the US to be an obligation of the army of the United States. It was beginning to be less of a joke to Doris now.

Bill Graff, pilot, 389th BG, Hethel

Doreen Ivy Seabourn was brought up in Belvoir Street, Norwich. After leaving the Model School on Dereham Road nearby, she worked at Harmers shoe factory and then at the post office. Later she went to Luton on war work. During a weekend leave to Norwich in October 1943 she went to the Odeon cinema and was offered a cigarette by an American, Charles Holston, a cook in the 44th BG at Shipdham, who was sitting next to her. As she didn't smoke, Ivy pretended to smoke it. Charles and Ivy arranged to meet later outside the post office but there were dozens of Americans there in the blackout. Ivy says, 'It was hard to see. I said, "Is that you?"'. Ivy and Charles corresponded and met in London or Norwich when they could get leave. Charles, who worked twenty-four hours on, forty-eight hours off, would cycle the 18 miles from Shipdham to Norwich. 'The first day I thought I'd never get there,' he recalls, 'but each day it got shorter'.

Ivy Seabourn and Charles Holston married on 20 May 1944 at St Philip's Church, Heigham Road. A year later their eldest daughter was born in Thorpe Nursing Home three days before VE Day. Six weeks later Charles returned to the States and Ivy, with baby Diane, followed on the *Queen Mary* in February 1946.

Below: *Ivy Seabourn and Charles Holston on their wedding day, 20 May, 1944. (Holston)*

I met my husband-to-be, Corporal Herman Canfield (later sergeant) of the 577th Squadron, 392nd BG, in May 1944 at a friend's home at Crane's Corner near Wendling. He'd arrived in November 1943 and was a clerk in the Group Operations office where his work included the scheduling of practice missions over The Wash, North Sea, and eastern England for the flight crews. When we got engaged in August 1944, we immediately began the necessary procedures to obtain permission to marry. He had to write a letter to the chaplain at the base, giving my reasons for wanting to get married and that I was single, of good character, etc. My aunt, who was responsible for my upbringing after I'd lost my mother when I was four years old, was also required to write, confirming her approval and giving her permission. Herman had to go for a personal interview with the 392nd Group base chaplain: Why did he want to marry? Was he being coerced in any way? How long had he known me, etc, etc. Then began the waiting while Herman's record was investigated to see if he really was single or married or divorced, etc. We went ahead and planned our wedding for early December, as we knew it would take some time for official permission to filter through. Our banns were published in the local paper and we made all the necessary arrangements with the vicar and the

Below: With the war coming to its conclusion, spring romances flourished and many a village church near the fighter and bomber bases witnessed weddings between GIs and English girls. Servicemen had to seek the approval of their commanding officers two months in advance of a proposed wedding. By October 1943 some 60,000 GI brides were still waiting to be transported to the States. (via Richards)

WANDERING WANDA AND IRIS

Wandering Wanda led a charmed life. She completed 117 air combat bombing missions. She always came back. A solemn tribute to the dedicated ground crew who gave her tender, loving care and to the Power who was with her on each mission she flew. Henry Barker was *Wandering Wanda's* co-pilot, at Old Buckenham, the 453rd BG base, flying Liberators. His crew had some close calls. On Henry's first mission the B-24 on their left wing was shot down by an Me 163 Komet rocket aircraft. On a subsequent mission, he saw three bombers in the lead squadron just ahead shot down in a matter of seconds by two Me 262s. The Luftwaffe jets took out the lead and deputy lead crews on that attack. On another mission his crew had to fly back to England alone after being hit by flak in the No. 3 engine, rendering their aircraft unable to keep up with the formation.

After flying a number of missions, Hank Barker got a 48-hour pass and while at a dance at London's Covent Garden one evening met an attractive English girl, Iris Borrett. She was a great dancer with a sparkling personality and was a WAAF in Air Intelligence at RAF Headquarters. Hank and Iris became close friends. While they dated in London she told him that she had been seeing an RCAF Hurricane pilot, who she knew had been shot down in combat over the continent. Iris would on occasion come up to Hank's base for social events there, and she would take him on tours of London during several of his London '48s'. They saw the sights, went to dances and even went

sexton of my local church. In mid-November, permission was granted and we were married on 2 December 1944.

Nora Norgate, eighteen-year-old English girl who married Herman Canfield. Nora and Ivy Seabourn both lived on Belvoir Street and Nora borrowed Ivy's wedding dress to wear. Nora and Ivy went to London together to register at the American Embassy. Nora also called Shipdham to tell Charles

By 1942, the Americans had arrived and Bedford became a very lively town to live in. Most of the local boys, including my brother Tony and his best friend, Curly Fensome, were soon called up for active service in the forces.

I had been sorting out dividend cheques all day and by 5.30 p.m. I was more than ready to go home. We were always rushed off our feet to get those cheques ready for the Bedford Co-op members to pick up on divi day. They looked forward to it all through the year and by 9 a.m. we knew they would be queuing in their hundreds all the way down the stairs and out along Midland Road.

Above: *453rd BG pilot Hank Barker and attractive English girl Iris Borrett, at Old Buckenham. (via Pat Ramm)*

row boating on one of London's park lakes.

After VE Day they parted. *Wandering Wanda* was flown back to the United States. Iris rejoined her Canadian boyfriend after he returned to England, having survived his bailout and imprisonment as a POW. They were later married and had two sons. Henry met his late wife, Marilyn Ackerson, shortly after the war. They were married for forty-eight years and raised their three children in Knoxville, Tennessee. Hank and Iris still correspond, exchanging Christmas cards each year.

Holston he had a daughter. When the war was finally over in 1945 she was given permission by the manager of her office to go to the train platform and say goodbye to Herman, who that July, was returning to America. It was a very emotional parting, as they really had no idea when they would see each other again. They began their lives together eight months later when Nora arrived in America.

I was in a tearing hurry that evening. I ran headlong down the steep office stairs and out through the big street door to bump straight into the tall, khaki-clad figure of a GI.

'Well hello there!' he said as he put out an arm to steady me in my rush to collect my old bicycle from the back of the building. 'Where are you going in such a hurry?'

I blushed and when I looked up into the young GI's amused eyes, I knew that this was the start of something which I would remember for the rest of my life. It was the feeling that we all had during the war, that we had to live every day to the full while there was time because time could suddenly run out without warning.

Burnell Hoffacer was only nineteen years old. We walked back to my parents' home at 43 Dents Road together that late afternoon pushing my bike between us over the town bridge, along St Mary's and St John's Streets and finally over London Road bridge before turning into Dents Road. My head was in the clouds every step of the way. I was really smitten and I stayed that way for the next two-and-a-half years.

When he wasn't on duty Burnell, who was a gunner on a B-17, spent his time with me. He

Above: *Lt. Romsca, mess officer, 392nd BG, and lady friend in Weasenham woods near Wendling, Norfolk in 1944. (Joe Micksch via Ben Jones)*

(MWB)

Below: *Unrequited love in wartime – Burnell Hoffacer and Jean Harpur. (via Richards)*

think, 'Well he's a gunner; will he be here tomorrow? Will we be doing this tomorrow?'

Every night we used to say goodbye because you never knew what was going to happen the next day. We sat in a pub one night and he said, 'I'll come back for you in five years time.'

I said, 'Five years is a very long time.'

He said, 'I will be back for you because I love you.'

Burnell, who came from a large family back in the States, told me he had nothing to offer me then. I am certain he meant it at the time, but he never made it back across the Atlantic once he left the army.

always treated me with great respect and was a real gentleman. Dad, in his turn, treated him like another son and liked to polish his service shoes along with the rest of the family's early on the morning of his visits. We walked our feet off all along the river in Bedford and in the evenings there was a choice of four cinemas to visit locally where we sat in the back stalls and watched black and white American movies. I thought they were marvellous!

We went to the Corn Exchange where Glenn Miller used to play. We loved going to the pictures and dancing and we went frequently. I spent two days in London with him. We stayed the night together at the Red Cross. We managed to get a room. We went sightseeing. We went to the Windmill Theatre; 'the theatre that never closed.' Then there was dancing at Hammersmith Palais where I learned to jitterbug with the best of them, and the Lyceum. We danced, and danced, and danced.

'Every time we say Goodbye' will always be a memory for me, particularly in London, where it was played quite a lot. You'd look at your GI and

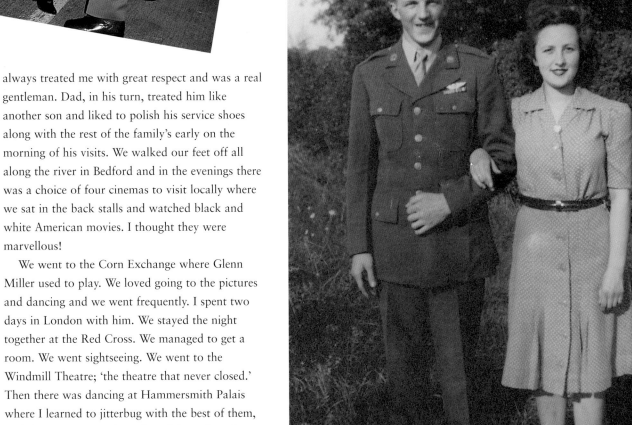

On VE night, when war was declared over, we stood on the town bridge with our arms round each other. Everyone was cheering. There were balloons. There were fireworks. At that moment it never entered my head that he'd go.

Soon after he came over to our house. I sat outside while he went straight in and spoke to my mum and dad. Then my sister came out and she sat down next to me. I said, 'What's the matter?'

She said, 'Well, you've got to be very, very brave.'

I asked, 'Why?'

She said, 'Burnell's going home tomorrow.'

I broke down.

He said, 'I will come back for you.'

I watched him walk away along Dents Road. He turned right but he never looked back.

Jean Harpur. On 24 February 1951 she married Curly Fensome at St John's church in Bedford, but, like many girls at that time, had to learn to put her wartime romance behind her. But in all the years she never quite forgot her GI.

Barbara lived with her family in Stratford Drive, Norwich. She went to the Notre Dame School and then worked in the education department of the County Council. Wally, a GI in the 96th BG at Snetterton Heath, and Barbara, met at an American Red Cross dance on 26 January 1944 at the Stuart Hall, Norwich. Barbara recalls, 'US servicemen could come to the Bishop's Palace, adjoining the cathedral, where the Red Cross had a place for them to sleep when on leave … I remember especially the band playing 'Paper Doll', originally by the Mills Brothers. We used to go to the Samson and Hercules ballroom and also the Lido on dates. Eventually I was called up and worked in the Foreign Office at Bletchley for a year until the end of the European war. I was billeted with families in Bedford. When on leave, I rode the train to Cambridge and Norwich. Wally would visit me in Bedford whenever he had leave. Whenever I was walking in Bedford, I can remember hearing Glenn Miller's orchestra playing for servicemen in one of the halls.

Barbara Woods and Wallace Porter married at St Stephen's Church on 3 August 1945. After their wedding and a reception in the restaurant at the Haymarket cinema they went to the Regent Palace Hotel in London for their honeymoon. While they were there, 5 August, the atomic bomb was dropped on Japan. Barbara followed Wally to the States in February 1946.

Above: *GI Wallace Porter and English girl Barbara Woods on their wedding day in 1945. (Wallace and Barbara Porter)*

Above: *Broken bridge across the Rhine during a 'Trolly' mission in May 1945. (Joe Micksch via Ben Jones)*

Right: *Wrecked house and shop in Germany at the end of the war. (Joe Micksch via Ben Jones)*

Below: *Duisburg Bahnhof (railway station) at the end of the war. (Joe Micksch via Ben Jones)*

Happy Days Ahead

'So here's to happy days ahead,
When you and I are free.
To look back on this interlude
And call it history.'

J. B. Boyle

We were convinced that nothing could be changed about the outcome of the war. The war was completely lost ... we knew it could only take a few more days. On the other hand, we had the most advanced, far superior aircraft ... the first operational jet. We saw that the German population had to suffer under horrifying attacks without any hope day and night. Having the best fighters in the world ready to take off we couldn't sit down and tell the people, no ... we won't take off any more because the war is lost. It was a moral question for us. We had to go into combat.

Above: *GIs among the ruins of a German city. (Joe Micksch via Ben Jones)*

Generalmajor Adolf Galland, CO, *Jagdverbande 44*, equipped with Me 262s. During the week 18–25 April 1945, missions were briefed and scrubbed almost simultaneously. The end came on 25 April when the 8th Air Force flew its last full-scale mission of the war. B-17s bombed the Skoda armaments factory at Pilsen and Liberators hit four rail complexes surrounding Hitler's mountain retreat at Berchtesgaden. On 26 April fighters destroyed a record 747 German fighters on the ground in one day. During April, 8th Air Force fighters attacked over forty Luftwaffe installations in Germany and Czechoslovakia. The Germans in Italy surrendered on 29 April, and on 7 May Germany unconditionally surrendered to the Allies. 8 May 1945 was VE (Victory in Europe) Day.

Left: *Lt. Chamberlain's crew and B-17* Leading Lady *in the 364th BS, 305th BG at Chelveston on 8 July 1944. This aircraft survived the war and on 20 May 1945 was transferred to the 401st BG at Deenthorpe. (USAF via Bill Donald)*

Above: *Corporal Herman Canfield of the 392nd BG and English girl Nora Norgate married in December 1944. While many GI marriages failed due to homesickness and cultural reasons, for them it was 'happy days ahead' and their fifty-eight years of married life have produced five sons and seven grandchildren. (Nora Canfield)*

'Get a load of those guys, high in the skies,
Winging to victory,
Up and at 'em in the fight for,
People like you and me ...'
'People Like You and Me', Mack Cordon and Harry Warren ©1942

All wars are senseless and yet, World War II was unavoidable. We had gained victory, not necessarily through superior intellect, but rather through the will to win and the belief that we were in the right. Like all human endeavors, we were fraught with frustration and at times, saddled with stupidity, but the love of man and the love of our country brought forth accomplishments and sacrifices beyond man's own comprehension.

The 100th BG was known throughout the land not because we were superhuman but rather because we were human. Our fame and notoriety spread not just because of Regensburg or Berlin or the Russian mission, but also because of our losses, and yes, even because of our 'faux pas'. We were famous and to some of the new flyers, infamous, both for what we did and what we gave. Mighty as we were with our seventy to eighty bombers and our 4,000 men, we were but a small fraction of the total force ultimately applied against the Axis powers. We contributed our part and it was our knowledge and belief that others were making an even greater sacrifice that assured us of ultimate victory.

Bill Carleton, engineering officer,
351st BS, 100th BG

'There was never a good war or a bad peace.'

Benjamin Franklin

Vonny:

I've been on a tour today that beats nearly anything I've ever seen. We flew a low-altitude sightseeing mission using a five-man crew and carrying ten ground men as passengers. The weather was beautiful over the continent ... We made landfall at Ostend, went over Brussels and down to Frankfurt. It's on the Rhine River and of course all the bridges had been blown or bombed out. We made a circle north and back to Frankfurt and then headed up the Rhine. All of the towns were bombed beyond belief. From Frankfurt we went past Mainz and Wiesbaden, then up to Bingen where the Rhine turns north, from there up to Koblenz ... I flew about 100 feet over the famous Remagen Bridge where our troops first crossed the Rhine. It gave me a funny feeling to see the American flag flying over the bridge. From there we continued up to Bonn and then Cologne which is undoubtedly the worst-bombed large city in Germany. The big cathedral, which is so often pictured, stood out like a mountain among the rubble and mess all around it ... We landed back here at base at 8 p.m. and were all agreed that the trip could never be duplicated for any amount of money. Coming on the eve of the war's end tomorrow, it's made a rather remarkable end to what has been a hectic ten months for the crew and me. When I once bombed places like that I never expected to 'tour' the same area someday. I'm glad it's over, to put it mildly, Vonny. It's a wonderful feeling.

Your loving husband, Ralph.

Captain Ralph H. Elliott, pilot, 467th BG, Trolley Mission, 7 May 1945

8 MAY 1945 – VE DAY!

'I cried as they fired flares and rockets to celebrate VE Day. My mother explained they were so happy to be going home. After the war, the base was used to store bombs, and in my teens, I went on the runway to pick cowslips. The runways stretched out into the distance, so empty yet so full … I swore out loud that I would never forget them.'

> **Pat Everson, twelve-year-old Norfolk schoolgirl. She has never forgotten 'her' Americans. Pat has had a leading role in the Station 146 Tower Association, which has restored the control tower at Seething. Her collection of memorabilia is popular with American and English veterans alike.**

'There'll be love and laughter, and peace ever after
Tomorrow when the world is free.
The shepherd will tend his sheep,
The valley will bloom again,
And Jimmy will go to sleep
In his own little room again.
There'll be bluebirds over the white Cliffs of Dover,
Tomorrow, just you wait and see.'
'The White Cliffs of Dover'
famously sung by Vera Lynn

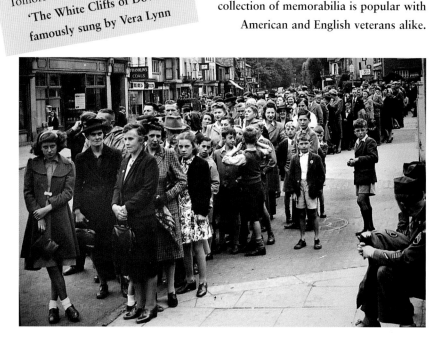

Above: *Children wait in lines in a Bedford street at the end of the war to board trucks to take them to a party at Thurleigh. (via Richards)*

We went to work as usual that morning, but as soon as the joyous news came through on the wireless that the war in Europe was finally over, we all left the office and went home to prepare for the celebrations. Everyone was so very happy at the almost unbelievable and momentous news. People were clambering on cars, lorries and buses, singing such wartime songs as 'We'll Meet Again', 'Bless 'em All', 'Lili Marlene' etcetera. Everyone letting themselves enjoy the moment which we'd all been hoping and praying for for almost six long years of war with its deprivations, heartache and suffering. Herman, my GI

husband, came over that night from Wendling and saw all the lights switched on in Norwich for the first time. All the principal buildings, County Hall, the big department stores, etc, were floodlit and searchlights swept the night sky, showing the 'V for Victory' sign. There were bonfires and fireworks displays all over the city in joyful celebrations, which continued during the following day and night. We all realized however, that although the war was finally over for us, there was still fighting, dying and much suffering in the Pacific theatre. In fact, when the GIs left Wendling in June and July 1945 they all thought that after a brief rest in America, they would probably go to the Pacific because we had no idea when that conflict would end. Little did we know that it would end, quite suddenly and terrifyingly, with the dropping of the two atomic bombs on Hiroshima and Nagasaki in August 1945. In addition to saving an estimated one million Allied casualties, the bombs also undoubtedly saved several million Japanese casualties, from battle, starvation, disease, epidemics etc, if the planned invasion of the Japanese mainland had taken place. I arrived in America by ship in late February 1946, and joined Herman at his home in Bloomingdale, In., after a lengthy train journey from New York. What impressed me most of all was the vast size of the United States compared to England.

Nora Norgate Canfield

'The only Yanks to leave 3rd SAD on VE Day was a group of four of us (Base Ordnance personnel) that the base CO directed to go to the bomb dump to get suitable fireworks. That we did, and had a huge blast that night! I'll never forget that trip to Elveden Hall area. The road was filled with men and women celebrating, and they would dash up to our jeep to kiss us, etc. Like to have not made it back home! You'll never believe the offers we had that day! And I am not talking about the fine wine and Scotch they so generously supplied!'

Technical Sergeant Wiley S. Noble, 31st HQ & HQ Sqn, assigned to Base Ordnance at Watton-Griston

Returning to home base, Wendling, the squadron commander told us to go on leave for about two weeks and then phone in to see if orders had been cut sending us stateside. It was early May and the war in Europe had not ended. We knew the normal routine was to be sent stateside for a thirty-day leave and then processed for another tour off in the south Pacific. Knowing this, Fergie and I went to London, our favourite town ... Dinner at the private Exhibition Club with drinking, dancing, and carousing until well into the night came after the show. Being a private club, it could stay open until 2 a.m. with continuous entertainment on three floors. VE (Victory in Europe) Day did occur during this time. London went wild and we partied for several days and nights. Lights came on and thankful prayers were said.

'Goodbye G.I., Bud. Now you know the way Come back and see us in a brighter day. When England's free and the Scotch is cheap but strong, And you can bring your pretty wives along.'
A. P. Herbert, the famous English historian, for the closing of the American Red Cross club in London in 1945

Below: *'Cheerio Yanks!' Locals wave goodbye to the crew of Alice Blue Gown of the 851st BS, 490th BG, at Eye, 8 July 1945. (via Eric Swain)*

Above: *VE Day fireworks (via Pat Everson)*

After ten days of the good life in London, I phoned the base and orders had been cut returning us to the ZOI (Zone of the Interior). Back to Wendling, we went to prepare to go home.

Robert H. Tays, pilot, 392nd BG

With most of the German armies surrendered it will really be over soon. We're DONE combat flying, Vonny, so you don't need to worry about that any longer. With twenty-six missions I have a tour in, so you needn't worry either about my going to the South Pacific. I have no idea of the job I'll get, but as long as we're together it won't matter. I've waited a long time to tell you we're through, darling, and how good it seems to be able to. I wish we could have gotten in four more but then it doesn't matter. Most of these last ones have been milk runs in a way, and we've seen a lot to remember. It's going to be fun telling you about it. That will take twenty-five years at least ... It's getting a bit warmer here now, but it rains about ten times a day, off and on. What a country!

You asked about coming over after the war is over ... I don't think I'll ever want to come back. I've seen a lot and of course wartime England isn't at it's best, but there's 'no place like home' and I do mean it. So I think your idea of Bermuda sounds OK ... or just a cabin up among the pines and lakes ...

Captain Ralph H. Elliott, pilot, 467th BG, letter to his wife Vonny, May 1945. (They did visit England after the war.)

HOW I SWAPPED WAR STORIES WITH JIMMY STEWART

We were on a bus riding through the English countryside headed for an American cemetery near Cambridge. We had a special passenger that day on the bus, one whom I had seen many times before, but not in this environment. That passenger was Jimmy Stewart, who was sitting with his lovely wife up front. I was seated about ten rows back. I had seen Stewart years before in *Mr Smith Goes to Washington* and others of his famous films, but I had only heard of his wartime experience. Here on this bus on a cold, damp English day I got a real close-up of him. We talked briefly and he asked me what group I was in during the war. When I said the 44th BG he replied, 'Oh, you mean the Eight Balls.' He knew that much about my group and I admired him for remembering.

As we got off the bus at Madingley Cemetery we walked toward the memorial flagpole area where a great many memorial wreaths and various 8th Air Force groups including Stewart's group had placed tributes. What I recall most about Stewart was his tall, angular frame and his kindly face, but even more impressive was the manner in which he spoke. It appeared to be at that time as a softly American voice shadowed by the most peaceful kind of intonations. He spoke like a kindly uncle would to everyone. He walked tall and straight with the particular gait and posture so familiar to movie goers the world over. I remember how he stood with his head bared to the cool English breeze from the nearby fens. He stood before the memorial and spoke quietly yet eloquently about the sacrifices of the thousands of American men who lay at rest beneath the white crosses all about us. He spoke lovingly of past times and youth, when all of us were virile and passionate, as he was in that time fifty years ago. He gave the memorial tribute that day. Afterward I walked silently and alone to the grooviest of one of my fallen comrades, Lieutenant David Edmonds, and I saw afar off the tall figure of Jimmy Stewart, linking us all and linking me to this past and to my fallen comrade.

Edmonds was a graduate of the Valley Forge Military Academy and was brought up by a prominent Pennsylvania family in the Philadelphia area. He was tall, good looking and had a moustache, making him look exactly like an RAF pilot. He was our bombardier but he loved to go pub crawling so much that often we had to sober him up by putting him into a cold shower. Before one mission he was missing and found unconscious along the roadside where his bike had cracked up on his way back from a pub. But despite all this Edmonds went

Above: *Madingley Cemetery. (MWB)*

on flying missions until on Friedrichshafen in March 1944, the B-24 he was on with Lieutenant Scarborough's crew crashed at Woodchurch on return. He had made his final mission and is buried in Madingley.

Later that night at a crowded reception in the guildhall of that ancient medieval city of Norwich, Stewart could be picked out of the crowd, towering above all others amid the glitter of bedecked officials and veterans of the air war. Stewart told of one day when he and another command pilot decided to buzz the group commander's living quarters at their base. They tried to awaken the commander from his usual nap. Stewart still chuckled over that episode of youthful exuberance and joy. We all told our favorite war stories that day. I think Stewart proved once again how close he was and how close he remains to his comrades of WWII. It was like flying again in the same formation. All considered it to be an honor. Keep 'em flying, Jimmy!

Technical Sergeant Forrest S. Clark, air gunner, 67th BS, 44th BG

My mother wrote to me that my cousin, Billy Elliott, also a radio-operator, was killed on 13 July in a crash landing of a B-24. He was in the 491st BG in the Second Air Divison. We had grown up together, lived across the street from each other when small, and later attended high school together. In my scrapbook I have the last letter he wrote. Dated 1 July 1944, and written to our aunt, it was written thirteen days before he died. He said, 'After this war, I am going to spend the rest of my life resting. Remember how lazy we used to be – well, you haven't seen nothing yet.' They had been flying continuously.

… Billy and his friends were buried in the beautiful American Cemetery at Cambridge where 3800 Americans, almost all of them airmen, sleep the sleep of heroes.

Chick's Crew, 'Billy's Death', Ben C. Smith. Solon 'Billy' Elliott was killed on 13 July 1944 when *Delirious Dolores*, flown by Second Lieutenant Max R. Shea, was lost returning from a mission to Saarbrucken. The B-24 Liberator which had two engines feathered, clipped the tops of trees and crashed in a field at Morningthorpe near Hardwick airfield and caught fire. Elliott, Shea and three others died in the crash.

THEY CAME TO MADINGLEY

It chanced I wandered Hardwick way
From Cambridge on a sunny day,
By pleasant lanes in early May
And here I parked, an hour to stay,
Then o'er the trees against the sky
I saw Old Glory flying high
And remembered nearby lay
War Dead of the USA.

It was Madingley I'd chose to stay
Where often aged couples stray
From several thousand miles away
And at a grave to stand and pray;
Maybe o'er their only son
And clasp the medal that he won
As he was on his fateful way
To come to Madingley to stay.

He may have come from Santa Fe,
He may have known the Great White Way,
Some came who knew Pacific spray
Blowing in from 'Frisco Bay
They came from North, East, South and West
Certain their own state was best;
Reckless too with love or pay
Then came to Madingley to stay.

By various paths they made their way
To come to Madingley to stay,
Some bombed Schweinfurt in the day
And, in air-combat's lethal fray
A bullet does not ask what race,
Not even colour of a face
And some could fall to friendly stray
Then come to Madingley to stay.

And these at Madingley do stay
Are very much the same as they
Our Brits: in France or in Malay,
And Senseless slaughter some may say
But such are easy words to speak
For Belsen's chimney ceased to reek
Due to young men such as they
Who came to Madingley to stay.

Oh do not let the Dead March play
O'er these at Madingley do stay
For they were young and old-style gay,
Play their music of the day;
Tunes of Dorsey, songs of Bing,
Let them hear Glenn Miller's swing
Then too the crosses well may sway
With those at Madingley do stay.

Although, in truth, those boys don't stay
I've 'Knowledge' and I hereby say
The empty bodies are not They
Below in that cold Cambridge clay;
Such happy souls don't stick around
In that well-tailored burial ground
But you be sure they see you pray
And pray for you, as you for they.

Jasper Miles

'The atmosphere was ghostly, building doors left open, some furniture still left in situation, curtains blowing in the wind, ashes in the tortoise stoves. Magazines on the floor, roadways deserted, the hospital empty; nothing remained alive ... Daily we visited our old haunts, the control tower, the fire station, where a few weeks earlier we had enjoyed coffee and eggs. All was silent. We walked the whole airfield hoping we were wrong; they would be back. Alas, it was not to be. Realization eventually came but still we visited our beloved Thorpe Abbotts.'

Billy Taylor, Suffolk schoolboy

When the Americans went home we spent many weekends and school holidays playing on the deserted base. It was like a ghost town. However, it wasn't long before some of the buildings were in use again. The old briefing building was opened as a village cinema, where we spent many enjoyable evenings watching westerns. After I left school I worked for Corbatch Canners whose factory was at communal site No. 4., which included the former American Red Cross building. In 1945 we moved into the former officer's club building, our home for the next eight years. This building still stands and there are murals, which remain to this day.

John Gilbert, Norfolk schoolboy

Above: *Ground Officers' Mess at Wendling in 1944. This building, which is still in use today, contains the B-24 silhouettes and eagle and is the same building occupied by the Gilbert family who were bombed out in Norwich during the Baedeker Blitz. (Joe Micksch via Ben Jones)*

'The big airbases, with which the 8th Air Force punctuated the British landscape, have just about disappeared. Residents of east England, whose daily lives were regulated by the roar of fighter and bomber formations continually shuttling across the channel, now are scarcely aware of the dozen or so

planes which pass overhead daily. The personnel have vanished, too, for of the more than 300,000 men and women who served under the banner of the 8th from August 1942 to April 1945, only 30,000 remained in late October – and even they had their bags packed ...'

'Goodbye, Big 8th Air Force', **December 1945**

In the parish church at Kimbolton, there is a touching tribute to the American visitors. At the altar there is a leather-bound volume, dedicated to the memory of the American airmen stationed at Kimbolton who lost their lives during the war. In careful script the name and rank of each dead airman is entered on the pages of the book. Sad to say, the entries were many. These were the men of the 91st and 379th Heavy Bombardment Groups.

At the old Saxon church at Quidenham in Norfolk there is a magnificent stained glass window which was dedicated as a memorial to the airmen of the 96th BG, which was stationed at nearby Snetterton Heath. It depicts an American airman in flight uniform looking at the ascended Christ, a glorious and appropriate tribute to our comrades who fell.

The following incident shows the bond that bound the English and Americans together. In the summer of 1944, a young man, Staff Sergeant Bill Brockmeyer, was flight engineer on a B-17 crew of the 92nd BG at Podington. On their first mission as they became airborne, they suddenly lost altitude and crashed into a wood at the end of the runway. A young farmer named Walter Nottage was working in the wood and ran to the crash site. There he saw Brockmeyer, the only survivor, walking around in the wreckage, dazed, his clothes on fire. Nottage dashed into the flames, scooped up the young American flyer, and ran with him. He kept going until he was some distance from the crash, and luckily so; the bombs began to explode.

In August 1977, through English friends in an association called Friends of the Eighth, we located Nottage! A group of us, Brockmeyer included, went over to see him. He had no idea what we wanted with him. Bill introduced himself, related the

incident, and told the now middle-aged Englishman that he was the living proof of this heroic feat. The two men, overcome with emotion, embraced and stood in silence for a long moment thinking of that fateful day in the long ago.

These poignant instances underscore the nature of the Anglo-American relations far better than the trite phrase: 'Overpaid, oversexed, and over here'.

Chick's Crew, 'The Ties that Bind', Ben C. Smith

I found my hut down a concrete path that pretended to be a concrete roadway leading somewhere. Huge tufts of grass, knee-high to the hedgerow, coarse, triumphant, winning grass, sprouting out of spits and cracks, creating natural disorder and chaos of neglect where once we sailed free on cycles so long ago ... The hut was in the grip of bramble in the silence of a site where once there was no silence. I knew it as site 5, now an abandoned wood where a walk can bring the sudden panic of a woodpigeon, slapping the air, cracking the branches and freezing the spine in plunging fear.

The site, the cleared patches, the faint outline of a barrack hut in the trees – just a concrete patch, moss-covered, long forgotten. At my hut the shape is there, the number too, flaky white spots on the

green stained wall. Bramble and nettle thick around the door, ever open. Windows bursting out in small trees and branches framing the intruders like aboreal paintings. Inside, like rebellious plants they run amok, tall, heavy, bursting through roofs and windows ... The skeleton framework of the roof

Above: *On 1 August 1945 the remaining bases in England were opened to the British public. Among them was King's Cliffe, wartime home of the 55th FG, a number of whose Mustangs can be seen. The two Fortresses are from the 96th BG at Snetterton Heath. (via Michael L. Gibson)*

Left: *A former* Cap'n and the Kids *crewmember in the 452nd BG returns to Deopham Green in the 1980s. (MWB)*

Above: *A cowboy and his bucking bronco, one of several images painted on walls at the 14th Wing HQ at Shipdham by Jack Loman in 1943. This picture was taken thirty-eight years later. (MWB)*

Below: *Attlebridge control tower in 1953. (Mort Meintsma)*

against the sky, leaking in the sunlight in the wrong places and in corners that seemed forever dark. Nearby, on closer look, the ghosts in the abandoned wood emerge. Lumpy mounds of blast shelters, bearing trees like battle standards, merging into the landscape, withdrawing into the comfort of obscurity yet showing their tails. Patches of shiny brickwork beyond the nettles. The abandoned buildings given like gifts to nature, gutted, windowless, rusting deep-brown sagging roofs.

Thick undergrowth and trees, smothering, engulfing, blurring the outline except the memory, hiding my past like a hand against a photograph.

My hut – where in youth I felt fear, anxiety and a love of life in all that aim of death, that held the purpose.

My hut within a space that had no meaning, walls that framed a patch of ground that was like no other.

My hut, sad, decaying, still holding my space and for the young men that have gone forever. Here in a wood, buried in time like the site, half a century on, fading into nothingness amid the trees in an English countryside.

This article by Geoffrey Goreham is a collective expression of comments, memories, feelings and correspondence of former 2nd Air Division personnel whom the author met and escorted on visits to the old bases during the 1987 reunion in Norwich.

There's a 'Ghost American airfield' in England, just down the road from the modern US jet base at Alconbury, and it's fast becoming a favourite Yank tourist haunt.

The installation – Polebrook, sixty miles north of London – was a beehive of activity during World War II – when it served as the HQ of an American outfit. Today, it is as deserted as a haunted house.

Jet-age Yank airmen with a hankering to be transported back into history have only to visit the to get a hair-raising reminder of how things must have been there during the war.

Some fifty buildings stand empty and deserted on the erstwhile busy base, their windows shattered and their doors creaking eerily on rusted hinges. Pigeons dart insanely about the bare interiors, with bats and field mice their only company. Inside the barracks, grass has forced its way up through the warped floorboards. Out by the runway, a tattered windsock still flutters above the old wartime flightline but has fallen prey to weeds. The roar of B-17s has long since gone. Polebrook, like many of the RAF bases hastily erected during the early World War Two days, has lain idle and uninhabited since the war.

Everything remains just as it was left back at war's end in 1945, the huge hangars standing black and foreboding amid their silent surroundings and scores of old bomb shelters dot the landscape like rows of tombs.

Strange, incongruous signs like 'Barbershop' and 'Chapel' dangle from the prefabricated huts here and there, but the sounds of snipping shears and hymnal voices have long been silent.

In a huge building that apparently served as the officers' mess, the ghosts virtually come alive as paintings on the wall evoke memories of yesteryear. A sign over a dusty counter identifies one room as the 'Oasis Bar' and the insignia identifies the last tenant as the 351st BG. On the walls are listed the raids the 351st participated in against the Germans, along with the date and number of Nazi aircraft destroyed. Names like Amiens and Hamburg and Berlin are repeated often and alongside a Schweinfurt raid on 17 August 1943 are painted twenty-five swastikas, one for each Messerschmitt shot down. Another insignia of the 351st hangs over the door – a golden eagle with bombs clutched in its talons – and against the opposite wall is the familiar emblem of the US 8th Air Force.

Above: *'... against the opposite wall is the familiar emblem of the US 8th Air Force.'* Stars and Stripes (MWB)

It was like a dream come true for me to go back to England and see the people who had meant so much. You become close to people very quickly when you're in a life and death situation.

Now there are no planes on the hardstand at Snetterton Heath. The old runway is a racing circuit with the roar of racing cars and cycles replacing the roar of our engines as we lined up to take off on a mission. The living quarters have been demolished and that land is now used for farming. Only three

Below: *'Now there are no planes on the hardstand at Snetterton Heath. The old runway is a racing circuit with the roar of racing cars and cycles replacing the roar of our engines as we lined up to take off on a mission.' Peder Larsen (MWB)*

Above: *The raids the 351st participated in against the Germans. (Stars & Stripes)*

The haunting atmosphere of the abandoned B-17 base so excites the imagination of some visitors that they swear they are able to detect the roar of Flying Fortresses coming in for a landing – mission completed.

***Stars and Stripes*, 6 October 1958**

bomb shelters remain. These were used when our field was strafed or when a buzz bomb engine stopped overhead – it was then that we ran for cover!

The motor pool building, the parachute rigging silo, the operations building and a pile of large timbers stored in the woods are all that remain of the old base.

St Andrew's Church meant a great deal to me during the war and also played an important part in our missions. On our return we knew when we saw the church steeple that we were almost home safe.

Snetterton Heath echoes to the roars of racing cars and the cheers of crowds, but the volume of all that will never drown those two years 40 years ago.

That's part of our heritage as much as it is yours. It's always going to be that way, and if you doubt that the association will last, then go out to Snetterton Heath in the dark hours as dawn is breaking and the first light of day cracks the eastern horizon, and the mists wrap themselves around the old Norfolk oaks and there's a pinch in the air. Then, in your mind's eye, you can see them – you can see *5 Grand*, *Wabbit Tracks*, *Fertile Myrtle* and all the other bombers roaring their way into the sky over the Norfolk fields, carrying their lethal loads. That's an association that will never die – those ghosts will be there long after you and I have been gone for generations.

Peder Larsen, 96th BG

(MWB)

Below: *'Helton's Hellcats' (493rd BG) return to Debach in the summer of 2001. (MWB)*

GHOSTS OF THE RUNWAYS

'I was alone in the Tower in the ground floor front room, at about 1.45 p.m., paint brush in hand. A breeze came through the room, then noises started, aircraft engines and radios (RT) followed by men shouting. I was oblivious to anything else other than the noise, but I must say that prior to this, five minutes before, I had glanced out of the window and thought what a wonderful day it was. What seemed ages, was but a few seconds or so. I left the Tower at 1.55 p.m. and headed straight home. My wife Jane was surprised to see me home so early. I did not tell her at that time but did tell her later. Mike Harvey, Ron Batley and I have all experienced an unusual atmosphere at the Tower prior to the dedication.'

Sam Hurry (Diss schoolboy in World War II), 100th BG Memorial Museum, Thorpe Abbotts

English flowers bloom along the runways of the old airbase using each and every crack to germinate their yellow, blue, and red blossoms. Yet other things take root. There are ghosts that bloom along the runways, silent for years but now stirring in the east-west wind, the same wind that echoes about the ruined control tower. There is a corner of the old airbase at Shipdham that is particularly haunted. Friends of the Eighth tell of weird sounds and an icy feeling as they pass this corner. The bomber of a green crew rested there in dispersal during 1944. One day returning from a mission the bomber had damage to one engine and made a turn into that side resulting in a spin that sent them down. All died in that crash. But the place where their plane rested is now haunted.

There is a mighty bird that sometimes on fog-bound nights, roars along the runway, skimming the concrete cracks and the distant hedgerows.

When I stand on an old abandoned runway or control tower and look out across the old base I

hear many sounds: engines warming up, the roar of takeoffs, the squeal of landing wheels as they hit the runway after a long mission, and that peculiar squeaking sound and the whisper as the engines were cut off and the bomber came to rest. However, above all these sounds there are the faint words of a song that comes back on the slight wind across the English fields like a whisper from our youth, summoning the past. We would be coming back from a mission, tired, disgusted, many times ill from the cold and high-altitude flying. Suddenly, over the intercom, silent on most returns from a mission, we would hear a voice singing, 'Roll me over, Roll me over, Lay me down and do it again.' It's the voice of our navigator, Lieutenant Robert Weatherwax, his flight cap pushed far back on his forehead.

That song, a favourite of bomber crews, still haunts me and is to me the essence of my combat flying experience.

I remember the words of our radio operator coming on the wind: 'This damn English weather. I can't wait to get out of here and back to the Bronx.'

English weather often played tricks on bomber crews and more than one mission was scrubbed by the weather. But despite all, to see again the rows of walls, the village churchyards, and the patterns of fields and woodlands of England was always a welcome sight to bomber crew eyes. I can see and feel the time a friend, a radio operator, ran into a

moving prop one early dawn before takeoff. The time a bomber burst into flames on the flight line. The time a rookie crew crashed on landing, and the times thick fog shrouded the runways, even through the flare paths.

However, the most enduring and most vivid ghosts are the friends and fellow crewmembers left behind in the skies – Sergeant Sofferman and Lieutenant Dave Edmonds among many others. They too haunt the runways and mix like sighs with the wind and the quiet.

Who can forget these ghosts of the airfields?

Technical Sergeant Forrest S. Clark

Above left: *Crews of the 467th BG heading for briefing at Rackheath. In the background is one of the T-2 hangars, which still stands today. (James J. Mahoney via Brian H. Mahoney)*

Above: *Men of the 470th sub-depot, 467th BG working on the Liberators' Pratt & Whitney Wasp engines at Rackheath. (James J. Mahoney via Brian H. Mahoney)*

(MWB)

Twelve O'Clock High

'You're not going home. You're going to die. In fact, consider yourselves already dead!'

General Frank Savage, from the movie *Twelve O'Clock High*

In 1946, while many people's thoughts turned to peace, others were still thinking of war. In the famous opening scene of the movie *Twelve O'Clock High*, veteran American screen and stage actor Dean Jagger in his all-important role of Major Harvey Stovall returns to England to revisit his wartime base. Stovall leans his bicycle against the wooden gate at the entrance to the disused and deserted wartime airfield at Archbury and the bespectacled former executive officer surveys the overgrown dispersals where just a few years earlier mighty Forts of his beloved 918th BG had stood. He squints across the English meadow where cows are grazing. In the wind Stovall can hear the roar of the engines and for a moment he is transported back to the war when the 918th BG had

dominated this now quiet pastoral scene. After reminiscing, Stovall re-mounts his bicycle, rides off, and by chance sees in a shop the Toby jug that once had pride of place on the mantelpiece in the officers' mess. When a mission was scheduled for the next day the jug would be turned around and the officers would head for their barracks and bed.

The fictionalized 918th BG was created by writer Beirne Lay Jr. – one of Eaker's original six staff officers in World War Two. (He came up with the name by multiplying the 306th by three.) In 1946 Lay was working for MGM on *Above and Beyond*, another aviation film, when he received an interesting approach from Sy Bartlett who, as a major, had been General Carl Spaatz's aide. Bartlett was now working as a screenwriter at

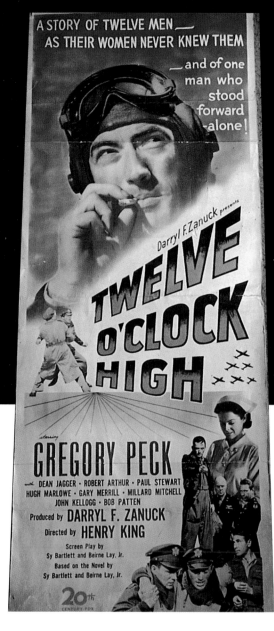

A STORY OF TWELVE MEN —
AS THEIR WOMEN NEVER KNEW THEM

... and of one
man who
stood
forward
—alone!

Darryl F. Zanuck presents

**TWELVE
O'CLOCK
HIGH**

starring

GREGORY PECK

with DEAN JAGGER • ROBERT ARTHUR • PAUL STEWART
HUGH MARLOWE • GARY MERRILL • MILLARD MITCHELL
JOHN KELLOGG • BOB PATTEN

Produced by **DARRYL F. ZANUCK**

Directed by **HENRY KING**

Screen Play by
Sy Bartlett and Beirne Lay, Jr.
Based on the Novel by
Sy Bartlett and Beirne Lay, Jr.

20th
CENTURY-FOX

Twentieth Century Fox Studios. He wanted Lay to co-write a book and screenplay about the air war called *Twelve O'Clock High*. Lay initially thought they did not stand a chance with a book about the war, but Bartlett's determination eventually persuaded him. A thrilling storyline owed much to the events – often tragic – that were experienced by the 306th BG at Thurleigh in 1943. *Twelve O'Clock High* draws upon the 306th's troubled early combat history and its effect on the combat crews. Allusions to real events and representations of actual wartime personnel abound. (The names of targets were actually 'smoked' – traced with the smoke of a candle flame – onto the ceilings of briefing rooms, as seen in the movie). The film is also significant for the use of real combat footage

(shot over Europe), and of real incidents.

'General Frank Savage', the commander and the movie's central character, was modelled on Brigadier General Frank Armstrong, a West Pointer with whom Bartlett had struck up a close friendship during the war. Armstrong, a cool, tough, no-nonsense North Carolinian, was one of Eaker's original staff officers. Early in the war, Armstrong took over the 97th BG at Grafton Underwood, a 'lackadaisical, loose-jointed, fun-loving, badly trained outfit', and he inherited much the same at Thurleigh with the 306th BG. Armstrong commanded the respect of those who served with him. He worked his new crews hard and he soon turned both groups into very effective outfits.

In 1948, with the novel *Twelve O'Clock High* nearing publication, Louis O. 'Bud' Lighton, a producer at Fox, became very interested in the screenplay. Lighton sounded out studio head Darryl F. Zanuck who promptly purchased the

Above: *Traditional 'smoking' of the ceiling of the 306th BG officers' club at Thurleigh with candles. Maj. Harry Holt, CO, 367th BS until 4 March 1943 (left); Captain John L. Ryan (with candle); Captain John L. Lambert, 367th BS, later CO, 423rd BS (left); and Captain George Buckey 367th CO, 19 August 1943 to 2 May 1944, lend support. Ryan took command of the 367th on 5 March 1943, and was shot down the next day. He evaded capture and returned to England after forty-two days. This stunt was used in* Twelve O'Clock High. *(Richards Coll)*

movie rights. The central theme in the movie version would be the gradual and ultimate destruction of General Savage (played superbly by Gregory Peck). Zanuck hired Henry King, an accomplished pilot, as the movie's director. King, Bartlett and Lay refined the overlong script, which had already seen the removal of Savage's love interest, and together they produced a highly-polished final draft.

Twelve B-17s were used in the making of *Twelve O' Clock High* which was filmed largely at Eglin Air Force Base, Florida, and Ozark, Alabama. Shooting lasted from February to July 1949 and when edited the picture ran for 133 minutes. This most celebrated of black and white aviation movies premiered at Grauman's Chinese Theatre in Hollywood on Christmas Day 1949.

Above: *General Savage (Gregory Peck) 'chews out' Ben Gately in a poster of the period. (via Richards)*

Left: *The famous scene in* Twelve O'Clock High *where General Savage (Gregory Peck) is unable to summon enough strength to climb aboard a B-17 for his mission. (via Philip Kaplan)*

Right: *Madingley Cemetery is located three miles west of Cambridge. The sloping site covers over thirty acres and has the graves of over 3,800 of our military dead. The 'great wall of the missing' records the names of 5,126 who gave their lives in the service of their country, but whose remains were never recovered or identified. Most of these men died in the battle of the Atlantic or in the strategic air bombardment of north-west Europe. (MWB)*

'Only the dead have seen the end of war.'
Plato

Acknowledgements

ACKNOWLEDGEMENTS: First and foremost, I would like to thank editor Ian Drury for making this project possible, Caroline Cambridge for her dedicated editing and Rod Teasdale for his superb layouts. I am also most grateful to the following: Steve Adams, T. R. Anderson Jr., Robert S. Arbib, John Archer, Christine Armes; May Ayers; Richard E. Bagg, Mike Bailey, Mickey Balsam; Henry 'Hank' W. Barker; Marvin Barnes, Harold Belkin; Lieutenant Colonel Tom S. Belovich, Virginia Bergman, Theo Boiten, Martin Boswell, Mel Bourne; William A. Boutelle, Bob Browne, William Bruce, Lilian Burnett, John W. Butler. Camera ship pilots: Jim Avis, Philip Back, John Carter, Dale Featherby, Captain Steve Graham AAC, Gerry Honey OBE, Bruce Monk, Ian Robins, John Romaine, Squadron Leader Dave Thomas BBMF, and the crews of *Diamond Lil'*, BBMF Avro Lancaster, *City of Lincoln* and C-47 Dakota, *Fuddy Duddy*, *9-0-9*, *Sentimental Journey*, *Texas Raiders*, and *Tico Belle*. Colonel William B. Cameron, Nora and Herman Canfield; Bill Carleton; Raphael F. Carrow, James Chainey, Tony Chardella, Don. V. Chase; Forrest S. Clark; Bob Clements, Wilbur Clingan, R. D. Clover, Muriel Colborn; Franklin H. 'Pappy' Colby, Bob Collis, George M. Collar, Father Joe Collins; Andy J. Coroles, Frank Cotner, Art Crandell; Frank Crosby, IWM Duxford, Clyde Crowley, Colonel John Crump, Tom Cushing, Harry H. Darrah; Rob Davies OBE, Squadron Leader Paul Day OBE AFC, Gerald Deacon, Abel L. Dolim, Bill Donald, Michael R. Downes, Charles 'Bud' Doyle, Tommy Dungar, Bill Eagelson; Robert P. Eberwein, Christopher R. Elliott, the late Major Ralph H. Elliott; Mrs Daisy Elmar, Bill Espie; George Evans, Mrs Pat Everson; Robert L. Ferrell; The Fighter Collection, Neville Firman; Thomas J. Fitton, Robert Foose, Ian Frimston, Friends of the Eighth, Carmelo Frontino, Mike Fuenfer; Gene Gaskins; Michael L. Gibson, John Gilbert; Molly Giles; Jim Gintner; Colonel Harry D. Gobrecht, Ken Godfrey, Lieutenant Colonel James F. 'Goody' Goodson, J Gogle; Laurence S. 'Goldie' Goldstein; Lee C. Gordon, Geoffrey Goreham; Steve Gotts; Bill and Doris Graff; Don and Peggy Garnham; George Greengrass; Carl W. Groshell, Alan Hague, the late Charles 'Holly' Hall. Cliff Hall, Cliff Hatcher; Greg Hatton, Russ D. Hayes, Hershel J. Hausman; the late Allan Healy, A. P. Herbert, Howard F. Hernan, Herman Hetzel; Sidney Hewett, John A. Holden, Ivy and Charles Holston; John L. Hurd, Sam Hurry, Glenn B. Infield, Edward J. Israel, Dan Jacobs, Robert A. Jacobs, Loren F. Jackson, Steven Jefferson; Emily and Allen Johnston, Richard 'Dick' Johnson, Ben Jones; Sidney Jrueger; Philip Kaplan, John Edward Kerns, David Kibble-White; Jim Kidder, Norm Kiefer, Walt Konantz, Ronald V. Kramer, Jack Krause, Peder Larsen, Corporal Ellsworth B. Laurence, Muriel Lawrence; the late Beirne Lay Jr., Mary Carroll Leeds; the late General Curtis E. LeMay, Clement L. Lockwood, Roger Lovelace, Will Lundy, Floyd H. Mabee, Estate of the late Colonel James J. Mahoney, Brian H. Mahoney, Delbert Mann, Robert T. Marshall, Jim Matsell; Mort Meintsma; Jasper Miles, Anona Moeser, John W. McClane; Brian S. McGuire, Newton L. Mclaughlin; Frank M. Mead Jr., Armand Miale, Joe Micksch, John A. Miller; Robert L. Miller; Joseph Minton, Bill Mulroney, Lloyd Murff, Theodore J. Myers, Wiley S. Noble, Tony North, Frances Nunnally, James E. O'Brien, Merle C. Olmsted, Robert 'Bob' O'Hearn, Old Flying Machine Company, Mike O'Shea, Ralph K. Patton, Stanley Peterson; Norman R. Pickstone, Kenneth M. Pieffer, Barbara and Wallace Porter; John D. Preston, Cliff Pyle, Pat Ramm; Vince Reed; Russell A. Reeve; Reflections Photographic Studio; Jean Lancaster-Rennie, Connie and Gordon Richards, Rick Rokicki; Bill Rose, The Second Air Division Memorial Library, Norwich; Joseph H. Saling; Dean H. Sanner, Emmett D. Seale, David Schmitt, Donald J. Schmitt, Martin H. Schreck, Tom J. Shepherd; Colonel Albert J. Shower, Anne and Graham Simons, Gene Skaggs, Les Skitterall; Phyllis Smales; Ben C. Smith; Griswold Smith; Tom Smith, Steve Snelling, Sam Sox, General Delmar Spivey, Ann K. Spredbury; Fred Squires; Hans-Heiri Stapfer, Rocky Starek, George Stebbings; Al Steller, Doris Stephens; William Sterrett, Bert Stiles, Francis (Frank) W. Stokes, Beryl M. Sutton; Eric Swain, Paul G. Tardiff, Billy Taylor, Robert H. Tays, Leslie G. Thibodeau, Mary Thompson; Miriam Thorpe, Thorpe Abbotts Memorial Museum, Paul W. Tibbets, Walt Truax, William W. Varnedoe Jr.; John W. Voght, Douglas D. Walker, Lowell Watts, Perry Watts, Karl Wendel, Dick Wickham; Paul Wilson, Truett Woodall, Lisa and Peter Worby, Russell J. Zorn.

Glossary

Big-B	Berlin	KIA	Killed in Action
BG	Bomb Group	Liberty run	night off into town
BS	Bomb Squadron	Little friend	fighter aircraft
Buzz job	attack base etc., at very low level	MIA	Missing in Action
Carpetbagger mission	clandestine night operation in support of underground forces in occupied lands	Milk run	easy mission
		Non-com	NCO (non-commissioned officer)
		Piccadilly commando	prostitute
Chug-a-lug	drink vast quantities of beer	Poop	information
Dear John	a letter from a girl back home saying she's found someone else	POM	Preparation for Overseas Movement
		Pubbing mission	pub crawl
ETO	European Theatre of Operations	PX	Post Exchange
FG	Fighter Group	SAD	Second Air Division
Flak	flieger abhwer kannonen: anti-aircraft fire	Sack	bed
		Shuttle	long bombing mission via stop en route
Flak alley	heavily defended bomb run		
Flak happy	state of victim of combat fatigue	Snafu	situation normal all f***** up
Flak house	rest home	Snowdrop	military policeman, so-called because of his white helmet
Flak shack	rest home		
FTR	Failed to Return	Short snorter	a bill of currency autographed to prove one had been in that country
Funny money	pounds sterling		
Furlough	leave	Tour	series of missions
GI	Government Issue: American soldier	Trolley mission	carrying of ground peronnel on sightseeing missions over Germany after hostilities ceased
Happy Valley	Ruhr Valley		
Heavies	bombers		
IP	initial point at the start of the bomb run	ZOI	Zone of the Interior (USA)

Select Bibliography and Further Reading

In the titles below, (H) stands for Heavy.

34th Bomb Group Association, *34th Bomb Group (H) 1944–45*, Turner Publishing, 1988

352nd Fighter Group Association, *The Blue Nosed Bastards of Bodney: A Commemorative History*, Taylor Publishing, Texas

Advisory Board for *Reporting World War II*, Part One, Library Classics of the United States, 1995

Andrews, Paul M., *Courage, Honor, Victory: An Operational Record of the 95th Bomb Group (H)*, privately published

Andrews, Paul M. and Adams, William H., *Heavy Bombers of the Mighty Eighth*, Eighth Air Force Museum Foundation Project, Bits & Pieces, 1995

Appleby, John T., *Suffolk Summer*, East Anglia Magazine, Ipswich, 1948

Arbib, Robert S. Jr., *Here We Are Together: notebook of an American soldier in Britain*, Longmans, Green, London, 1946

Bailey, Mike and North, Tony, *Liberator Album: B-24s of the 2nd Air Division, USAAF*, Midland, Leicester, 1998

Barnes, Marvin E., *A History of the 452nd Bomb Group (H)*, privately published, 1987

Bendiner, Elmer, *The Fall of Fortresses*, G. P. Putnam's Sons, New York, 1980

Birdsall, Steve, *The B-17 Flying Fortress*, Morgan, 1965

Birdsall, Steve, *Fighting Colors: B-17 Flying Fortress*, Squadron Signal, Carrollton, 1986

Birdsall Steve, *Hell's Angels: B-17 Combat Markings*, Grenadier Books, 1969

Birdsall, Steve, *Log of the Liberators*, Doubleday, New York, 1973

Birdsall, Steve, *Pride of Seattle: The Story of the First 300 B-17Fs*, Squadron Signal, Carrollton, 1998

Blakebrough, Ken, *The Fireball Outfit: the 457th Bomb Group*, Aero, Fallbrook, 1968

Blue, Allan C., *B-24 Liberator*, Charles Scribner's Sons, New York, 1977

Blue, Allan C., *The Fortunes of War*, Aero, Fallbrook, 1967

Bowden, Ray, *Plane Names & Fancy Noses: the 91st Bomb Group (H)*, Design Oracle Partnership, Bridport, 1993

Bowers, Peter M., *Fortress in The Sky*, Sentry, Granada Hills, 1976

Bowman, Martin W., *The 8th Air Force At War: Memories and Missions 1942–45*, PSL, Sparkford, 1994

Bowman, Martin W., B-17 *Flying Fortress Units of the 8th AF*, Osprey, Oxford, 2002

Bowman, Martin W., *The B-24 Liberator 1939-1945*, Wensum Books, Norwich, 1979

Bowman, Martin W. and Boiten, Theo, *Battles with the Luftwaffe*, Jane's Publishing, London, 2001

Bowman, Martin W., *The Bedford Triangle*, Sutton, Stroud, 1996

Bowman, Martin W., *Boeing B-17 Flying Fortress*, Crowood, Marlborough, 1998

Bowman, Martin W., *Castles In The Air*, PSL, Cambridge, 1984

Bowman, Martin W., *Consolidated B-24 Liberator*, Crowood, Marlborough, 1998

Bowman, Martin W., *Fields of Little America*, Wensum Books, Norwich, 1977

Bowman, Martin W., *Flying To Glory*, PSL, Sparkford, 1992

Bowman, Martin W., *Four Miles High*, PSL, Sparkford, 1992

Bowman, Martin W., *Great American Air Battles of WWII*, Airlife, Shrewsbury, 1994

Bowman, Martin W. and Woodall, Truett Lee Jr., *Helton's Hellcats: A Pictorial History of the 493rd Bomb Group*, Turner, Padvcah, 1998

Bowman, Martin W., *Home By Christmas?*, PSL, Cambridge, 1987

Bowman, Martin W. and Boiten, Theo, *Raiders of the Reich: Air Battle Western Europe 1942–45*, Airlife, Shrewsbury, 1996

Bowman, Martin W., *USAAF Handbook 1939–1945*, Sutton, Stroud, 1997

Bowman, Martin W., *The USAF At War*, PSL, Sparkford, 1995

Bowman, Martin W., *The US Eighth Air Force In Camera 1942–44*, Sutton, Stroud, 1997

Bowman, Martin W., *The US Eighth Air Force In Camera 1944–45*, Sutton, Stroud, 1998

Caidin, Martin, *Black Thursday*, E. P. Dutton, New York, 1960

Caidin, Martin, *Flying Forts: the B-17 in WWII*, Ballantine, New York, 1968

Clark, Forrest S., *44th BG stories*, unpublished

Collar, George M., *Reflections of a Bombardier*, unpublished

Colman, Penny, *Rosie The Riveter: Women Working on the Home Front in WWII*, Crown Publishers, New York, 1995

DeWitt, Hugh, *Bawdy Barrack-room Ballads*, Universal-Tandem, London, 1970

Doherty, Robert E. and Ward, Geoffrey D., *Snetterton Falcons: The 96th Bomb Group in WWII*, Taylor Publishing, Texas, 1989

Donald, William, *305th BG*, unpublished

Elliott, Major Ralph H., *Letters Home and Other Stuff*, unpublished

Ethell, Jeffrey L. and Simonsen, Clarence, *The History of Aircraft Nose Art: WWI to Today*, Motorbooks, 1991

Freeman, Roger A., *Airfields of the Eighth*, Battle of Britain Prints International, London, 1978

Freeman, Roger A. with Osborne, David, *The B-17 Flying Fortress Story*, Arms & Armour, London, 1998

Freeman, Roger A., *B-17 Fortress At War*, Ian Allan, Hersham, 1977

Freeman, Roger A., *The Mighty Eighth*, Macdonald, London, 1970

Freeman, Roger A., *The Mighty Eighth In Art*, Arms & Armour, London, 1996

Freeman, Roger A., *The Mighty Eighth War Diary*, Jane's Publishing, London, 1981

Galland, Adolf, *The First And The Last*, Ballantine, New York, 1954

Gann, Ernest K., *Fate Is The Hunter*, Simon & Schuster, New York, 1961

Gaskins, Gene, *Crew 64*, privately published

Gibson, Michael L., *Aviation in Northamptonshire*, Northamptonshire Libraries, Northampton, 1982

Good Brown, James, *The Mighty Men of the 351st: Heroes All*, Publishers Press, 1984

Harvel, Ursel P., *Jaws Over Europe*, privately published

Havelaar, Marion H. with Hess, William N., *The Ragged Irregulars of Bassingbourn*, Schiffer Military History, 1995

Hawkins, Ian L., *B-17s Over Berlin: Personal Stories from the 95th Bomb Group (H)*, Brasseys, London, 1990

Healy, Allan, *The 467th Bombardment Group*, privately published, 1947

Hess, William, *B-17 Flying Fortress*, Ballantine, New York, 1974

Huntzinger, Edward J., *The 388th At War*, privately published, Cape Coral, 1979

Jablonski, Edward, *Airwar*, Doubleday, New York, 1971

Jablonski, Edward, *America in the Air War*, Time Life Books, Alexandria, 1982

Jablonski, Edward, *Flying Fortress*, Doubleday, New York, 1965

Johnsen, Fred, *Winged Majesty*, PNAHF, 1980

Johnson, Robert S. with Caidin, Martin, *Thunderbolt*, Ballantine Books, New York, 1958

Kaplan, Philip and Smith, Rex Alan, *One Last Look: a sentimental journey to the Eighth Air Force heavy bomber bases of World War II in England*, Cross River Press, 1983

Lande, D. A., *From Somwhere in England*, Airlife, Shrewsbury, 1991

Lay, Beirne Jr. and Bartlett, Sy, *Twelve O'Clock High*, Ballantine Books, New York, 1948

LeMay, General Curtis E. and Kantor, MacKinlay, *Mission with LeMay*, Doubleday, New York, 1965

Le Strange, Richard assisted by Brown, James R., *Century Bombers: The Story of the Bloody Hundredth*, 100th Bomb Group Memorial Museum, Thorpe Abbotts, 1989

Logan, Ian and Nield, Henry, *Classy Chassy*, Mathews Miller, Dunbar, 1977

MacKay, Ron, *381st Bomb Group*, Squadron Signal, Carrollton, 1994

Mahoney, Colonel James J. and Brian H., *Reluctant Witness: Memoirs from the last year of the European Air War 1944–45*, Trafford Publishing, Victoria, 2001

Marshall, Technical Sergeant Robert T., *The Flight From Boyhood*, unpublished

McClane, First Lieutenant John W., *An Army Air Force Navigator*, unpublished

McCrary, John R. and Scherman, David E., *First of the Many*, Simon and Schuster, New York, 1944

McDowell, Ernest R., *Flying Fortress in Action*, Squadron Signal, Carrollton, 1987

McLachlan, Ian, *Eighth Air Force Bomber Stories*, PSL, Sparkford, 1991

McLachlan, Ian, *Final Flights*, PSL, Sparkford, 1989

McLachlan, Ian, *Night of the Intruders*, PSL, Sparkford, 1994

Members of the 490th Bomb Group (H), *Historical Record of the 490th Bomb Group (H)*, unpublished

Merrill, Sandra D., *Donald's Story*, Tebidine, Berlin (US), 1996

Miles, Jasper, *Echoes: A Tribute In Verse to the U.S. Army Corps 1942–1945*, privately published

Olsen, Jack, *Aphrodite: Desperate Mission*, G. P. Putnam's Sons, New York, 1970

Peaslee, Budd I., *Heritage of Valor*, J. B. Lippincott, Philadelphia, 1963

Redding, Major John M. and Leyshon, Captain Harold I., *Skyways to Berlin*, Bobbs-Merrill, Indianapolis, 1943

Rennie, Jean Lancaster-, *And Over There*, privately published, 1976

Shirer, William L., *The Rise and Foil of the Third Reich*, Simon and Schuster, New York, 1960

Slater, Harry E., *Lingering Contrails of The Big Square A: a history of the 94th Bomb Group (H) 1942–45*, 94th Bomb Group Memorial Association, Nashville, 1980

Slater, Harry E., ed., *Nostalgic Notes: the 94th BG Newsletter*

Sloan, John S., *The Route As Briefed*, Argus Press, Cleveland, 1946

Smith Jr., Ben, *Chick's Crew: A Tale of the Eighth Air Force*, privately published, New York, 1978

Smith, John N., *Airfield Focus 37*, GMS Peterborough, 1999–2001

Stapfer, Hans-Heiri, *Strangers in a Strange Land*, Squadron Signal, Carrollton, 1988

Stiles, Bert, *Serenade to the Big Bird*, Lindsay Drummond, London, 1947

The Story of the 390th Bomb Group (H), privately published, 1947

Strong, Russell A., *First Over Germany: A History of the 306th BG*, Hunter Publishing, 1982

Sweetman, John, *Schweinfurt: Disaster in the Skies*, Ballantine Books, New York, 1971

Target: Germany – The Army Air Forces' official story of the VIII Bomber Command's first year over Europe, Simon and Schuster, New York, 1943

Tays, Robert H., *Country Boy – Combat Bomber Pilot*, privately published

Woolnough, John H., *The 8th Air Force Yearbook*, The 8th Air Force News, Hollywood, 1981

Woolnough, John H., *Journal of the 8th Air Force Historical Society*, The 8th Air Force News, Hollywood, 1976–1983

Vargas, Alberto and Reid, Austin, *Vargas*, Plexus, London, 1978

Varnedoe, W. W. Jr., *B-17s of the 385th Bomb Group, 8th AF*, privately published, 1996

Varnedoe, W. W. Jr., *A Navigator in World War II*, privately published, 1997